ORGANIZING AND THE LAW

ORGANIZING AND THE LAW

REVISED EDITION
by
Stephen I. Schlossberg
*General Counsel, United Automobile,
Aerospace & Agricultural Workers of America (UAW)*

and

Fredrick E. Sherman
*Assistant Professor, School for Workers
The University of Wisconsin*

A
BNA
BOOK

The Bureau of National Affairs, Inc.   Washington, D.C.

Printed in the United States of America
Library of Congress Catalog Card Number: 70-140189
Standard Book Number: 87179-116-1 (hardcover)
87179-117-X (paper)

31

Organizing And The Law

Chief Justice Charles Evans Hughes, of the Supreme Court of the United States, said in *NLRB* v. *Jones & Laughlin Steel Corp.*, 301 U.S. 1 at 33:

> Long ago we stated the reason for labor organizations. We said that they were organized out of the necessities of the situation; that a single employee was helpless in dealing with an employer; that he was dependent ordinarily on his daily wage for the maintenance of himself and family; that if the employer refused to pay him the wages that he thought fair, he was nevertheless unable to leave the employer and resist arbitrary and unfair treatment; that union was essential to give laborers opportunity to deal on equality with their employer.

TO THE MEN AND WOMEN OF THE UAW

Acknowledgments

Pat Greathouse, Vice-President of the UAW and its Director of Organization, is responsible, in a very real sense, for this book. He is the one who saw the value of a legal-organizing team approach and who implemented it in the UAW. I am greatly indebted to him for his inspiration and advice.

Joseph L. Rauh, Jr., my friend and former general counsel of the UAW, encouraged the writing of this book. I acknowledge an incalculable debt to him.

Frank Winn, special assistant to UAW President Walter P. Reuther, was kind enough to read each page and to make valuable suggestions. Frank kept this book from the disease of "lawyerese" when I would, occasionally, lapse into it.

The research assistance of Michael Friedman, assistant general counsel of the UAW, and law clerks Erwin Adler and Robert Weinberg was most appreciated. I also acknowledge the cooperation of my colleagues, John A. Fillion, associate general counsel of the UAW, and Jordan Rossen and Bernard F. Ashe, both assistant general counsel of the UAW.

Finally, this book could not have been written without the understanding and the wonderful help of my wife, Nancy K. Schlossberg.

*   *   *

Phyllis J. Oster of the School for Workers, University of Wisconsin, provided invaluable and untiring assistance in the preparation of the revised edition.

Foreword

Taft-Hartley may, indeed, be, as some have said, a "slave labor law," but you won't find proof either way in this publication. This book is about the law—not a debate as to its merits and demerits—but what it is, how it helps, and how it hurts. It represents a try at setting out in usable and readable form the major legal principles affecting union organization. It is not, however, written without a point of view. *This book is based on the simple premise that the unionization of workers is a social and economic necessity.* It is hoped that it will help to take some of the mystery and mumbo-jumbo out of the basic law in the field and, in so doing, permit the acceleration of organization. In the last analysis, that is why the book was written.

The task of organizing workers into unions has never been easy. It has always been, by definition, a "rugged" staff assignment. An ideal organizer combines essential talents of a variety of occupational specialties. He should be part missionary, part salesman, part politician, part counselor, part teacher, part psychologist and, most relevant here, part lawyer.

This book aims to help the organizer become more familiar with the law because the better the organizer understands the law, the more he will be able to make it work for him. This volume will *not* make lawyers out of organizers, but, if carefully followed, it may permit organizers to make intelligent choices under the law and to know when they need lawyers. Properly used, with an understanding of its character and limitations, and not treated as an authoritative word that must be followed in every single case, this handbook should prove extremely useful. No organizer should assume that this volume can substitute for legal advice.

The main source for the material in this volume is the Labor Management Relations Act, as amended (originally "The Wagner Act" and now called "The Taft-Hartley Act"), and the decisions of the Labor Board and the courts interpreting that law. Where

ix

relevant, to the organizer, unions, or the workers, however, other matters will be mentioned.

Attention to detail, the avoidance of mistakes and violations of law, and the careful use of tools provided by the law can be tremendously important to the organizer and the workers he seeks to help.

It must be kept in mind that lawyers usually get a case after it has been made. That is, the facts are already determined. No matter how clever an attorney may be, he cannot change the facts he "inherits."

Forearmed with a basic knowledge of Board procedure and some of the more important rules of law announced by the NLRB and the courts, an alert organizer can make more meaningful decisions as to timing, can tailor situations to the law, and can keep the kind of detailed records that will enable lawyers, both partisan and government, to prove the best possible case.

Policy is inextricably bound up with advice for most effective performance under the law, so this book is bound to include some admonitions and suggestions of a policy nature, although the major thrust is toward understanding law and procedure. Policy is, of course, made by the union's organizing department and not its legal department, so, in the unlikely event of a policy conflict, the organizer should look to the union rather than to this book.

This book does not cover the law applicable to municipal, state, and federal employees; nor does it deal with state labor relations law or the Railway Labor Act. Organizers concerned with these laws will have to look elsewhere for guidance.

Finally, to state what is presumed to be already obvious, there is no legal trick or bag of tricks that will organize workers. While this book can, it is hoped, make the task somewhat easier, workers can be organized into unions only by their own efforts and the efforts of union leaders.

Laws cannot substitute for hard work. The job of an organizer —professional or amateur—will always be tough, and there is no quick and easy gimmick available to change that.

STEPHEN I. SCHLOSSBERG

January 1967

Foreword to the
Revised Edition

We have not made major changes in the first edition of Organizing and the Law with respect to its basic design and organization. Revisions have been made to reflect changes in the law in the last three years and to clarify and expand discussion in a number of areas where we thought it might be useful. As in the earlier edition there is no attempt at comprehensive citation of authority and, by and large, new cases have been added only where they stand for changed principles or seem particularly interesting.

STEPHEN I. SCHLOSSBERG
FREDRICK E. SHERMAN

October 1970

TABLE OF CONTENTS

AN OVERVIEW OF THE LAW

Labor relations are not matters of mere
local or private concern.

Mr. Justice Murphy,
Thornhill v. *Alabama*,
310 US 88, 103 (1940)

Introduction

Most of the basic law affecting union organization is set out
here in Chapter I. But these bare bones of the law are only
the framework upon which the legal principles are built.

Labor law, and specifically the law that governs union organizing, is state and federal law, statutory and case law. By far
the most significant statutory law is the federal National Labor
Relations Act. Likewise, the most important labor case law is
made by the National Labor Relations Board, which administers
the Act, and by the federal courts. The federal law plays the
paramount role it does because of a doctrine known as preemption: generally, if the Federal Government acts in a particular area where it has the authority to act, the states are precluded from acting in that same area. In the labor field this
has meant that by and large the states have been limited to
acting in those areas where the federal law has not gone (either
because of statutory or Board-created exclusion) or in those
areas where specific allowances are made for state regulation
(as with right-to-work laws). Because of the preeminence of
the federal law and the impossibility of treating briefly the
varying regulatory schemes of some 50-odd jurisdictions, this
text will concern itself almost exclusively with the national law.

But organizers should be aware that in some situations state law will govern entirely or in some detail, and in those situations the organizer would do well to inform himself of the local legal pattern.

The "charter" of organization is the federal labor act—originally the Wagner Act, now the Taft-Hartley Act and officially the Labor Management Relations Act, as amended. In this chapter you will find relevant portions of that Act printed along with a brief summary analysis or illustrative examples for each relevant section. The analysis is followed by a brief summary of the Labor Board's jurisdictional standards, and a quick digest of the Board's unfair-labor-practice procedure.

While the Act is certainly the core of most of the law in the field, other materials of possible relevance have been condensed and included so that, in proper cases, organizers may call upon union "law" or reporting-and-disclosure law for a needed assist.

One word of caution. The material in this chapter is only the skeleton. Until subsequent chapters supply the flesh, the creature is unfinished. The sole purpose of this part of the book is to give the reader the benefit of an overview of the main law. After the more pertinent parts of the law, such as organizing ground rules and election rules, have been covered in some depth, however, occasional reference to the definitions and other original language of the statute may help keep the whole picture in perspective.

It is important to remember that some of the seemingly simple words written by Congress back in 1935, as well as the later amendments, are still being interpreted by the United States Supreme Court. Read those words carefully, know them, and relate them directly to the material in later chapters. These legislative words, these laws, are the tools of your trade.

Analysis of Selected Portions of the Taft-Hartley Act

Findings and Public Policy of the Act [Section 1]

The law aims at removing obstructions to interstate com-	"The denial by some employers of the right of employees to organize and the refusal by some employers to accept the procedure of collective bargaining lead to strikes and other forms of

merce resulting from strife caused by the refusal of employers to accept collective bargaining and the *denial of the right to organize.*

industrial strife or unrest, which have the intent or the necessary effect of burdening or obstructing commerce by (a) impairing the efficiency, safety, or operation of the instrumentalities of commerce; (b) occurring in the current of commerce; (c) materially affecting, restraining, or controlling the flow of raw materials or manufactured or processed goods from or into the channels of commerce, or the prices of such materials or goods in commerce; or (d) causing diminution of employment and wages in such volume as substantially to impair or disrupt the market for goods flowing from or into the channels of commerce.

Inequality of bargaining power between unorganized workers and powerful employers tends to cause depressions and low wages.

"The inequality of bargaining power between employees who do not possess full freedom of association or actual liberty of contract, and employers who are organized in the corporate or other forms of ownership association substantially burdens and affects the flow of commerce, and tends to aggravate recurrent business depressions, by depressing wage rates and the purchasing power of wage earners in industry and by preventing the stabilization of competitive wage rates and working conditions within and between industries.

We have learned that it is necessary to protect by law the right to organize and bargain collectively.

"Experience has proved that protection by law of the right of employees to organize and bargain collectively safeguards commerce from injury, impairment, or interruption, and promotes the flow of commerce by removing certain recognized sources of industrial strife and unrest, by encouraging practices fundamental to the friendly adjustment of industrial disputes arising out of differences as to wages, hours, or other working conditions, and by restoring equality of bargaining power between employers and employees.

"Experience" has taught Congress that there is also a need

"Experience has further demonstrated that certain practices by some labor organizations, their officers, and members have the intent or the necessary effect of burdening or obstruct-

to protect against unfair practices by some unions.

ing commerce by preventing the free flow of goods in such commerce through strikes and other forms of industrial unrest or through concerted activities which impair the interest of the public in the free flow of such commerce. The elimination of such practices is a necessary condition to the assurance of the rights herein guaranteed.

It is the declared policy of the United States to encourage collective bargaining.

"It is hereby declared to be the policy of the United States to eliminate the causes of certain substantial obstructions to the free flow of commerce and to mitigate and eliminate these obstructions when they have occurred by encouraging the practice and procedure of collective bargaining and by protecting the exercise by workers of full freedom of association, self-organization, and designation of representatives of their own choosing, for the purpose of negotiating the terms and conditions of their employment or other mutual aid or protection."

The policy portion of the Act was printed in full because it, along with Section 7, forms the keystone of the Act. Despite the claims of employer organizations and conservative critics, you must never forget that the public policy of the United States favors the right of union organization and the encouragement of collective bargaining. Many workers do not understand this simple truth. Organizers should deliver the message.

Some Definitions [*Section 2*]

Employer

Agents of employers are also considered employers, but government, nonprofit hospitals, and railroads are not covered.

Section 2 (2)

"The term 'employer' includes any person acting as an agent of an employer, directly or indirectly, but shall not include the United States or any wholly owned Government corporation, or any Federal Reserve Bank, or any State or political subdivision thereof, or any corporation or association operating a hospital, if no part of the net earnings inures to the benefit of any private shareholder or individual, or any person subject to the Railway Labor Act, as amended from time to time, or any labor organization (other than when acting as an employer), or anyone acting in the capacity of officer or agent of such labor organization."

Employee

People on strike or unfairly discharged are included under the term "employee." In other words, one need not be *working* for a particular boss.

Agricultural laborers, domestics, independent contractors, those employed by a parent or spouse, supervisors, and those who work for someone not included in the above definition of employer are not considered employees and are not covered by the Act.

Taken together, the definitions of "employer" and "employee" detail the statutory exclusions from the Act's coverage.

Section 2 (3)

"The term 'employee' shall include any employee, and shall not be limited to the employees of any particular employer, unless the Act explicitly states otherwise, and shall include any individual whose work has ceased as a consequence of, or in connection with, any current labor dispute or because of any unfair labor practice, and who has not obtained any other regular and substantially equivalent employment, but shall not include any individual employed as an agricultural laborer, or in the domestic service of any family or person at his home, or any individual employed by his parent or spouse, or any individual having the status of an independent contractor, or any individual employed as a supervisor, or any individual employed by an employer subject to the Railway Labor Act, as amended from time to time, or by any other person who is not an employer as herein defined."

Supervisor

Those who act for

Section 2 (11)

"The term 'supervisor' means any individual

the employer, using their own "independent judgment," in dealing with other employees, especially those who hire, fire, and handle grievances, are supervisors.

having authority, in the interest of the employer, to hire, transfer, suspend, lay off, recall, promote, discharge, assign, reward, or discipline other employees, or responsibly to direct them, or to adjust their grievances, or effectively to recommend such action, if in connection with the foregoing the exercise of such authority is not of a merely routine or clerical nature, but requires the use of independent judgment."

Professionals

Section 2 (12)

Employees whose main work is intellectual, who exercise discretion, and who usually are specially trained at professional schools, or those who train with other professionals, such as interns, are professionals. Examples are nurses, pharmacists, lawyers, doctors, graduate engineers and accountants.

"The term 'professional employee' means—

"(a) any employee engaged in work (i) predominantly intellectual and varied in character as opposed to routine mental, manual, mechanical, or physical work; (ii) involving the consistent exercise of discretion and judgment in its performance; (iii) of such a character that the output produced or the result accomplished cannot be standardized in relation to a given period of time; (iv) requiring knowledge of an advanced type in a field of science or learning customarily acquired by a prolonged course of specialized intellectual instruction and study in an institution of higher learning or a hospital, as distinguished from a general academic education or from an apprenticeship or from training in the performance of routine mental, manual, or physical processes; or

"(b) any employee, who (i) has completed the courses of specialized intellectual instruction and study described in clause (iv) of paragraph (a), and (ii) is performing related work under the supervision of a professional person to qualify himself to become a professional employee as defined in paragraph (a)."

Agent

Section 2 (13)

For one person to be the agent of another, it is not necessary

"In determining whether any person is acting as an 'agent' of another person so as to make such other person responsible for his acts, the question of whether the specific acts performed

that he receive either actual authorization for the acts he performs or approval after he performs them (ratification). This definition becomes important where illegal acts have been committed by persons employed by or related to a union or an employer and prior authorization or subsequent approval of acts cannot be shown.

were actually authorized or subsequently ratified shall not be controlling."

Labor Organization

Any kind of group of employees which does any bargaining, or has the goal of doing any bargaining, is a labor organization under this law.

Section 2 (5)

"The term 'labor organization' means any organization of any kind, or any agency or employee representation committee or plan, in which employees participate and which exists for the purpose, in whole or in part, of dealing with employers concerning grievances, labor disputes, wages, rates of pay, hours of employment, or conditions of work."

Rights of Employees [Section 7]

The key to worker rights is Section 7, which reads as follows:

Examples of Section 7 rights:
1. Helping to organize a union.
2. Striking.
3. Protesting in unison.

"Employees shall have the right to self-organization, to form, join, or assist labor organizations, to bargain collectively through representatives of their own choosing, and to engage in other concerted activities for the purpose of collective bargaining or other mutual aid or protection, and shall also have the right to refrain from any or all of such activities except

4. Joining a union.
5. Refusing to act for a union.
6. Acting together to improve working or safety conditions.

The crucial words are "concerted activities," *i.e.,* acting together, and the "right to self-organization."

to the extent that such right may be affected by an agreement requiring membership in a labor organization as a condition of employment as authorized in section 8(a)(3)."

Employer Unfair Labor Practices [Section 8(a)]

The following are employer unfair labor practices:

Examples of 8(a)(1) violations:

1. Threatening to fire for union or concerted activity.
2. Threatening to demote, reprimand, or punish in any way because of union activity.
3. Conducting widespread antiunion interrogation.
4. Threatening to move to escape the union.
5. Threatening loss of benefits if union comes in.
6. Promising benefit to employees in return for anti-

Section 8(a)(1)
". . . to interfere with, restrain, or coerce employees in the exercise of the rights guaranteed in section 7 . . ."

union activities.
7. Interfering with communication among employees or with attempts to organize by such means as unduly restrictive no - solicitation rules.
8. Spying on union meetings.
9. Granting benefits or wage increases timed to defeat union organization.

Examples of 8 (a) (2) violations:
1. The boss forming a company union to beat or keep out a real union, or to control employees.
2. Pressuring employees to join a company - preferred union.
3. Paying a company union's expenses.
4. Blatantly favoring one union over another in an organizing campaign by permitting the favored union special privileges.

Section 8(a)(2)
". . . to dominate or interfere with the formation or administration of any labor organization or contribute financial or other support to it: *Provided,* That subject to rules and regulations made and published by the Board pursuant to section 6, an employer shall not be prohibited from permitting employees to confer with him during working hours without loss of time or pay . . ."

A few examples of 8(a)(3) violations: Refusing to hire, firing, demoting, or in any way punishing an employee to "encourage or discourage" union membership.

This is the section protecting workers from discharge or other employer discrimination because of union activity.

This section also permits the union shop.

Section 8(a) (3)

". . . by discrimination in regard to hire or tenure of employment to encourage or discourage membership in any labor organization: *Provided,* That nothing in this Act, or in any other statute of the United States, shall preclude an employer from making an agreement with a labor organization (not established, maintained, or assisted by any action defined in section 8(a) of this Act as an unfair labor practice) to require as a condition of employment membership therein on or after the thirtieth day following the beginning of such employment or the effective date of such agreement, whichever is the later, (i) if such labor organization is the representative of the employees as provided in section 9(a), in the appropriate collective-bargaining unit covered by such agreement when made, and (ii) unless following an election held as provided in section 9(e) within one year preceding the effective date of such agreement, the Board shall have certified that at least a majority of the employees eligible to vote in such election have voted to rescind the authority of such labor organization to make such an agreement: *Provided further,* That no employer shall justify any discrimination against an employee for non-membership in a labor organization (A) if he has reasonable grounds for believing that such membership was not available to the employee on the same terms and conditions generally applicable to other members, or (B) if he has reasonable grounds for believing that membership was denied or terminated for reasons other than the failure of the employee to tender the periodic dues and the initiation fees uniformly required as a condition of acquiring or retaining membership . . ."

This is the section that protects those who testify or file charges at the NLRB from any punishment by the vengeful employer.

Section 8(a)(4)

". . . to discharge or otherwise discriminate against an employee because he has filed charges or given testimony under this Act . . ."

Examples of 8 (a) (5) violations:
1. Refusing to bargain with a majority union.
2. "Bad faith" bargaining, *e.g.,* going through the motions but not really desiring to reach agreement.
3. Refusing to bargain on a required (mandatory) subject.

Section 8(a)(5)
". . . to refuse to bargain collectively with the representatives of his employees, subject to the provisions of section 9(a)."

Union Unfair Labor Practices [Section 8(b)]

The following are union unfair labor practices:

Examples of 8(b)(1) (A) violations:
1. Mass picketing barring employees from entering workplace.
2. Acts of force against nonstrikers.
3. Threatening nonunion or antiunion employees.

Section 8(b)(1)
". . . to restrain or coerce (A) employees in the exercise of the rights guaranteed in section 7: *Provided,* That this paragraph shall not impair the right of a labor organization to prescribe its own rules with respect to the acquisition or retention of membership therein; or

8 (b) (1) (B) makes it unlawful for a union to refuse to bargain with a particular person or agency chosen by an employer as his representative.

(B) [to restrain or coerce] an employer in the selection of his representatives for the purpose of collective bargaining or the adjustment of grievances;"

Causing or trying to cause, an employer to fire, demote, or treat badly an employee because of lack of union membership is violative.

The single exception is that where a valid union-security provision has been negotiated (*e.g.*, a union-s h o p provision), and an employee has failed to make the payments required by t h a t provision, the union may require the employer to terminate the delinquent employee.

Section 8(b)(2)
". . . to cause or attempt to cause an employer to discriminate against an employee in violation of subsection (a) (3) or to discriminate against an employee with respect to whom membership in such organization has been denied or terminated on some ground other than his failure to tender the periodic dues and the initiation fees uniformly required as a condition of acquiring or retaining membership ..."

Insisting on illegal conditions or otherwise refusing to bargain in good faith is unfair.

Section 8(b)(3)
". . . to refuse to bargain collectively with an employer, provided it is the representative of his employees subject to the provisions of section 9(a) . . ."

The law of Section 8 (b) (4) would fill a volume, but because it is not too relevant in industrial organizing, it is very briefly summarized here. Stated simply, Section 8 (b)

Section 8(b)(4) (i)
". . . to engage in, or to induce or encourage any individual employed by any person engaged in commerce or in an industry affecting commerce to engage in, a strike or a refusal in the course of his employment to use, manufacture, process, transport, or otherwise handle or work on any goods, articles, materials, or commodities or to perform any services; or (ii) to threaten, coerce, or restrain any person engaged in commerce or in an industry affecting

(4) makes it an unfair labor practice for a union to strike, threaten to strike, or encourage others to do so, or to threaten, coerce, or restrain an employer for the following purposes:

1. To force an employer to join a union or employer organization or to enter into a "hot cargo" agreement.

2. To force one employer not to deal with another employer or to force or require *another* employer to deal with an uncertified union.

3. To force an employer to deal with one union when another union has been certified.

4. To force the assignment of work (in a jurisdictional dispute) .

But nothing in the Act makes it *illegal* for employees to observe a lawful picket line.

commerce, where in either case an object thereof is:

"(A) forcing or requiring any employer or self-employed person to join any labor or employer organization or to enter into any agreement which is prohibited by section 8(e);

" (B) forcing or requiring any person to cease using, selling, handling, transporting, or otherwise dealing in the products of any other producer, processor, or manufacturer, or to cease doing business with any other person, or forcing or requiring any other employer to recognize or bargain with a labor organization as the representative of such employees under the provisions of section 9: *Provided,* That nothing contained in this clause (B) shall be construed to make unlawful, where not otherwise unlawful, any primary strike or primary picketing;

"(C) forcing or requiring any employer to recognize or bargain with a particular labor organization as the representative of his employees if another labor organization has been certified as the representative of such employees under the provisions of section 9;

"(D) forcing or requiring any employer to assign particular work to employees in a particular labor organization or in a particular trade, craft, or class rather than to employees in another labor organization or in another trade, craft, or class, unless such employer is failing to conform to an order or certification of the Board determining the bargaining representative for employees performing such work:

"*Provided,* That nothing contained in this subsection (b) shall be construed to make unlawful a refusal by any person to enter upon the premises of any employer (other than his own employer), if the employees of such employer are engaged in a strike ratified or approved by a representative of such employees whom such employer is required to recognize under this Act: *Provided further,* That for the purposes of this paragraph (4) only, nothing contained in such paragraph shall be construed to prohibit publicity, other than picketing, for the purpose of truthfully advising the public, including consumers and members of a labor organization, that a product or products are produced by an employer with whom the labor organization has a primary dispute and are distributed by another employer, as long as such publicity does not have an effect of inducing any individual employed by any person other than the primary employer in the course of his employment to refuse to pick up, deliver, or transport any goods, or not to perform any services, at the establishment of the employer engaged in such distribution . . ."

Excessive fees and dues are prohibited.

Section 8(b)(5)

". . . to require of employees covered by an agreement authorized under subsection (a)(3) the payment, as a condition precedent to becoming a member of such organization, of a fee in an amount which the Board finds excessive or discriminatory under all the circumstances. In making such a finding, the Board shall consider, among other relevant factors, the practices and customs of labor organizations in the particular industry, and the wages currently paid to the employees affected . . ."

Featherbedding is outlawed.

Section 8(b)(6)

". . . to cause or attempt to cause an employer to pay or deliver or agree to pay or deliver any money or other thing of value, in the nature of an exaction, for services which are not performed or not to be performed; and . . ."

Recognition picketing is unlawful where:

1. Another union has recognition rights which cannot be challenged at that time (*e.g.*,

Section 8(b)(7)

". . . to picket or cause to be picketed, or threaten to picket or cause to be picketed, any employer where an object thereof is forcing or requiring an employer to recognize or bargain with a labor organization as the representative of his employees, or forcing or requiring the employees of an employer to accept or select such labor organization as their collective bargaining representative, unless such labor or-

because a contract bar exists).

2. There was a valid election in the past year.
3. No election petition is filed within a reasonable time—outer limit: 30 days.

Note that "standards" picketing and consumer boycotts are permitted, provided the picketing does not cause a stoppage of services or a refusal to pick up or deliver goods.

ganization is currently certified as the representative of such employees:

"(A) where the employer has lawfully recognized in accordance with this Act any other labor organization and a question concerning representation may not appropriately be raised under section 9 (c) of this Act,

"(B) where within the preceding twelve months a valid election under section 9 (c) of this Act has been conducted, or

"(C) where such picketing has been conducted without a petition under section 9(c) being filed within a reasonable period of time not to exceed thirty days from the commencement of such picketing: *Provided,* That when such a petition has been filed the Board shall forthwith, without regard to the provisions of section 9(c)(1) or the absence of a showing of a substantial interest on the part of the labor organization, direct an election in such unit as the Board finds to be appropriate and shall certify the results thereof: *Provided further,* That nothing in this subparagraph (C) shall be construed to prohibit any picketing or other publicity for the purpose of truthfully advising the public (including consumers) that an employer does not employ members of, or have a contract with, a labor organization, unless an effect of such picketing is to induce any individual employed by any other person in the course of his employment, not to pick up, deliver or transport any goods or not to perform any services.

"Nothing in this paragraph (7) shall be construed to permit any act which would otherwise be an unfair labor practice under this section 8 (b)."

"Free Speech" Provision [Section 8(c)]

The "free speech" provision of the Act reads as follows:

Views, arguments and opinions (free speech) that do not threaten or promise

Section 8(c)
"The expressing of any views, argument, or opinion, or the dissemination thereof, whether in written, printed, graphic, or visual form, shall not constitute or be evidence of an unfair

may not be used as evidence of *unfair labor practices.*

labor practice under any of the provisions of this Act, if such expression contains no threat of reprisal or force or promise of benefit."

Good-Faith Bargaining [Section 8(d)]

Bargaining in "good faith," which is required of both sides, is defined as follows:

8 (d) requires that bargaining be in "good faith." Here, too, are the notice requirements for striking on contract reopeners or for new contract provisions.

"For the purposes of this section, to bargain collectively is the performance of the mutual obligation of the employer and the representative of the employees to meet at reasonable times and confer in good faith with respect to wages, hours, and other terms and conditions of employment, or the negotiation of an agreement, or any question arising thereunder, and the execution of a written contract incorporating any agreement reached if requested by either party, but such obligation does not compel either party to agree to a proposal or require the making of a concession: *Provided,* That where there is in effect a collective-bargaining contract covering employees in an industry affecting commerce, the duty to bargain collectively shall also mean that no party to such contract shall terminate or modify such contract, unless the party desiring such termination or modification—

"(1) serves a written notice upon the other party to the contract of the proposed termination or modification sixty days prior to the expiration date thereof, or in the event such contract contains no expiration date, sixty days prior to the time it is proposed to make such termination or modification;

"(2) offers to meet and confer with the other party for the purpose of negotiating a new contract or a contract containing the proposed modifications;

"(3) notifies the Federal Mediation and Conciliation Service within thirty days after such notice of the existence of a dispute, and simultaneously therewith notifies any State or Territorial agency established to mediate and conciliate disputes within the State or Territory where the dispute occurred, provided no agreement has been reached by that time; and

"(4) continues in full force and effect, without resorting to strike or lockout, all the terms and conditions of the existing contract for a period of sixty days after such notice is given or until the expiration date of such contract, whichever occurs later:

"The duties imposed upon employers, employees, and labor organizations by paragraphs (2), (3), and (4) shall become inapplicable upon an intervening certification of the Board, under which the labor organization or individual, which is a party to the contract, has been superseded as or ceased to be the representative of the employees subject to the provisions of section 9(a), and the duties so imposed shall not be construed as requiring either party to discuss or agree to any modification of the terms and conditions contained in a contract for a fixed period, if such modification is to become effective before such terms and conditions can be reopened under the provisions of the contract. Any employee who engages in a strike within the sixty-day period specified in this subsection shall lose his status as an employee of the employer engaged in the particular labor dispute, for the purposes of sections 8, 9, and 10 of this Act, as amended, but such loss of status for such employee shall terminate if and when he is reemployed by such employer."

Election Provisions [Section 9]

A union chosen by a majority is entitled to exclusive recognition. A union's majority status may be proved by

Section 9(a)
"Representatives designated or selected for the purposes of collective bargaining by the majority of the employees in a unit appropriate for such purposes, shall be the exclusive representatives of all the employees in such unit for the purposes of collective bargaining in respect

an NLRB election or through other means.

Even though there is a union in a plant, an employer *may* be permitted to settle grievances brought to him directly by employees if the union is allowed to be present.

to rates of pay, wages, hours of employment, or other conditions of employment: *Provided,* That any individual employee or a group of employees shall have the right at any time to present grievances to their employer and to have such grievances adjusted, without the intervention of the bargaining representative, as long as the adjustment is not inconsistent with the terms of a collective-bargaining contract or agreement then in effect: *Provided further,* That the bargaining representative has been given opportunity to be present at such adjustment."

The Board shall decide bargaining-unit questions. However, it may not include professional and nonprofessional employees in a single unit unless the professionals vote separately for inclusion.

The Board may not refuse to carve out a craft unit *solely* on grounds of a previous unit determination unless the members of that unit vote against being represented separately.

The Board may not include plant guards in a unit with other employees, nor may it certify a union to represent plant police if that union al-

Section 9(b)

"The Board shall decide in each case whether, in order to assure to employees the fullest freedom in exercising the rights guaranteed by this Act, the unit appropriate for the purposes of collective bargaining shall be the employer unit, craft unit, plant unit, or subdivision thereof: *Provided,* That the Board shall not (1) decide that any unit is appropriate for such purposes if such unit includes both professional employees and employees who are not professional employees unless a majority of such professional employees vote for inclusion in such unit; or (2) decide that any craft unit is inappropriate for such purposes on the ground that a different unit has been established by a prior Board determination, unless a majority of the employees in the proposed craft unit vote against separate representation or (3) decide that any unit is appropriate for such purposes if it includes, together with other employees, any individual employed as a guard to enforce against employees and other persons rules to protect property of the employer or to protect the safety of persons on the employer's premises; but no labor organization shall be certified as the representative of employees in a bargaining unit of guards if such organization admits to membership, or is affiliated directly or indirectly with an organization which admits to membership, employees other than guards."

so represents other employees besides p l a n t - protection people.

On petition of a union, an employee, a group of workers, or an employer, t h e Board shall investigate representational questions and, in proper cases, direct elections.

Section 9(c)(1)

"Whenever a petition shall have been filed, in accordance with such regulations as may be prescribed by the Board—

"(A) by an employee or group of employees or any individual or labor organization acting in their behalf alleging that a substantial number of employees (i) wish to be represented for collective bargaining and that their employer declines to recognize their representative as the representative defined in section 9(a), or (ii) assert that the individual or labor organization, which has been certified or is being currently recognized by their employer as the bargaining representative, is no longer a representative as defined in section 9(a); or

An employer may petition for an election only after a demand for recognition has been made upon him by a union.

"(B) by an employer, alleging that one or more individuals or labor organizations have presented to him a claim to be recognized as the representative defined in section 9(a);

the Board shall investigate such petition and if it has reasonable cause to believe that a question of representation affecting commerce exists shall provide for an appropriate hearing upon due notice. Such hearing may be conducted by an officer or employee of the regional office, who shall not make any recommendations with respect thereto. If the Board finds upon the record of such hearing that such a question of representation exists, it shall direct an election by secret ballot and shall certify the results thereof."

Not more than one election may be held in a unit in a year.

Section 9(c)(3)

"No election shall be directed in any bargaining unit or any subdivision within which, in the preceding twelve-month period, a valid

Economic strikers may vote in elections.

Runoff elections shall be held where there is no majority on the first ballot.

election shall have been held. Employees engaged in an economic strike who are not entitled to reinstatement shall be eligible to vote under such regulations as the Board shall find are consistent with the purposes and provisions of this Act in any election conducted within twelve months after the commencement of the strike. In any election where none of the choices on the ballot receives a majority, a run-off shall be conducted, the ballot providing for a selection between the two choices receiving the largest and second largest number of valid votes cast in the election."

Parties may waive investigations and hearings and agree to NLRB elections voluntarily.

Section 9(c)(4)
"Nothing in this section shall be construed to prohibit the waiving of hearings by stipulation for the purpose of a consent election in conformity with regulations and rules of decision of the Board."

The Board may not rely *solely* on the number and kind of employees the union has "signed up" in deciding the appropriate unit.

Section 9(c) (5)
"In determining whether a unit is appropriate for the purposes specified in subsection (b) the extent to which the employees have organized shall not be controlling."

Statute of Limitations [Section 10(b)]

There is a six-month statute of limitations on unfair labor practice charges. Anything that happened more than six months before the filing of an unfair labor practice charge is insulated

"Whenever it is charged that any person has engaged in or is engaging in any such unfair labor practice, the Board, or any agent or agency designated by the Board for such purposes, shall have power to issue and cause to be served upon such person a complaint stating the charges in that respect, and containing a notice of hearing before the Board or a member thereof, or before a designated agent or agency, at a place therein fixed, not less than five days after the serving of said complaint: *Provided,* That no complaint shall

and may not be considered by the Board.

issue based upon any unfair labor practice occurring more than six months prior to the filing of the charge with the Board and the service of a copy thereof upon the person against whom such charge is made, unless the person aggrieved thereby was prevented from filing such charge by reason of service in the armed forces, in which event the six-month period shall be computed from the day of his discharge. Any such complaint may be amended by the member, agent, or agency conducting the hearing or the Board in its discretion at any time prior to the issuance of an order based thereon. The person so complained of shall have the right to file an answer to the original or amended complaint and to appear in person or otherwise and give testimony at the place and time fixed in the complaint. In the discretion of the member, agent, or agency conducting the hearing or the Board, any other person may be allowed to intervene in the said proceeding and to present testimony. Any such proceeding shall, so far as practicable, be conducted in accordance with the rules of evidence applicable in the district courts of the United States under the rules of civil procedure for the district courts of the United States, adopted by the Supreme Court of the United States pursuant to the Act of June 19, 1934 (U.S.C. title 28, secs. 723-B, 723-C)."

Injunctions Against Unfair Practices [Section 10(j)]

The Board has the *discretion* to seek injunctions against unfair labor practices in federal court, *after* it has issued its complaint.

"The Board shall have power, upon issuance of a complaint as provided in subsection (b) charging that any person has engaged in or is engaging in an unfair labor practice, to petition any district court of the United States (including the District Court of the United States for the District of Columbia), within any district wherein the unfair labor practice in question is alleged to have occurred or wherein such person resides or transacts business, for appropriate temporary relief or restraining order. Upon the filing of any such petition the court shall cause notice thereof to be served upon such person, and thereupon shall have jurisdiction to grant to the Board such temporary relief or restraining order as it deems just and proper."

Priority of Charges [Section 10(m)]

Discrimination charges are given priority.

"Whenever it is charged that any person has engaged in an unfair labor practice within the meaning of subsection (a)(3) or (b)(2) of section 8, such charge shall be given priority over all other cases except cases of like character in the office where it is filed or to which it is referred and cases given priority under subsection (1)."

No Ban on Strikes [Section 13]

The Act protects the right to strike.

"Nothing in this Act, except as specifically provided for herein, shall be construed so as either to interfere with or impede or diminish in any way the right to strike, or to affect the limitations or qualifications on that right."

Supervisors in Unions [Section 14(a)]

Supervisors may join unions, but the Act does not *require* employers to recognize unions of supervisors or bargain with a union which purports to represent them.

"Nothing herein shall prohibit any individual employed as a supervisor from becoming or remaining a member of a labor organization, but no employer subject to this Act shall be compelled to deem individuals defined herein as supervisors as employees for the purpose of any law, either national or local, relating to collective bargaining."

State Union-Security Laws [Section 14(b)]

States may forbid union-shop agreements and other union-security arrangements, despite federal law and even if both the union and the employer desire to make such agreements.

"Nothing in this Act shall be construed as authorizing the execution or application of agreements requiring membership in a labor organization as a condition of employment in any State or Territory in which such execution or application is prohibited by State or Territorial law."

Suits in Federal Courts [Section 301]

Unions and employers may sue in federal courts to enforce collective bargaining agreements.

Section 301(a)
"Suits for violation of contracts between an employer and a labor organization representing employees in an industry affecting commerce as defined in this Act, or between any such labor organizations, may be brought in any district court of the United States having jurisdiction of the parties, without respect to the amount in controversy or without regard to the citizenship of the parties."

Unions and employers are bound by acts of their agents. They may be sued in federal courts. Money judgments against unions may not, however, under any condition, be recovered from individual members.

Section 301(b)
"Any labor organization which represents employees in an industry affecting commerce as defined in this Act and any employer whose activities affect commerce as defined in this Act shall be bound by the acts of its agents. Any such labor organization may sue or be sued as an entity and in behalf of the employees whom it represents in the courts of the United States. Any money judgment against a labor organization in a district court of the United States shall be enforceable only against the organization as an entity and against its assets, and shall not be enforceable against any individual member or his assets."

Jurisdiction of the NLRB

The NLRB has the power to assert jurisdiction over activities in "interstate commerce," but it decides the standards which determine whether it will accept or decline jurisdiction over particular enterprises. Usually strictly local or very small businesses are not covered, but most medium-size and large ones are.

The Board considers the following enterprises to affect interstate commerce sufficiently for it to assert jurisdiction in cases involving them:

1. Nonretail concerns (*e.g.,* factories) where $50,000 or more worth of goods and services flow indirectly (that is, to or from other in-state employers clearly in "interstate commerce") or directly across state lines.

2. Office buildings where gross revenues total $100,000 and at least $25,000 comes from any other enterprise meeting the direct inflow and outflow standards set by the Board.

3. Retail concerns where the gross volume of annual business receipts hits $500,000.

4. Public utilities having $250,000 or more gross volume, or $50,000 outflow or inflow, direct or indirect.

5. Transit systems having $250,000 or more gross volume, except for taxicabs, for which the gross volume requirement is $500,000.

6. Newspapers having a gross volume of $200,000 or more.

7. Apartment-house projects which receive at least $500,000 in gross revenue per year.

8. Proprietary hospitals with gross revenues of $250,00 per year and proprietary nursing homes with gross revenues of $100,000 per year.

9. Any business having a substantial impact on national defense.

10. Associations (treated as single employers), if total gross business receipts of all member enterprises are large enough to meet any of the other standards.

11. Any employer whose business touches interstate commerce

in any way, and who refuses to furnish jurisdictional data to the NLRB.

In addition to the quantitative discretionary declinations of jurisdiction made according to the "yardsticks" outlined above, the Board has in the past declined certain cases because assertion of jurisdiction "would not effectuate the purposes of the Act." Perhaps the most important category excluded on this ground consists of noncommercial, nonprofit organizations. Just recently, however, the NLRB reversed itself and asserted jurisdiction over private universities. This decision may presage a general change in attitude toward nonquantitative jurisdictional declinations.

Summary of NLRB Unfair Labor Practice Procedure

Because of its direct relevance and importance to the organizer's job, representation procedure will be discussed at length in a subsequent chapter of this book. This overview of the law would not, however, be complete without a brief sketch of the more significant aspects of the Board's unfair labor practice procedures as they bear on organization.

The Charge

Any "person" can file a charge. Of course, a union, a company, or an employee can file a charge. Organizers are primarily concerned with the charge against an employer. This charge is filed on a form provided by the Board, NLRB Form 501. (See Appendix D.) A charge should be filed at the regional office of the Board serving the area in which the case arose.

The charge includes a sworn statement to the effect that its allegations are true to the best of the knowledge of the one who signs it. Willful false statements in a charge violate federal criminal law and can be punished by fines and imprisonment.

Two tips are worth bearing in mind when an organizer writes up a charge against an employer. First, it is best to file the charge in the name of the union, rather than in the names of employees who might have been treated unfairly. The reason for this is obvious. When the charge is filed in the union name, you have much greater control over it. Copies of pertinent correspondence will be sent to *you* and the Board will have to deal with *you* in any attempted settlement. Additionally, you may at some future date, for tactical reasons, want to file a "Request to Proceed" form (See Appendix, D) (in effect a promise not to try to upset an election on the basis of the charge), so you can have an election despite pending unfair labor practice charges. Of course, if the union did not file the charge, it is in no position to request the Board to proceed with the election.

A second important consideration in filling out a charge form is the technique of supplying the "basis of the charge," item 2 on the form. In most cases the basis of the charge should be stated in a general way—what some have called a "shotgun" style. This technique helps to prevent you from tipping your complete hand to the employer too early. It is not necessary to spell out the intricate details of your case, the names of witnesses and all the rest, to the employer at that early stage.

An example of a specific case helps make the point. Let's assume that an employer called seven or eight individual employees into his office and threatened each of them with discharge unless he abandoned the union; called in two others and promised them raises if they would help him fight the union; and actually fired the leader of the in-plant committee, a fellow named Joe Blow, for union activity. Assume too, that he refused your request for recognition, despite your majority status.

Here's the way you would fill out that part of the charge:

On or about June 17, the above-named employer threatened employees with discharges and reprisals for union activity.

On or about June 19, the above-named employer promised benefits to employees conditioned upon the abandonment of union activity.

On or about June 20, the above-named employer discharged Joe Blow to discourage union membership.

On or about June 20, the above-named employer refused to recognize and bargain with the union despite its majority status, its demand, and the lack of a good-faith doubt as to majority status.

By these and other acts, the above-named employer has denied the employees Section 7 rights and otherwise violated the Act.

Notice that the charge is phrased in a general, conclusory way. The only name used is that of the discharged employee.

This type of charge does not lend itself to such an easy defense as one which spells out every fine point.

An original and four copies of the charge should be filed with the regional office of the NLRB. A copy should be mailed simultaneously to the employer.

Unless there is a great emergency and speed is required, it is a good idea to have, in the organizer's possession, a written account of what happened based on statements from the employees who are witnesses to employer unfair conduct. It is best to have these statements signed but *not* notarized; *and it is unwise to mail in or hand in to the Board* these statements along with the charge. Instead, it is better to write a *summary*, in letter form, signed by the organizer or, preferably, in complicated cases, by a lawyer, covering the important points made in the employee statements. The statements are best kept in the organizer's files or those of his lawyer because if they are in the Board's files they are subject to "discovery," that is, examination by the employer during a Board hearing. Often, innocent errors of fact will show inconsistencies in two sets of statements, and might lead to impeachment (that is to having the witness discredited on the stand) or, at least, embarrassment of the witness. It is a good practice to let the Board get its own statements. Incidentally, organizers should instruct each witness to ask the Board agent for a copy of any statement he signs at the time it is taken, as this copy may be needed later.

After the charge is filed, the Board's field staff will investigate it. Try to cooperate as fully as possible with the Board agent who investigates your charge. He may request copies of papers and ask you to arrange interviews with witnesses. Help him all you can; it may pay off. If the Board determines that there is merit to the charge it will first try to obtain a settlement and, failing in that, will issue a formal complaint and set the case down for hearing. During the investigation the case may be settled, withdrawn, dismissed or otherwise handled without formal action. If the Board regional office feels the charge involves a novel issue of law, it might send the case to the NLRB General Counsel in Washington for advice as to whether to proceed. If the union is made aware of the "advice" proceeding, tell your lawyer right away. He might be able to get a hearing in

Washington. Only about one of every 200 cases filed is sent to Washington for advice.

When the NLRB regional director decides a case has no merit, he calls the charging party and, if he fails to get a withdrawal, announces a refusal to issue a complaint. There is a limited right of appeal from these refusals to the General Counsel in Washington, but it is unusual, although not unheard of, for him to reverse the regional director. In recent years only a maximum of about 6 percent of these appeals from regional directors' refusals to issue complaints have been granted by the NLRB General Counsel.

Section 10 (j) of the Act provides for a discretionary injunction against unfair labor practices at the instance of the Board's General Counsel after he has issued a complaint, but the provision is seldom used. Despite a recent increase in the number of such petitions filed, they still total only 16 for the entire United States in fiscal year 1968.

After a complaint issues, the case is tried by a trial examiner who issues a decision and recommended order. The trial examiner's decision is *always* reviewed by the Board in Washington at the instance of any party. The Board then makes a final decision and any party "aggrieved"—employer or union—may seek review in a federal court of appeals, just as the Board may petition these courts to enforce its orders. Finally, there is the rare case important enough to merit review by the Supreme Court of the United States.

Interunion Arrangements

This review must include a fast look also at internal union rules that affect organizing.

Article XX of the AFL-CIO Constitution provides a procedure for the settlement of certain jurisdictional disputes. Normally these matters are handled by the presidents of the international unions involved and their official staff members. Any organizer who encounters a problem even remotely falling within the purview of Article XX should alert his union superior so that early and proper contact can be made with the office of the international president.

Article XX reads as follows:

Settlement of Internal Disputes

Section 1.   The principles set forth in this Article shall be applicable to all affiliates of this Federation, and to their local unions and other subordinate bodies.

Section 2.   Each affiliate shall respect the established collective bargaining relationship of every other affiliate. No affiliate shall organize or attempt to represent employees as to whom an established collective bargaining relationship exists with any other affiliate. For purposes of this Article, the term, "established collective bargaining relationship" means any situation in which an affiliate, or any local or other subordinate body thereof, has either (a) been recognized by the employer (including any governmental agency) as the collective bargaining representative for the employees involved for a period of one year or more, or (b) been certified by the National Labor Relations Board or other federal or state agency as the collective bargaining representative for the employees.

Section 3.   Each affiliate shall respect the established work relationship of every other affiliate. For purposes of this Article, an "established work relationship" shall be deemed to exist as to any work of the kind which the members of an organization have customarily performed at a particular plant or work site, whether their employer is the plant operator, a contractor, or other employer. No affiliate shall by agreement or collusion with any employer or by the exercise of economic pressure seek to obtain work for its members as to which an established work relationship exists with any other affiliate, except with the consent of such affiliate. This section shall not be applicable to work in the railroad industry.

Section 4.   In the event that any affiliate believes that such special and unusual circumstances exist that it would be violative of its basic jurisdiction or contrary to basic concepts of trade union morality or to the constitutional objectives of the AFL-CIO or injurious to accepted trade union work standards to enforce the principles which would apply to the absence of such circumstances, such organization shall nevertheless observe such principles unless and until its claim is upheld in the manner prescribed in Section 17 of this Article.

Section 5.   No affiliate shall, in connection with any organizational campaign, circulate or cause to be circulated any charge or report which is designed to bring or has the effect of bringing another affiliate into public disrepute or of otherwise adversely affecting the reputation of such affiliate or the Federation.

Section 6.   Dispute settlements and determinations under this Article shall not determine the general work or trade jurisdiction of any affiliate but shall be limited to the settlement or determination of the specific dispute on the basis of the facts and considerations involved in that dispute.

Section 7.   The President shall establish procedural rules for the handling of complaints under this Article so that all affiliates involved in or affected by a dispute will have notice thereof, will have an opportunity for the voluntary settlement of the dispute, and, in the event of a failure to reach a voluntary settlement, will have a full and fair hearing before an Impartial Umpire. The rules shall be such as to insure a speedy and early disposition of all complaints arising under this Article.

Section 8.   The President shall establish a panel of mediators composed of persons from within the labor movement. The members shall serve at the pleasure of the President. Any affiliate which claims that another affiliate has violated this Article may, by its principal officer, file a complaint with the President. Upon receipt of such complaint the President shall designate a mediator or mediators, selected by him from the mediation panel, and direct that all affiliates involved or affected meet with such mediator or mediators in an effort to effect a settlement.

Section 9.   A panel of Impartial Umpires composed of prominent and respected persons shall be established. The members of the panel shall be selected by the President with the approval of the Executive Council. If voluntary settlement of a dispute is not reached within fourteen days after the appointment of a mediator or mediators, a hearing shall be held before an Impartial Umpire selected from such panel. Impartial Umpires shall be assigned on a rotating basis, subject to their availability to conduct hearings. The terms of employment of the members of the panel shall be established by the President, with the approval of the Executive Council.

Section 10.   The Impartial Umpire shall make a determination, after hearing, based upon the principles set forth in this Article. He shall make such determination within a time specified by the President, unless an extension of time is agreed to by the parties. The President shall transmit copies of the determination to all affiliates involved. He shall, at the same time, request any affiliate which the Impartial Umpire has found to be in violation of this Article to inform him as to what steps it intends to take to comply with such determination. Any response received, or the fact that no response has been received within a time fixed by the President, shall be communicated to the other parties to the dispute.

Section 11.   The President may extend any time limit if, in his judgment, such extension will more readily effectuate an early settlement or determination of a dispute. Whenever, in the judgment of the President, pressing reasons require an accelerated settlement or determination, he may shorten or eliminate the mediation process or refer the dispute directly to an Impartial Umpire.

Section 12. If no appeal is filed from a determination of the Umpire, within five days as provided below the determination shall automatically go into full force and effect. Any affiliate which is adversely affected by a determination of the Umpire, and which contends that the determination is not compatible with this Constitution, or not supported by facts, or is otherwise arbitrary or capricious, may file an appeal with the President within five days after it receives the Umpire's determination. Any such appeal shall be referred by the President to a subcommittee of the Executive Council.

Section 13. The subcommittee of the Executive Council may disallow the appeal, in which event the determination of the Umpire shall be final, and subject to no further appeal and shall go into full force and effect; or the subcommittee may refer the appeal to the Executive Council, in which event the determination of the Umpire shall be automatically stayed pending disposition of the appeal by the Executive Council. The determination of the Umpire shall be sustained unless it is set aside or altered by vote of a majority of all the members of the Executive Council. The decision of the Executive Council where an appeal is granted shall be final, and shall be effective as of the date therein specified.

Section 14. Any affected affiliate may file a complaint with the President that another affiliate has not complied with an effective determination of the Impartial Umpire or of the Executive Council on appeal. Upon receipt of such a complaint the President shall immediately convene a meeting of the subcommittee of the Executive Council referred to above. If non-compliance with the determination is found at such meeting, notice of such non-compliance shall be issued by the President to each affiliated national or international union and department.

Section 15. Immediately upon the issuance of such notification, the following shall apply:

(1) The non-complying affiliate shall not be entitled to file any complaint or appear in a complaining capacity in any proceeding under this Article until such non-compliance is remedied or excused as provided in Section 16;

(2) The Federation shall, upon request, supply every appropriate assistance and aid to any organization resisting the action determined to be in violation of this Article;

(3) The Federation shall appropriately publicize the fact that the affiliate is not in compliance with the Constitution;

(4) No affiliate shall support or render assistance to the action determined to be in violation of this Article.

In addition, the Executive Council is authorized, in its discretion, to:

(1) Deny to such an affiliate the use of any or all of the services or facilities of the Federation;

(2) Deny to such an affiliate any protection under any of the provisions or policy determinations of the Federation;

(3) Apply any other authority vested in the Executive Council under this Constitution.

Section 16.   Any affiliate which has been found to be in non-compliance and which has been deprived of its rights under this Article may apply for restoration of such rights.   Notice of such application shall be given to all of the affiliates involved in the determination or determinations as to which there is non-compliance.   If such affiliates consent, the President shall be authorized to restore the rights of the non-complying affiliate after it states its intention in writing to comply thenceforth with the provisions of this Article.   If any affiliate involved in the cases of non-compliance opposes the application, the rights of the non-complying affiliate shall be restored only under the following conditions:

(a) The non-complying affiliate states its intention, in writing, to comply thenceforth with the provisions of this Article;

(b) The non-complying affiliate has undertaken whatever measures may be necessary and practicable to remedy the situation;

(c) The application for restoration of rights is approved by two-thirds vote of the Executive Council, or by a majority of the convention.

Section 17.   Any affiliate which claims justification under Section 4, for action, which would, in the absence of such justification violate the provision of this Article, shall process its claim, prior to taking action, under the provisions of this Section.   Such claim shall set forth the basis upon which the claim is made and the action which the affiliate proposes to take.   The claim shall thereafter be processed as provided in this Article except that the determination as to whether the facts justify the proposed action shall not be made by the Impartial Umpire.   The Impartial Umpire shall determine whether the proposed action would violate the provisions of this Article in the absence of justication, shall find the facts with respect to the claim of justification, and submit a report to the Executive Council.   The Executive Council shall determine on the report of the Impartial Umpire whether the proposed action would violate the provision of this Article in the absence of justification; and, if it concludes by majority vote that the proposed action would so violate it shall find such justification only by a vote of two-thirds of the membership of the Council.

Section 18.   The President shall be authorized to delegate to such person or persons as he may designate any of his powers or functions under this Article except the authority granted by Sections 12, 14, and 16.

Section 19.   Where a dispute between affiliates subject to resolution under this Article is also covered by a written agreement between all of the affiliates involved in or affected by the dispute, the provisions of such agreement shall be complied with prior to the invocation of the procedures provided in this Article. If such agreement provides for final and binding arbitration, and an affiliate party to such agreement claims that another such affiliate has not complied with a decision under that agreement, it may file a complaint under the provisions of Section 14 of this Article and the procedures provided in this Article in the case of non-compliance shall be applicable. Where a dispute between affiliates subject to resolution under this Article is also covered by a written agreement between affiliates but involves or affects an affiliate not a party to such an agreement, the affiliate not a party to such agreement may invoke the procedures provided in this Article for the settlement and determination of such dispute.

Section 20. The provisions of this Article with respect to the settlement and determination of disputes of the nature described in this Article shall constitute the sole and exclusive method for settlement and determination of such dispute and the provisions of this Article with respect to the enforcement of such settlements and determinations shall constitute the sole and exclusive method for such enforcement. No affiliate shall resort to court or other legal proceedings to settle or determine any disputes of the nature described in this Article or to enforce any settlement or determination reached hereunder.

Section 21. The provisions of this Article shall take effect on January 1, 1962. Upon such effective date, the provisions of Article III, Section 4, of this Constitution, except the first sentence thereof, shall be of no further force and effect. However any dispute which has become subject to a formal complaint under such provision prior to January 1, 1962, shall be disposed of under the procedures and principles theretofore applicable and not under the procedures or principles set forth in this Article, except that any recommendation of the Impartial Umpire issued subsequent to January 1, 1962, shall be subject to the provisions of Sections 14 through 16 of this Article.

Section 22. Notwithstanding any other provision of this Constitution this Article shall be subject to amendment by the convention by a majority vote of those present and voting either by a show of hands, or, if a roll call is properly demanded as provided in this Constitution, by such roll call.

It should be noted that the Industrial Union Department of the AFL-CIO has a comprehensive organization-disputes agreement covering former CIO affiliates. This deals with such matters as raiding and conduct of campaigns and provides for procedures to settle these kinds of disputes. Again, these matters are handled primarily by the international offices of the unions involved.

Finally, it should be noted that individual internationals often have agreements with one another providing for cooperation and the settlement of jurisdictional or organizational disputes. Union organizers, or their supervisors, should be thoroughly familiar with such arrangements, and no organizer should forget the existence of such pacts.

Analysis of Selected Portions of the Landrum-Griffin Act

This chapter would be incomplete if we did not deal with certain portions of the Labor-Management Reporting and Disclosure Act of 1959 (Landrum-Griffin Act) which are of interest to organizers.

Right to Copies of Collective Bargaining Agreements

If there is a company union or any other kind of union in the shop, you will need to see the contract it has in order to compare benefits and to avoid "contract bar" or timing problems (to be discussed later).

Your in-plant committee can put this section to good use, because this Act *requires* the union to furnish a copy of its collective bargaining agreement to any employee who requests it.

Section 104. "It shall be the duty of the secretary or corresponding principal officer of each labor organization, to forward a copy of each collective bargaining agreement made by such labor organization with any employer to any employee who requests such a copy and whose rights as such employee are directly affected by such agreement and in the case of a labor organization, to forward a copy of any such agreement to each constituent unit which has members directly affected by such agreement; and such officer shall maintain at the principal office of the labor organization of which he is an officer copies of any such agreement made or received by such labor organization, which copies shall be available for inspection by any member or by any employee whose rights are affected by such agreement.

Reports of Employers

An employer *must report:*

1. Any payments to unions or union officials o t h e r than normal and legal payments such as checkoffs.

Section 203. "(a) Every employer who in any fiscal year made— (1) any payment or loan, direct or indirect, of money or other thing of value (including reimbursed expenses), or any promise or agreement therefor, to any labor organization or officer, agent, shop steward, or other representative of a labor organization, or employee of any labor organization, except (A) payments or loans made by any national or State bank, credit union, insurance company, savings and loan association or other credit institution and (B) payments of the kind referred to in section 302(c) of the Labor Management Act, 1947 as amended;

2. Any payments to an employee or group to cause t h e m not to choose their own union or to persuade others not to do so, unless he had told the other employees of the payment.

"(2) any payment (including reimbursed expenses) to any of his employees, or any group or committee of such employees, for the purpose of causing such employee or group or committee of employees to persuade other employees to exercise or not to exercise, or as the manner of exercising, the right to organize and bargain collectively through representatives of their own choosing unless such payments were contemporaneously or previously disclosed to such other employees;

3. Payments t h a t have as an object the commission of unfair labor practices against employees.

"(3) any expenditure, during the fiscal year, where an object thereof, directly or indirectly, is to interfere with, restrain, or coerce employees in the exercise of the right to organize and bargain collectively through representatives of their own choosing, or is to obtain information concerning the activities of employees or a labor organization in connection with a labor dispute involving such employer, except for use solely in conjunction with an administrative or arbitral proceeding or a criminal or civil judicial proceeding;

4. A d e a l with a "consultant" or an agency to keep out a union or to bust a union.

"(4) any agreement or arrangement with a labor relations consultant or other independent contractor or organization pursuant to which such person undertakes activities where an object thereof, directly or indirectly, is to persuade employees to exercise or not to exercise, or persuade employees as to the manner of exercising, the right to organize and bargain collectively through representatives of their own choosing, or undertakes to supply such employer with information concerning the activities of employees or a labor organization in connection with a labor dispute involving such employer, except information for use solely in conjunction with an administrative or arbitral proceeding or a criminal or civil judicial proceeding; or

5. Any payments to such consultants or agencies.

" (5) any payment (including reimbursed expenses) pursuant to an agreement or arrangement described in subdivision (4) ; signed by its president and treasurer or corresponding principal officers showing in detail the date and amount of each such payment, loan, promise, agreement, or arrangement and the name, address, and position, if any, in any firm or labor organization of the person to whom it was made and a full explanation of the circumstances of all such payments, including the terms of any agreement or understanding pursuant to which they were made.

Persons who receive employer payments shall also file reports.

"(b) Every person who pursuant to any agreement or arrangement with an employer undertakes activities where an object thereof is, directly or indirectly—

(1) to persuade employees to exercise or not to exercise, or persuade employees as to the manner of exercising, the right to organize and bargain collectively through representatives of their own choosing, or

(2) to supply an employer with information concerning the activities of employees or a labor organization in connection with a labor dispute involving such employer, except information for use solely in conjunction with an administrative or arbitral proceeding or a criminal or civil judicial proceeding;

shall file within thirty days after entering into such agreement or arrangement a report with the Secretary, signed by its president and treasurer or corresponding principal officers, containing the name under which such person is engaged in doing business and address of its principal office, and a detailed statement of the terms and conditions of such agreement or arrangement. Every such person shall file annually, with respect to each fiscal year during which payments were made as a result of such an agreement or arrangement, a report with the Secretary, signed by its president and treasurer or corresponding principal officers, containing a statement (A) of its receipts of any kind from employers on account of labor relations advice or services, designating the sources thereof, and (B) of its disbursements of any kind, in connection with such services and the purposes thereof. In each case such information shall be set forth in such categories as the Secretary may prescribe.

Bona fide persons hired by employers to help in legal, arbitration, or administrative cases or in collective bargaining are excepted from the reporting requirements.

"(c) Nothing in this section shall be construed to require any employer or other person to file a report covering the services of such person by reason of his giving or agreeing to give advice to such employer or representing or agreeing to represent such employer before any court, administrative agency, or tribunal of arbitration or engaging or agreeing to engage in collective bargaining on behalf of such employer with respect to wages, hours, or other terms or conditions of employment or the negotiation of an agreement or any question arising thereunder.

Reports need only be filed where such arrangements and payments were made; that is, if no such payments were made it is not necessary to file reports saying that.

"(d) Nothing contained in this section shall be construed to require an employer to file a report under subsection (a) unless he has made an expenditure, payment, loan, agreement or arrangement of the kind described therein. Nothing contained in this section shall be construed to require any other person to file a report under subsection (b) unless he was a party to an agreement or arrangement of the kind described therein.

Regular compensation to managers and supervisors need not be reported.

"(e) Nothing contained in this section shall be construed to require any regular officer, supervisor, or employee of an employer to file a report in connection with services rendered to such employer nor shall any employer be required to file a report covering expenditures made to any regular officer, supervisor, or employee of the employer as compensation for services as a regular officer, supervisor, or employee of such employer."

Attorney-Client Communications Exempted

In a *true* lawyer-client relationship, where the lawyer acts as a professional and not a union buster, no reports need be filed. Sometimes there is a fine line between these two lawyer roles in labor law.

Section 204. "Nothing contained in this Act shall be construed to require an attorney who is a member in good standing of the bar of any State, to include in any report required to be filed pursuant to the provisions of this Act any information which was lawfully communicated to such attorney by any of his clients in the course of a legitimate attorney-client relationship."

Reports Made Public Information

All of these reports are public; you can inspect copies of them free, and you may purchase copies. This opportunity could be of great value in an organizational campaign. Where illegal payments to employees or agents of an employer are suspected, organizers would be well advised to have the union's research department or other administrative arm check with the Labor Department.

Section 205. "(a) The contents of the reports and documents filed with the Secretary pursuant to sections 201, 202, 203, and 211 shall be public information, and the Secretary may publish any information and data which he obtains pursuant to the provisions of this title. The Secretary may use the information and data for statistical and research purposes, and compile and publish such studies, analyses, reports, and surveys based thereon as he may deem appropriate.

"(b) The Secretary shall by regulation make reasonable provision for the inspection and examination, on the request of any person, of the information and data contained in any report or other document filed with him pursuant to section 201, 202, 203, or 211.

" (c) The Secretary shall by regulation provide for the furnishing by the Department of Labor of copies of reports or other documents filed with the Secretary pursuant to this title, upon payment of a charge based upon the cost of service. The Secretary shall make available without payment of a charge, or require any person to furnish, to such State agency as is designated by law or by the Governor of the State in which such person has his principal place of business or headquarters, upon request of the Governor of such State, copies of any reports and documents filed by such person with the Secretary pursuant to section 201, 202, 203, or 211, or of information and data contained therein. No person shall be required by reason of any law of any State to furnish to any officer or agency of such State any information included in a report filed by such person with the Secretary pursuant to the provisions of this title, if a copy of such report, or of the portion thereof containing such information. is furnished to such officer or agency. All moneys received in payment of such charges fixed by the Secretary pursuant to this subsection shall be deposited in the general fund of the Treasury."

Investigations

The Secretary of Labor has wide investigatory powers.

Section 601. "(a) The Secretary shall have power when he believes it necessary in order to determine whether any person has violated or is about to violate any provision of this Act (except title I or amendments made by this Act to other statutes) to make an investigation and in connection therewith he may enter such places and inspect such records and accounts and question such persons as he may deem necessary to enable him to determine the facts relative thereto. The Secretary may report to interested persons or officials concerning the reasons for failure or refusal to file such a report or any other matter which he deems to be appropriate as a result of such an investigation.

"(b) For the purpose of any investigation provided for in this Act, the provisions of sections 9 and 10 (relating to the attendance of witnesses and the production of books, papers, and documents) of the Federal Trade Commission Act of September 16, 1914, as amended (15 U.S.C. 49, 50), are hereby made

applicable to the jurisdiction, powers, and
duties of the Secretary of any officers designated by him."

Welfare and Pension Plans Disclosure Act

A brief mention of the Welfare and Pension Plans Disclosure
Act will complete the survey of the statutory law affecting
organizing.

This Act, while not directly relevant to organizing, is a useful
tool in certain situations. The Act requires, among other things,
the filing of detailed information with respect to health and
welfare, insurance, accident, disability, retirement, and death
benefit plans. This filing, with the Department of Labor, is
required of all such plans—whether unilateral employer plans
or negotiated plans. Furthermore, under this law, copies of the
description of the plan and the latest annual report must be
made available to any covered employee.

The obvious value of this Act to organizers is that it furnishes a vehicle for obtaining detailed information with respect
to the benefit plans provided by a particular employer. An
analysis of a nonunion benefit plan can furnish organizers with
valuable economic ammunition in an organizing campaign.

Finally, a number of states have similar laws governing benefit
plans and filings are often public records available to organizers
for comparison or any other purposes.

CHAPTER II

GROUND RULES FOR ORGANIZERS

Substantive rights and duties in the
field of labor-management do not depend on verbal ritual reminiscent of
real property law.

Mr. Justice Jackson in
NLRB v. *Rockaway News,*
345 US 71, 74 (1953)

Introduction

Nine times out of 10, the organizing campaign at a nonunion
shop begins in one of two ways. Either a worker in the shop contacts the union and asks for help; or the organizer finds out about
the shop and gets in touch with the workers through either
handbilling or personal contact. In any event, the first problem
is the establishment of a two-way communication system so that
the unorganized workers can enlighten the union as to the problems in the particular shop and so that the union can give the
necessary organizational know-how to the workers.

The next step is to use those lines by beginning the process
of education. The organizer must educate himself to the shop
problems, and then he must educate the workers by showing
them how and why the union can help. The purpose of everything that has taken place up to this point is to convince unorganized workers to "join" the union and to get the shop organized. These two objectives necessarily involve contacting the
employees, "signing them up," and, perhaps, contacting the employer. This chapter deals with the initial stages of the organizing campaign—what can and should be done and what to watch

41

out for *before* a demand for recognition is made or a representation petition is filed with the NLRB.

This chapter deals primarily with the proscriptions by way of unfair labor practices, on employers and unions, in the early stages of the campaign. It should be kept in mind, however, that most unfair labor practice conduct will also constitute adequate ground for objection to an election—even though the reverse is often not true.

Later, in Chapter IX, we discuss in more detail the Board's rules covering employer and union conduct as it may affect elections.

Local and State Laws

Local ordinances and state laws that prohibit organizing unless permits or licenses are obtained are unconstitutional because they constitute prior restraints on free speech,[1] and because of the supremacy of federal law—called preemption.[2]

Nevertheless, organizers frequently encounter such statutes and ordinances, particularly in the South. Inasmuch as time is often of the essence in organizing campaigns, it is sometimes decided, as a practical matter, to get the license where the fees are nominal, rather than to fight the offensive law through the courts.[3]

There is no real question of the right to organize in any community. This chapter will begin the discussion of how the right may be exercised.

Distribution and Solicitation—In General

The Labor Board has different rules covering the *distribution* of literature and the *solicitation* of membership or authorization cards. Moreover, there is one set of rules for employee organizers and another for nonemployee or professional organizers.

---

[1] Thomas v. Collins, 323 US 516 (1945), 15 LRRM 777; Staub v. Baxley, 355 US 313 (1958), 41 LRRM 2307.
[2] Hill v. Florida, 325 US 538 (1945), 16 LRRM 734.
[3] *See Steelworkers* v. *Bagwell*, 383 F.2d 492 (CA 4, 1967), 66 LRRM 2257, for an example of a case where offensive ordinances were successfully attacked through the courts.

It is important to understand the distinction between distribution and solicitation. "Distribution of literature" is best exemplified by the wholesale handing out of leaflets. Handbilling is a classic example of the distribution of literature. Distribution may be done in person or by mail, and it may or may not be accompanied by conversation. "Solicitation," on the other hand, is defined as "the practice, act, or instance of approaching with a request, a plea, or strongly urging another to take certain action and of trying to obtain a result by asking." In simpler, understandable terms, solicitation occurs when one person asks another to do something. One can be "solicited" entirely orally, entirely in writing, or by a combination of both. In union organizing, typically, workers are "solicited" to sign authorization cards, which entitle the union to represent them, or membership cards to join the union. The difference really is that distribution is primarily informative, whereas solicitation seeks specific action by a specific person.

For our purposes, the handing out of a union newspaper, handbill, or leaflet should be considered to be "distribution of literature," but the handing out of union cards for signature (with or without conversation) is "solicitation."

Distribution and Solicitation by Outside Organizers

Of course, professional organizers are free to hand out literature and to solicit workers on public property. Subject, naturally, to the requirements of local authorities to keep the traffic conditions safe and to avoid litter, the nonemployee organizer may hand out leaflets at plant gates, on public sidewalks, and at driveways. The First Amendment to the United States Constitution, guaranteeing free speech, protects the organizer's rights to disseminate information about the union.

When it comes to union activity on the employer's private property, however, the Supreme Court has, up to now, taken a narrow view of the rights of nonemployee organizers and a correspondingly broad view of the property rights of employers. The Court held in *NLRB* v. *Babcock & Wilcox Co.*,[4] that the employer lawfully could refuse the use of his property to nonemployee organizers for the distribution of literature, if the union

---

[4] 351 US 105 (1956), 38 LRRM 2001.

had open to it "other channels of communications" through which it could get its message to the employees and if the employer did not discriminate against the union by allowing distribution of *other* types of literature. So far most of the cases in which the Board has found "other channels of communications" closed to unions have been live-in employment situations such as lumber camps, resorts and ships, or company towns where the whole community is the property of the employer.[5] In a non-live-in situation, a showing that union access to employees is impossible because of such factors as location of the plant, the fact that employees' residences are scattered over a large area, and the unavailability of a single medium (*e.g.*, a newspaper or a radio or television station) through which all of the employees can be reached may result in the invalidation of a company's bar on solicitation and distribution by nonemployees on company property.[6]

Where an employer's private property has been so dedicated to public use that it has lost its private-property characteristics—as, for example, in the case of a shopping center—the constitutional free-speech right of the organizers has been held to take precedence over any private-property rights.[7]

If a professional organizer hands out union literature on the ordinary employer's property over the employer's objection, in the absence of the exceptional circumstances mentioned above, he does so without the protection of the Labor Act. The employer does not violate the law by posting his property. He is permitted to call the police to cause an arrest for trespassing, and finally he can, by self-help, use reasonable means to eject the organizer from the property. There is, however, no section of the Taft-Hartley Act available to the employer in this situation.

These are stiff rules and they make it pretty difficult for union organizers to communicate their message to the unorganized. But most union organizers have lived under these conditions long enough to have adjusted to them. The professional, therefore, makes contact as quickly as possible with the workers in the plant, for, as every experienced organizer

---

[5] *See, e.g.*, Interlake Steamship Co., 174 NLRB No. 55 (1969), 70 LRRM 1177.

[6] Solo Cup Co., 172 NLRB No. 110 (1968), 68 LRRM 1385.

[7] Food Employees, Local 590 v. Logan Valley Plaza, Inc., 391 US 308 (1968), 68 LRRM 2209.

knows, the rules are different for in-plant, employee organizers. While an employer, in the ordinary case, may bar outsiders from any distribution or solicitation on his property, he may not impose such a sweeping ban on his own employees.

A final word needs to be said about company prohibitions against nonemployee solicitation on company property. If an employer permits nonemployees other than union organizers to solicit his employees on company property without interference, he may not bar professional organizers from soliciting membership on his premises. In *Priced-Less Discount Foods, Inc.,*[8] the Board held that a company that permitted other solicitation but barred outside union solicitation on its parking lot was guilty of interference in violation of Section 8 (a) (l). The Board also held that the company committed a further violation of the law by having the union representative arrested.

Distribution and Solicitation by Employees

When employees of a particular employer are assisting unions to organize, they are much better protected than professional organizers. The Supreme Court has said: "No restrictions may be placed on the employees' right to discuss self-organization among themselves, unless the employer can demonstrate that such a restriction is necessary to maintain production or discipline." [9]

An elaborate set of *general* rules has been worked out by the Labor Board on the subject of employee distribution and solicitation. We emphasize *general* rules because these rules apply only where there is no discrimination, favoritism, or other special circumstances. In the unusual case, the facts become most important.

The General rules governing employee distribution and solicitation:

1. A company rule that prohibits employees from distributing union literature in *nonwork* areas on the employees' own time is "interference" with employee rights and violates Section 8 (a)

---

[8] 162 NLRB 872 (1967), 64 LRRM 1065.
[9] NLRB v. Babcock & Wilcox Co., above, note 4.

(1) of the Act, in the absence of special circumstances making the rule necessary to maintain discipline or production.[10]

2. A company rule prohibiting the distribution of union literature in *working areas*, even on free time, is presumed valid by the Board and does not violate Section 8 (a) (1), unless, of course, it is discriminatorily enforced.

3. An employer can ban both distribution and solicitation anywhere in the plant *on working time.*

4. An employer may not ban union solicitation, even in work areas, during the employees' *free time.*

5. The handing out, with or without conversation, of authorization or membership cards is *solicitation,* not distribution, and cannot be prohibited anywhere in the plant during nonworking time, in the absence of unusual circumstances. [11]

6. A company rule which is vague or ambiguous, so that the average employee might have a difficult time knowing when and where he is allowed to engage in solicitation and distribution, is invalid even if it is susceptible of a valid interpretation. [12]

7. A valid company rule limiting distribution and solicitation may not be discriminatorily enforced—for example, enforced against employees favoring the union and not against those opposing the union. [13]

8. Workers entering or returning to the plant area during their nonworking time are governed by the rules for employees and not those for outside organizers.[14]

Employers' unlawful bars against proper distribution and solicitation by employees not only amount to unfair labor practices; they are good grounds for setting aside a representation election if the union loses. A more thorough discussion of election

---

[10] Stoddard-Quirk Mfg. Co., 138 NLRB 615 (1962), 51 LRRM 1110; Gale Products Corp., 142 NLRB 1246 (1963), 53 LRRM 1242; Rose Co., 154 NLRB 228 (1965), 59 LRRM 1738; Republic Aluminum Co. v. NLRB, 394 F.2d 405 (CA 5, 1968), 68 LRRM 2090.

[11] Gale Products Corp., above, note 10, NLRB General Counsel's Quarterly Report, July 28, 1966.

[12] *See, e.g.,* Fasco Industries, Inc. v. NLRB, 412 F.2d 589 (CA 4, 1969), 71 LRRM 2894.

[13] *See, e.g.,* Shepherd Laundries Co., 176 NLRB No. 113 (1969), 71 LRRM 1366.

[14] Diamond Shamrock Co., 181 NLRB No. 43 (1970), 73 LRRM 1348.

conduct and of other typical employer unfair practices will follow later.

Sometimes an organizing union is confronted with a contract between an incumbent union and an employer containing a broad ban on distribution and solicitation. The Board has taken the position that such a ban is unlawful if it is more stringent than that allowed by the general rules outlined above, but the courts of appeals have split on the issue.[15] The final determination of this question will probably have to await Supreme Court action.

A few examples will help round out the picture. Regardless of plant rules, a supervisor may not order employees not to solicit for a union on their own time.[16] Employees may wear union buttons or union T-shirts. But outsize buttons or flashy jewelry, shirts, or insignia present a somewhat different case; the Board has held, on occasion, that such distractions might adversely affect production or discipline or safety.[17]

Organizational Literature

Many union organizing campaigns have involved substantial amounts of harsh language, invective, charges, and counter-charges. Whether this kind of talk really convinces anyone is another question. However, because of some of the legal consequences of the use of certain rough language in campaign literature, it is necessary to discuss, at least briefly, the content of union organizing literature. A fuller discussion of various aspects of election propaganda will be found in Chapter IX.

The Labor Act, of course, bans union restraint and coercion. It hardly needs saying that it is considered a violation of the Act's Section 8 (b) (1) (A) to say orally or in a leaflet that "those who don't join the union will eventually lose their jobs." [18]

Then there is the problem of attacks on the employer and his

---

[15] *Compare* NLRB v. Gale Products, 337 F.2d 390 (CA 7, 1964), 57 LRRM 2164 and General Motors Corp. v. NLRB, 345 F.2d 516 (CA 6, 1965), 59 LRRM 2080 with Steelworkers v. NLRB, 377 F.2d 140 (CA DC, 1966), 64 LRRM 2009 and NLRB v. Mid-States Metal Products, Inc. (Chemical Workers, Local 738), 403 F.2d 702 (CA 5, 1968), 69 LRRM 2656.

[16] NLRB v. Dixie Shirt Co., 176 F.2d 969 (CA 4, 1949), 24 LRRM 2561.

[17] Republic Aviation v. NLRB, 324 US 793 (1945), 16 LRRM 620; Standard Oil Co., California, 168 NLRB No. 28 (1967), 66 LRRM 1276.

[18] Seamprufe, Inc., 82 NLRB 892 (1949), 23 LRRM 1646.

agents. At one end of the spectrum is the case of the employer who really tries to censor union literature and employee conversation. Obviously, an employer may not insulate himself from criticism. One employer went too far, for instance, when he established a rule specifying discharge as the penalty for "criticizing company rules and policies so as to cause confusion or resentment between employees and management." That broad rule inhibited union organizing by violating Section 8 (a) (1), said the NLRB, and the Court agreed.[19] But an employer who had, in the past, permitted the distribution of union literature did not commit an unfair labor practice when he stepped in to forbid the distribution of plainly libelous and scurrilous leaflets. [20] And another employer was upheld by a circuit court when he discharged an employee who likened him to Fidel Castro.[21]

A union unfair labor practice can be troublesome—it may embarrass the union, set back an organizing campaign, or even cause a union-won election to be set aside. Even more dangerous than any possible or probable violations of the Act, however, are the possible financial consequences of disseminating written or printed material that might be held libelous, or of uttering defamatory statements. The Supreme Court in *Linn* v. *United Plant Guards*,[22] held that where either party to a labor dispute maliciously circulates false statements injuring a complainant, the federal Labor Act does not preempt the jurisdiction of the state courts in damage suits for defamation.

The alleged libel of a Pinkerton manager in *Linn* occurred in the context of a union organizing campaign, and the union contended that the Labor Act superseded state law with respect to defamatory statements published during labor disputes. The U.S. Court of Appeals at Cincinnati had, reluctantly, agreed, but was overruled by the Supreme Court.

Previously, the Supreme Court had held consistently that labor disputes were governed exclusively by federal labor law except where violence and intimidation were involved. But under this decision, where false statements are made with malice—that is,

---

[19] NLRB v. Lexington Chair Co., 361 F.2d 283 (CA 4, 1966), 62 LRRM 2273.
[20] Maryland Drydock Co. v. NLRB, 183 F.2d 538 (CA 4, 1950), 26 LRRM 2450.
[21] Boaz Spinning Co. v. NLRB, 395 F.2d 512 (CA 5, 1968), 68 LRRM 2393.
[22] 383 US 53 (1966), 61 LRRM 2345.

with knowledge that they are false or with reckless disregard of whether they are true or false—and the person about whom the statements are made is injured by them, there can be a recovery of damages in the state courts. Injury is often not difficult to prove, so that, for all intents and purposes, the only requirement is that of "malice"—a loose standard indeed for potentially hostile juries.

Among the injuries for which the Court holds that state courts may compensate the victims of labor-dispute defamations are "general injury to reputation, consequent mental suffering, alienation of associates, specific items of pecuniary loss or whatever form of harm would be recognized by state court law." Punitive damages may also be recovered.

The government had urged the Court to confine liability to "grave defamations," such as accusations of criminal, homosexual, treasonable, or other infamous acts. But the Court refused to limit liability to these more flagrant kinds of defamation. Plainly, false accusations such as the above are actionable. So too, under some circumstances, might be the calling of names such as liar, cheat, and thief.

Even "truthful" derogatory charges about an employer representative are hazardous, for the obvious reason that it is not always easy to prove that a statement is true. A good, safe rule for organizers would be to make oral and written statements *positive* and *affirmative* rather than *negative* and *abusive*. If it becomes "necessary" to attack an employer, the organizer or representative should have *positive proof of the derogatory matter before using it*. All documents establishing conclusive proof of statements made should be retained in case they are needed later.

One does not have to be *named* to be the object of defamation. In the *Linn* case, the defamatory matter, for instance, referred to "managers" and Linn, an assistant general manager, filed the suit.

Special care should be exercised in the preparation of written matter and, particularly, in connection with mailings to employees on lists supplied by an employer under the auspices of the NLRB.

We have discussed libel thus far, but it should be remembered that both libel and slander are actionable in the courts under the reasoning of the *Linn* case. A good organizer is as careful of what he says as of what he writes. Libel is usually printed or written, but it includes all defamation in permanent form— cartoons, paintings, effigies, and the like. Slander is oral. The courts have said that defamation consists of the communication by one person to another of matter which causes a third person to be regarded with hatred, contempt, or ridicule, or tends to injure him in his business or profession.

There is *no* reason for an experienced organizer, or any other mature person, to libel or slander another person.

Authorization Cards

Early in the campaign the organizer begins to "sign up" the workers. Some unions use membership cards, but most seek authorization cards.

An "authorization" card is one that signifies the desire of a worker to be represented by a union in collective bargaining. The signer authorizes the union to represent him with his employer. The card may be used as proof of majority representation and, therefore, as a predicate to a demand for recognition from an employer or as evidence of the necessary showing of interest (30 percent) in an appropriate unit to support a representation petition at the NLRB.

A "membership" card used in organizing is actually an application for membership in the union. Such a card also usually carries with it an authorization to the union to represent the signer.

Finally, some unions use "check-off" cards, which actually combine representational authority and membership application while at the same time authorizing the employer to deduct union dues from wages. We are concerned here primarily with "authorization" cards.

There are two principal types of authorization cards. A "pure" authorization card states that the signer has designated the union as his exclusive collective-bargaining representative. A "dual purpose" card authorizes exclusive union representation and also includes a statement to the effect that the card may be used to demand recognition or to obtain an NLRB election. At present, the NLRB will accept dual-purpose cards to determine majority status of a union, but the courts of appeals are split on the issue. One court has said that such cards are "ambiguous" in that they mention elections and should, therefore, be confined to use in establishing a showing of interest to get an election.[23] But other courts have agreed with the NLRB that such cards may be counted to establish a union majority.[24] The Supreme Court has so far reserved judgment on dual-purpose card issues.

The solicitation of authorization cards is a crucial part of almost every organizing campaign. Great care must be exercised in the acquisition of these cards. For instance, a letter stating that cards will be used only for an election will render those cards ineffective for determining majority status.[25] And so will a legend printed on the cards stating, "THIS DOES NOT OBLIGATE ME IN ANY WAY."[26]

The methods of obtaining recognition based on a card majority are discussed in Chapter V; but some of the legal considerations with respect to cards can be usefully sketched in here. Of course, the first legal consequence of a union's possession of a card majority is that the union, at that point, legally may demand recognition from the employer.

One important holding in the Supreme Court's recent *Gissel* decision[27] was that an employer who refuses to recognize a union which presents him with a majority of cards (and which actually has a majority at the time of the presentation and demand for recognition) and who commits independent and substantial unfair labor practices that interfere with the election processes and tend to preclude the holding of a fair election, will be or-

---

[23] NLRB v. Peterson Bros., Inc., 342 F.2d 221 (CA 5, 1965), 58 LRRM 2570.
[24] UAW v. NLRB (Aero Corp.), 363 F.2d 702 (CA DC, 1966), 62 LRRM 2361, cert. denied 385 US 973 (1966), 63 LRRM 2527; IUE v. NLRB, 352 F.2d 361 (CA DC, 1965), 59 LRRM 2232, cert. denied 382 US 902 (1965), 60 LRRM 2353; NLRB v. C.J. Glasgow Co., 356 F.2d 476 (CA 7, 1966), 61 LRRM 2406; Bauer Welding and Metal Fabricators v. NLRB, 358 F.2d 766 (CA 8, 1966), 62 LRRM 2022.
[25] Cumberland Shoe Corp., 144 NLRB 1268 (1964), 54 LRRM 1233, affirmed 351 F.2d 917 (CA 6, 1965), 60 LRRM 2305; Levi Strauss and Co., 172 NLRB No. 57 (1968), 68 LRRM 1338. The Board's *Cumberland Shoe* standards for determining when employees have been misled as to the intended use of cards was approved by the Court in *NLRB* v. *Gissel Packing Company, Inc.,* 395 US 575 (1969), 71 LRRM 2481. *See also* John S. Barnes, 180 NLRB No. 139 (1970) , 73 LRRM 1215.
[26] Silver Fleet, Inc., 174 NLRB No. 141 (1969), 70 LRRM 1316.
[27] NLRB v. Gissel Packing Co., 395 US 575 (1969), 71 LRRM 2481.

dered to recognize and bargain with the union, either without an election being held or after the union has lost an election.

Under the Board's *Bernel Foam* doctrine,[28] a bargaining order may be obtained even after a union has lost an election if both unfair labor practice charges and objections to the election are filed and if the unfair labor practices were of sufficient magnitude to have destroyed the union's majority and their continuing effect is likely to interfere with the holding of a rerun election.

Another rule is that even where there is no request for recognition and no formal refusal to bargain, a union with majority support may in a proper case of massive interference [8 (a) (1)] or discrimination [8 (a) (3)] win a bargaining order as a remedy for sweeping employer unfair labor practices which have cost the union most or many of its supporters.[29]

Interest Showing

The showing-of-interest requirement in election cases should be met by a petitioning union when a petition is filed, but in cases where timing of the petition is at issue, the Board will allow an interest showing to be made within 48 hours after a petition is filed.

The following are the Board's interest-showing requirements:

1. A petitioning union needs 30 percent of the eligible employees in the unit. In strikes, 30 percent of the normal complement of employees will suffice. The showing may be made among strikers, nonstrikers, replacements, or any combination of these groups.

2. Where a union has petitioned and another union wishes to intervene and to urge a *different* unit, the second union must have 30 percent in the unit it seeks.

3. Where a union petitions and another union wishes to inter-

---

[28] Bernel Foam Products Co., Inc., 146 NLRB 1277 (1964), 56 LRRM 1039.

[29] D. H. Holmes v. NLRB, 179 F.2d 876 (CA 5, 1950), 25 LRRM 2408; NLRB v. Caldarera, 209 F.2d 265 (CA 8, 1954), 33 LRRM 2492; Northwest Engineering Co., 148 NLRB 1136 (1964), 57 LRRM 1116, affirmed 376 F.2d 770 (CA DC, 1967), 64 LRRM 2650.

vene in the *same* unit to the extent of blocking a consent-election agreement, it must have a 10 percent showing.

4. A showing of only one or two cards will normally suffice to permit a second union to intervene only to the extent of appearing on a ballot and participating in a hearing.

5. A current or recently expired contract will always provide a sufficient showing for a union fully to participate in an election case.

The determination of whether a petitioning union has made an adequate interest showing is purely an administrative matter for the Board. The employer has no *right* to litigate this subject, so that if such a question is raised at a hearing, the Board will investigate on its own but will not interrupt the hearing. Cards used to show interest are presumed valid and the Board ordinarily will not question them unless they appear faulty on their face or there is a specific allegation or evidence of fraud. Fraud, such as forgery of signatures on cards is a very serious matter, a felony punishable by imprisonment and fine.

General Rules in Soliciting Authorization Cards

Some general observations will help to place the handling of cards in perspective.

Whether cards are used to prove a majority or an interest showing, the Board has these rules:

1. If cards are used to prove a majority, they must be introduced into evidence at a public hearing. Such cards should never be considered "confidential." Cards can be termed confidential only if a union determines, early in the game, that under no circumstances will it use the cards for anything but an interest showing. Even in this instance, there is at least a public-relations risk in labeling cards "confidential," because a wily employer can point to literally strings of case citations where cards were introduced into evidence as public records. It is difficult to explain to workers that where the union makes a firm decision, it can control confidentiality. Nevertheless, some unions, particularly those organizing white-collar, technical and professional employees, never seek recognition except via an NLRB election. They never demand card checks or employer recognition with-

out certification. Cards obtained by these unions may be kept confidential, although there remains the difficulty of explaining the different effect of the union's tactical decision. One court has held that an employer lawfully may rebut a union's claim of confidentiality of authorization cards.[30]

2. The cards must be fresh or timely. There is no hard and fast rule as to weeks or months, but obviously, cards must have been obtained in a current campaign. The best proof of timeliness is, of course, a date, preferably in the handwriting of the card signer. Cards more than a year old generally are not counted,[31] but there are exceptions.[32]

3. The signature should be legibly written, not printed.

4. It might be necessary to prove in an unfair labor practice case that the signature is authentic. Precautions taken in securing signatures may prove helpful later.

When organizers personally sign up people they should, whenever possible, ask the signer to date the card. An organizer should initial each card he actually sees signed, so that if the signator is unavailable he can testify that he saw it signed. When cards are mailed in, they should be stapled to the postmarked envelopes and initialed by the person opening the envelopes. In-plant committeemen should be instructed carefully as to dates and asked to initial cards they see signed.

The words used by the solicitor to obtain a card are important. Regardless of the printed language of the card, if the organizer says that the card will be used *only* to secure an election, the card will not be counted by the NLRB for majority purposes. Of course, if employees are promised benefits, such as reduced dues, for signing a card or are threatened with increased dues or loss of work if they don't sign, the cards might well be held to have been obtained under duress and therefore to have no legal significance.

The UAW has issued to all of its organizers a "policy on organization." It reads as follows:

---

[30] NLRB v. Hobart Bros. Co., 372 F.2d 203 (CA 6, 1967), 64 LRRM 2289.
[31] Grand Union Co., 122 NLRB 589 (1958), 43 LRRM 1165.
[32] Blade Tribune Publ. Co., 161 NLRB 1512 (1966), 63 LRRM 1484.

UAW POLICY ON ORGANIZATION

The National Labor Relations Act gives employees the right to organize into a union of their own choosing and makes it an unfair labor practice for the employer to refuse to bargain with such union.

Over the years we have gotten into the habit of petitioning the National Labor Relations Board for an election as a means of proving that we represent a majority of the employees. The holding of an election is one procedure which may be used to prove a majority status, however, it is not a requirement of the Act.

Pertinent sections of the National Labor Relations Act are as follows:

"Sec. 7. Employees shall have the right to self-organization, to form, join, or assist labor organizations, to bargain collectively through representatives of their own choosing, and to engage in other concerted activities for the purpose of collective bargaining or other mutual aid or protection . . .

"Sec. 8. (a) It shall be an unfair labor practice for an employer—
"(1) to interfere with, restrain, or coerce employees in the exercise of the rights guaranteed in Section 7;

"(2) to dominate or interfere with the formation or administration of any labor organization or contribute financial or other support to it;

"(3) by discrimination in regard to hire or tenure of employment or any term or condition of employment to encourage or discourage membership in any labor organization;

"(4) to discharge or otherwise discriminate against an employee because he has filed charges or given testimony under this Act;

"(5) to refuse to bargain collectively with the representatives of his employees, subject to the provisions of section 9 (a).

"Sec. 9 (a) Representatives designated or selected for the purposes of collective bargaining by the majority of the employees in a unit appropriate for such purposes, shall be the exclusive representatives of all the employees in such unit for the purposes of collective bargaining in respect to rates of pay, wages, hours of employment, or other conditions of employment."

The Act then proceeds to outline procedure to be followed "wherever a petition shall have been filed." However, it does not require the filing or processing of a petition.

As you know, the UAW has the *policy of seeking recognition when we have obtained a majority of authorization cards.* It is important that we make this policy clear to employees of plants we are attempting to organize. If the employer accedes to our request for bargaining (on the basis of our majority claim or after a card check by an impartial third party) there are no problems, but if he does not, the cards can become very important.

On the assumption that we have to prove our majority, as of the date of our recognition demand, in a subsequent 8 (a) (5) hearing, we instruct you as follows:

1. *Workers should be told that as soon as we have a clear majority of authorization cards, we will demand recognition.* It is not necessary to discuss at all the possibility that if the employer refuses to recognize the union we might seek an election —this is a tactical decision that the Union may make later. In every case, however, we will seek recognition when we have a clear card majority and workers should know that.

2. When an organizer personally signs up a worker, he should *make certain that the card is properly dated and he should initial the back* so that he can later testify that he saw the card signed.

3. In-plant organizers should be told to see that cards are properly dated and they should initial cards they see signed or handed to them by signatories. The organizer who receives a card from an in-plant committee should also initial the card.

4. When cards are mailed in, the envelope bearing the postmark should be stapled to the card and initialed by the person opening it.

5. If a card, even though not signed in the presence of the organizer, is handed to him by the signer, the organizer should put the date and his initials on the card.

In order to make sure that employees of the company understand our position, you may want to put out a leaflet from time to time advising them of our objective.

REMEMBER

The purpose of signing up people is to get a majority and obtain recognition. In other words, we are not trying "to get an election"— we are trying to establish a union in the shop.

The above was the policy at the time of this writing. Union policy, of course, frequently changes to meet current needs.

What the organizer says at union meetings can have an important bearing on how the Labor Board treats cards. If there is any chance that the union may decide or be forced by circumstances to seek a bargaining order, organizers would be well advised at union meetings and in discussions with workers to emphasize that the purpose of signing up people is to bring union recognition and representation. If a situation develops where the union sees any possibility of the necessity of unfair labor pratcice charges as a route to recognition, the less said about NLRB elections the better. Of course, if at a hearing a union leaflet is produced proclaiming that the *sole* purpose of the cards is to secure an election, the cards, no matter how obtained, cannot be used to establish majority.

First Communication With Employer

Sometimes it is a good idea, early in an organizing campaign, for the organizer to write to the employer. Usually, this kind of letter officially (1) informs the employer of the union organizing campaign, (2) warns him against unfair labor practices, and (3) lists the names of the in-plant, employee organizing committee. A letter of this sort is useful because:

1. It actually may inhibit the commission of unfair labor practices, including assistance to another union, unilateral changes in working conditions calculated to interfere with employee rights, and other kinds of unlawful acts.

2. If the employer does discriminate against active union supporters, it may prove most valuable in a trial of the case to prove that he knew the people against whom he acted were active union supporters. Often company knowledge of union activity is difficult to prove.

In the initial communication to the employer, organizers should be careful not to demand recognition or to claim a majority unless, of course, they actually do have a majority. The Supreme Court has held that it is unlawful for an employer to recognize a minority union as an exclusive bargaining agent. [33]

Moreover, if litigation should follow because of later events and the employer can prove that a particular organizer claimed a majority when he did not, in fact, have such a majority, the organizer's testimony on all matters becomes highly suspect because he is discredited on this claim.

---

[33] NLRB v. ILGWU, 366 US 731 (1961), 48 LRRM 2251.

It should be remembered that the Board does not require that a demand for recognition precede the filing of a petition for certification.

Conclusion

The early stages of an organizing campaign—involving hand-billing, soliciting, meetings, and communication with the employer—are crucial to the success of the campaign. What happens initially determines what happens later, so that careful attention to detail in these matters can place the union in a position to exercise the widest possible discretion as to tactics, to capitalize on employer misconduct and unfair practices, and to use the law to good advantage.

CHAPTER III

EMPLOYER UNFAIR LABOR PRACTICES

The state must in some way come to
the aid of the workingman if democ-
ratization is to be secured.

Mr. Justice Brandeis in
Mason's book, *Brandeis,*
431

Introduction

Experience has taught that, as the organizing campaign begins to take shape, some employers are quick to respond in a hostile manner and, often, overstep the bounds of the law.

While it is impracticable to cover the almost infinite variety of unlawful employer conduct, this chapter will highlight instances of violations and will emphasize those kinds of violations most frequently found in organizing campaigns. Familiarity with some of the kinds of activity held to be illegal will permit organizers to maintain proper notes and records and, if necessary, consult the union's lawyer or file a charge.

The main thrust of a union in organizing a nonunion shop is to win recognition and bargaining, not to win a victory in charges before the NLRB. Sometimes, however, successful charges can stop unlawful conduct that, unchecked, would virtually kill any chance of success in the drive. Moreover, the legal consequences of certain unfair employer conduct can, in some instances, provide useful vehicles for successful unionization.

In most cases, despite the national policy favoring collective bargaining, employers resist the unionization of their employees and vigorously oppose the union. In these instances, organizing becomes a kind of contest. This chapter will sketch in the basic legal rules governing the employer's behavior during the course of the "contest."

One final word is in order before we launch into a discussion of the kinds of conduct forbidden to employers. Notes, records, dates, names, witnesses—the who, where, when, and why—become crucial in the trial of an unfair labor practice case. The organizer can't just "feel in his bones" that a boss broke the law to "bust" the union; he must be able to prove it. The organizer is the person on the firing line, and if he doesn't have the vital information to build a case, a lawyer cannot manufacture it. One of the most important aspects of an organizer's responsibility is the keeping of accurate and complete records. Write it down, fully, when it happens. Don't rely on your memory or on someone else's recollection.

Interference, Restraint, and Coercion [Section 8 (a) (1)]

All of the unfair labor practice prohibitions of Section 8 (a) are aimed at preventing erosion by employers of the protections and guarantees given to employees by Section 7 of the Act. Sections 8 (a) (2), (3), (4), and (5) speak to specific kinds of violations, but Section 8 (a) (1) makes it illegal in general terms "to interfere with, restrain, or coerce employees in the exercise of the rights guaranteed by Section 7." Because of the inclusiveness of the wording of 8 (a) (1) it is held that a violation of any other unfair labor practice section is automatically also a violation of 8 (a) (1). But the converse is not true: not all 8 (a) (1) violations are also violations of another section. There are many employer acts that violate the guarantees of Section 7 and yet do not transgress any of the specific prohibitions of Section 8 (a) (2) through (5). These are the "independent" 8 (a) (1) violations and it is with these that this section concerns itself.

In Section 7's guarantee of rights to self-organization, to form, join, or assist labor organizations, and to bargain through representatives of the employees' own choosing there is a heavy premium placed on free choice by employees—free choice of whether or not to organize into a union and of what union to choose.

Most of the actions that constitute independent 8 (a) (1) violations interfere with this free choice: by threatening some reprisal if the employees' free choice is exercised, by promising some benefit if it is not, by creating an atmosphere of distortion or intimidation that makes the concept of a free choice meaningless.

It is worth noting that the protective reach of Section 7 is broader than strictly union activity. Section 7 gives employees the affirmative right to engage in union activity and "in other concerted action for the purpose of collective bargaining or other mutual aid or protection." Section 7 covers combined employee action for mutual aid, even if there is no union in the picture.

It has been incorrectly said by some commentators and courts that an employer may "fire" an employee for good reason or no reason as long as he doesn't fire for *union* activity. Not true. An employer violates Section 8 (a) (1) when he fires two employees because together they sought to improve conditions or pay in the plant or for some other concerted activity—whether or not a union was on the scene. It is important to remember that Section 8 (a) (1) forbids discrimination against employees because of protected concerted activity—regardless of the presence or absence of a union—because, often when conditions in a particular shop are bad, workers may combine for mutual aid even before the union appears. If the employer responds by discriminating against them, an alert orgainzer can protect their rights by filing a charge when he gets there. The successful charge might also boost organizational chances.

Restrictions on Solicitation and Distribution

The general rule, set out in Chapter II, is that employers may bar distribution in work areas at all times and solicitation in nonwork areas during work periods. But where such company rules are adopted specifically to defeat organization and applied discriminatorily to the union, the company ban is unlawful under Section 8 (a) (1) .[1] Where a new company bar against employee communication is adopted immediately upon the em-

---

[1] Wm. H. Block Co., 150 NLRB 341 (1964), 57 LRRM 1531.

ployer's becoming aware of a union campaign, it is probably unlawful.[2]

Surveillance and Interrogation

Employers violate 8 (a) (1) when they spy on employees' union activities. The following are classic types of unlawful surveillance: taking still or motion pictures of employees distributing or receiving literature; sending supervisors or other employees to see who attends union meetings; and tapping telephones. Even creating the appearance of such surveillance may constitute a violation.[3]

Inducing a supervisor or an employee to furnish the employer with a list of union activists is unlawful.[4]

In certain circumstances an employer may question his employees as to their feelings about the organizing union. In 1967 in the case of *Struksnes Construction Co.*[5] the Board revised the standards it had announced in the 1954 *Blue Flash Express* case [6] for determining the legality or illegality of an employer's polling of his employees. While recognizing that "any attempt by an employer to ascertain employee views and sympathies regarding unionism generally tends to cause fear of reprisal in the mind of the employee if he replies in favor of unionism and, therefore, tends to impinge on his Section 7 rights," the Board noted that there are situations in which an employer is called upon to recognize a union without an election and that there are "clearly uncoercive methods for an employer to verify a union's majority status." Laying down general rules for determining the legality of an employer poll of employees, the Board said:

> Absent unusual circumstances, the polling of employees by an employer will be violative of Section 8 (a) (1) of the Act unless the following safeguards are observed:
> (1) The purpose of the poll is to determine the truth of a union's claim of majority,
> (2) this purpose is communicated to the employees,
> (3) assurances against reprisal are given,

[2] Ward Mfg., Inc., 152 NLRB 1270 (1965), 59 LRRM 1325.
[3] Puritana Mfg. Corp., 159 NLRB 518 (1966), 62 LRRM 1425.
[4] *See* NLRB Annual Reports 27 through 30 (1962-1965).
[5] 165 NLRB No. 102 (1967), 65 LRRM 1385.
[6] 109 NLRB 591 (1954), 34 LRRM 1384.

(4) the employees are polled by secret ballot, and
(5) the employer has not engaged in unfair labor practices or otherwise created a coercive atmosphere.

In the same decision the Board reaffirmed its longstanding rule that a poll taken while a petition for a Board election is pending does not serve any legitimate interest of the employer and is therefore a violation of Section 8 (a) (1).

The Board will not find interrogation illegal where information is needed to prepare a case before it. In such cases, however, the questions *must* be relevant to the issues and the data sought should be of sufficient probative value to justify the risk of intimidation involved.

An example of unlawful interrogation in connection with preparing for a Board case is *Guild Industries,*[7] where an employer's lawyer interrogated employees under oath with a court reporter taking statements, and asked questions that were coercive in result and may have tended to interfere with the employees' rights; and where, on another occasion, a team of lawyers interrogated *every* employee of the company over a period of five days.

Threats, Promises, and Material Misrepresentations

What an employer says in a union campaign—through supervisors, in speeches, or in written communications—must be viewed in light of the so-called "free speech" amendment to Taft-Hartley, Section 8 (c) of the Act. Under that section mere opinion, views, or argument cannot be used as evidence of an unfair labor practice. For example, if an employer expresses the view that he is opposed to having a union in his plant, without saying or doing more, this is not an unfair labor practice. But if the speech contains a threat of reprisal or force or a promise of benefit, 8 (c)'s shield does not apply and it may be an unfair labor practice. The key then for evaluating an employer's speech in the unfair-labor-practice context lies in determining whether it contains a threat or a promise, whether express or implied, crude or subtle, explicit or veiled. If professional organizers and employee organizers write down the exact

---

[7] 133 NLRB 1719 (1961), 49 LRRM 1101; 135 NLRB 971 (1962), 49 LRRM 1611.

words used, it is easier to determine later whether the language is forbidden or permitted.

Remember, however, that employer speech which is shielded by Section 8 (c) from being the subject of unfair labor practice charges may nonetheless, if it has a sufficiently distorting impact during the campaign, be a ground for setting aside an election. More on this in Chapter IX.

The Supreme Court, in the important *Gissel case*,[8] recently described the standard for determining the propriety of employer speech this way:

> . . . an employer is free to communicate to his employees any of his general views about unionism or any of his specific views about a particular union, so long as the communications do not contain a "threat of reprisal or force or promise of benefit." He may even make a prediction as to the precise effects he belives unionization will have on his company. In such a case, however, the prediction must be carefully phrased on the basis of objective fact to convey a management decision already arrived at to close the plant in case of unionization. If there is any implication that an employer may or may not take action solely on his own initiative for reason unrelated to economic necessities and known only to him, the statement is no longer a reasonable prediction based on available facts but a threat of retaliation based on misrepresentation and coercion, and as such without the protection of the First Amendment.

Certain conduct is so plainly violative of the Act that it needs no discussion here. If an employer, in no uncertain terms, says that a union victory will mean that (1) he will close or move; (2) there will be no further overtime; (3) he will take away benefits; or (4) he will get rid of the union activists, it is plainly unlawful. Also, it is illegal to promise that if the union is defeated, he will grant pay increases. The more difficult cases are those on the borderline where the employer says he is merely exercising his Section 8 (c) "free speech" rights. These are the cases in which the dividing line between legal and illegal activity is microscopically fine and ever changing. One philosopher has said that nothing is constant but change, and that is certainly true of decisions in the field of veiled employer threats and promises. A close look at two NLRB cases indicates the thin line of the boundary here.

---

[8] *See* NLRB v. Gissel Packing Co., 395 US 575 (1969), 71 LRRM 2481. A recent NLRB case in which the Board, applying the *Gissel* standard to an employer's speech, found a violation is *Yankee Trader, Inc.*, 184 NLRB No. 81 (1970), 74 LRRM 1595.

In *Graber Mfg. Co.*[9] the Board found an employer's preelection letters and speeches to contain veiled threats that the employees' choice of the union would have adverse consequences for them. The Board noted that, for the most part, Section 8 (c) protected the employer's views, opinions, and arguments in the letters and speeches, but it also noted that he overstepped the bounds by the following statements:

"This is a most important election for you. If *a majority of you vote for the Union, the existing easy relationship between you and your Company can no longer exist.* With a union, we can no longer treat you as an individual; you become a small part of a mass of people called "the Union." *Your individual interests become lost, because the Union officials must consider Union interests over and above your own interests. Thus, you give up part of the freedom you now have* in return for the promises which the Union makes, but which can be realized only if the Company agrees."

. . . .

"On Wednesday, you and other plant employees will decide an issue that will determine the basis on which you will deal with this Company for years to come. *Depending on the wishes of a majority* of the eligible employees who actually vote, *you will continue to talk about your own job affairs personally or a third party—the Union—will do your talking for you, to your exclusion; that is the law.*" (Emphasis added)

Comment: Of course that is not the law. Section 9 (a) permits the individual presentation of grievances if the union is offered the opportunity to be present. The Board held that this kind of talk was a threat to take away a substantial benefit (the statutory right to personal grievance presentation) if the union won. This kind of threat can be equated with the familiar chant: "Our door is always open to you, but it won't and can't be after the union comes in."

"How many plants have gone bankrupt or moved south because of excessive union demands? The Machinists Union itself lost 82,000 members between 1956 and 1962."

. . . .

"A Union might force a company to agree to *excessive wage rates, but that can only result in the destruction of the business and loss of jobs.* In such a situation the company can either quit as in the Prairie du Chien operation or move to a more favorable location."

Comment: Here the implication is that employers have gone

---

[9] 158 NLRB 244 (1966), 62 LRRM 1055, enforced NLRB v. Graber Mfg. Co., 382 F.2d 990 (CA 7, 1967), 66 LRRM 2269.

bankrupt or moved because unions demanded too much. There
is no factual basis for the assumption made, and the Board
concluded that the reasonable consequence of this statement was
to convince workers that this employer might quit business or
move if the union won.

> "A union can even cause you to lose pay by reducing flexibility
> within the plant. Now we have the right to assign people from one
> department to another wherever help is needed. Under union orga-
> nization this cannot be done, and when certain departments are out
> of work employees will have to be sent home. In the past this Com-
> pany produced unneeded inventories of products, in order to provide
> steady employment. Economic pressures from the union could well
> affect this method of operation and result in seasonal employment
> that is based on the number of customer orders we have."

Comment: The above amounts to a threat that employees
would lose pay because of reduced flexibility if the union won.
This is a distortion of the union's demands for protective work
and seniority practices.

It should be noted that Graber conducted a massive campaign, manifested great antiunion hostility, emphasized the importance of the above statements to employees, and also fired
two active unionists.

To see just how fine the line is drawn, *Graber* must be
compared with *Coors Porcelain Co.*,[10] decided by the *same* three-
member panel of the Board one month later. Here an aggressive
antiunion campaign by an employer was held not to exceed the
bounds of fair comment even though in a series of *preelection
bulletins* to workers, the employer reminded them of previous
bargaining history at the plant, which included strikes that resulted in the replacement of many employees. He also *noted
that a number of local employers had shut down their plants
after being unionized and made numerous references to other
strikes called by the union.* The employer mentioned "trouble
and suffering."

It would seem that, like Graber, Coors had instilled in the
employees' minds fear that inevitable trouble, bad relations,
unemployment, and strikes would unavoidably follow a union
victory. Not so, said the same Board panel (with one dissent) :

As is apparent from the above summary, the Employer waged an

---

[10] 158 NLRB 1108 (1966), 62 LRRM 1158.

aggressive campaign against the selection by its employees of the Petitioner as their bargaining representative. But its statements were factual in character and were relevant to the election issues before the employees. Further, while many of the Employer's assertions were strongly antiunion in character and were not limited to merely answering prounion propaganda, we believe that the employees could evaluate them as partisan electioneering.

Threats can take numerous forms. Although employer misrepresentation of facts in an election campaign is usually not found to be unlawful, the Board has held that if the facts misrepresented amount to a threat and have a sufficiently coercive effect on employees there will be an 8 (a) (1) violation. Where an employer untruthfully wrote to employees that clients in other cities had canceled contracts with it when the union got in, such a violation was found.[11] And where an employer told employees that no Negroes were to be hired unless the union won the election, in which case they would be hired, the Board found a threat to end racial discrimination and an 8 (a) (1) violation.[12]

The Board has distinguished cases of employer predictions of *union* misconduct. These, says the Board, are not threats by the employer, and therefore are not unfair labor practices.[13]

These examples illustrate that each case turns on its particular facts. A careful organizer will have witnesses, statements of the contents of employer speeches, and copies of company bulletins along with notes indicating the total substance and character of the employer's activity so that the union lawyer or Board agent can gauge the worth of a possible Section 8 (a) (1) charge.

Announcement or Conferral of Benefits During Campaign

Announcement or conferral of new benefits by an employer during an organizing drive or election campaign will constitute an 8 (a) (1) violation where the benefits are not part of an established program of increases and improvements but rather are specifically aimed at warding off the particular union campaign. In the leading case of *NLRB* v. *Exchange Parts Co.*[14]

---

[11] U.S. Gypsum Co., 130 NLRB 901 (1961), 47 LRRM 1436.
[12] Bush Hog, Inc., 161 NLRB 1575 (1966), 63 LRRM 1501, affirmed 405 F.2d 755 (CA 5, 1968), 70 LRRM 2070.
[13] *See, e.g.,* C.J. Pearson Co., 173 NLRB No. 228 (1969), 70 LRRM 1047.
[14] 375 US 405 (1964), 55 LRRM 2098.

the Supreme Court focused on how an implied threat underlay such a promise or conferral of benefits:

> [T]he danger inherent in well-timed increases in benefits is the suggestion of a fist inside the velvet glove. Employees are not likely to miss the inference that the source of benefits now conferred is also the source from which future benefits must flow and which may dry up if it is not obliged.

Showing Movies During Campaign

When an employer required all newly hired employees to see a controversial, strongly antiunion film ("And Women Must Weep"), the Board held that he violated Section 8 (a) (1) because the film contained threats to employees for engaging in union activity.[15] The Court of Appeals for the Fifth Circuit disagreed and reversed the Board, holding that the film was shielded by Section 8 (c).[16] (For a more complete discussion of movies, see Chapter IX.)

Firing of Prounion Supervisors

Supervisors are not protected by the Act, so an employer lawfully may fire a supervisor for joining or assisting a union.[17] However, the firing of a supervisor for permitting *workers,* who are covered by the Act, to engage in union activities or for refusing to spy on employees violates Section 8 (a) (1), and the employer will be ordered to reinstate the supervisor with back pay.[18] In such a case the union or worker must file the charges complaining of the supervisor's discharge.

Miscellaneous Section 8 (a) (1) Violations

Many kinds of employer conduct do not fall neatly into the categories that we have utilized in the above discussion but may still contain a threat of reprisal or otherwise interfere with the

[15] Southwire Co., 159 NLRB 394 (1966), 62 LRRM 1280.
[16] Southwire Co. v. NLRB, 383 F.2d 235 (CA 5, 1967), 65 LRRM 3042; *accord* NLRB v. Hawthorn Co., 404 F.2d 1205 (CA 8, 1969), 70 LRRM 2193.
[17] Leonard Niederriter Co., 130 NLRB 113 (1961), 47 LRRM 1249.
[18] Jackson Tile Mfg. Co., 122 NLRB 764 (1958), 43 LRRM 1195, enforced 272 F.2d 181 (CA 5, 1959), 45 LRRM 2239.

right to organize guaranteed by Section 7. The cases noted below represent but a sampling of the kind of situations that may raise questions of legality.

The Board does not consider that an employer-sponsored party or banquet for employees during a campaign violates Section 8 (a) (1).[19] Similarly, an employer may, immediately before an election, separate employees' pay into two envelopes—one containing the estimated amount of union dues and the other, the balance.[20]

When, however, an employer instituted a plant rule during a union drive which prohibited employees from "criticizing Company rules and policies so as to cause confusion or resentment between employees and management," both the Board and a court found a violation of Section 8 (a) (1).[21]

The Board and the courts have agreed that it is an unfair labor practice within the meaning of Section 8 (a) (1) for an employer to question employees as to the contents of statements given Board agents and to demand copies of these statements from employees.[22]

Conduct of Others

It is difficult to hold an employer responsible for the conduct of community vigilante groups, associations, newspapers, radio stations, and the like—difficult, but not impossible.

In *Lake Butler Apparel Co.*,[23] the Board held the employer responsible for threats by a "county development authority" which, in writing and orally, told employees the plant would not be expanded as planned and would, in fact, move if the union got in. The employer had asked the "authority" not to contact employees; he knew, however, that it had done so and he didn't disown it; the authority owned the land where the plant was

---

[19] *See* Peachtree City Warehouse Inc., 158 NLRB 1031 (1966), 62 LRRM 1169.

[20] Caressa, Inc., 158 NLRB 1745 (1966), 62 LRRM 1251.

[21] NLRB v. Lexington Chair Co., 361 F.2d 283 (CA 4, 1966), 62 LRRM 2273, enforcing 150 NLRB 1328 (1965), 58 LRRM 1263.

[22] *See, e.g.*, Texas Industries, Inc. v. NLRB, 336 F.2d 128 (CA 5, 1964), 57 LRRM 2046; NLRB v. Winn-Dixie Stores, Inc., 341 F.2d 750 (CA 6, 1965), 58 LRRM 2475, cert. denied 382 US 830 (1965), 60 LRRM 2234.

[23] 158 NLRB 863 (1966), 62 LRRM 1133, enforced in part 392 F.2d 76 (CA 5, 1968), 67 LRRM 2883.

situated and frequently had lent money to the employer; finally, the employer furnished an employee mailing list to the authority. In more recent cases an employer has been held responsible for the coercive actions of a local attorney-businessman not in the employ of the company,[24] and another employer was held to have violated the Act because of the actions during an organizing campaign of the town's mayor.[25]

Domination or Support of Union [Section 8 (a) (2)]

Section 8(a)(2) states that it is unfair for an employer
to dominate or interfere with the formation or administration of any labor organization or contribute financial aid or other support to it: *Provided,* That subject to rules and regulations made and published by the Board pursuant to section 6, an employer shall not be prohibited from permitting employees to confer with him during working hours without loss of time or pay.

There are two general categories of Section 8 (a) (2) violations: (1) domination of a labor organization by an employer, and (2) assistance or support of a labor organization by an employer that interferes with the organization's ability to function as an independent representative of employee interests. The remedy that the Board will order following the finding of an 8 (a) (2) violation depends on which of the two categories the offense falls into. If the union has been dominated by the employer, that is, it is truly a "company union," the Board will order the union's disestablishment. Disestablishment means that the employer must stop recognizing and dealing with the union and may not reestablish relations in the future. The essential finding underlying this remedy is that the union has been so completely controlled by management that it can never serve as a proper representative of the workers.

If the finding is that the violation was of the lesser illegal assistance or support variety the Board will not bar the union forever but will order the end of its bargaining rights until the effects of the illegality have disappeared and the union has then won a Board certification through an election.[26] And if

---

[24] NLRB v. General Metals Products Co., 410 F.2d 473 (CA 6, 1969), 70 LRRM 3327, cert. denied 396 US 830 (1969), 72 LRRM 2432.
[25] Henry I. Siegel, 172 NLRB No. 88 (1968), 69 LRRM 1094.
[26] Carpenter Steel Co., 76 NLRB 670 (1948), 21 LRRM 1232.

the illegality has been so minor that the union's capacity to represent the workers has not been damaged, the Board may not order even the temporary termination of bargaining rights.[27]

Section 8 (a) (2) violations arise in organizing campaigns where an employer is excessively cooperative and extends too much "help" to a union, particularly where there is another union in the picture. In a recent case the Board found 8 (a) (2) violations where, after moving his shop to avoid continued dealings with an existing union, the employer invited representatives of another union into the shop to speak to employees, assembled the employees on company time to be addressed by the union representative, and had supervisors assist the union in soliciting authorization cards from employees. When the employer recognized the union and entered into a contract with it following the presentation of a majority of cards thus obtained, it was another 8 (a) (2) violation.[28]

Other examples of 8 (a) (2) violations are:

1. While a bona fide union is organizing, the employer suggests the formation of an independent union to employees, helps them get started and grants benefits to the new "union." [29]

2. The employer recognizes and bargains with, as the exclusive representative, a minority union.[30]

3. The employer recognizes one union when two or more unions are seeking recognition.[31] But apparently when there is "no real question concerning representation," for example, when it is perfectly clear that one of the unions represents a majority of employees, and the employer has shown no favoritism, recognition will not be a violation.[32]

4. The employer bargains with an incumbent union when there is a real question concerning representation, such as a timely RC petition supported by the required interest showing.[33]

5. In a new plant situation the employer recognizes a union

[27] Lykes Bros., Inc., 128 NLRB 606 (1960), 46 LRRM 1347.
[28] Senco, Inc., 177 NLRB No. 102 (1969), 71 LRRM 1532; see also Keller Ladders Southern, 161 NLRB 21 (1966), 70 LRRM 2001.
[29] Southshore Packing Corp., 73 NLRB 116 (1947), 20 LRRM 1070.
[30] ILGWU v. NLRB, 366 US 731 (1961), 48 LRRM 2251.
[31] Midwest Piping & Supply Co., Inc., 63 NLRB 1060 (1945), 17 LRRM 40.
[32] American Bread Co. v. NLRB, 411 F.2d 147 (CA 6, 1969), 71 LRRM 2243.
[33] Shea Chemical Co., 121 NLRB 1027 (1958), 42 LRRM 1486.

and signs a contract before a "representative and substantial" number of employees has been hired.[34]

The Board's Annual Report for 1960 provides a good general discussion of the variety of situations that raise questions under Section 8 (a) (2) :

a. Domination of Labor Organization

A labor organization is considered dominated within the meaning of section 8 (a) (2) if the employer has interfered with its formation and has assisted and supported its administration to such extent that the organization must be regarded as the employer's creation rather than the true bargaining representative of the employees. Such domination is the result of a combination of factors and has been found where "the employer not only furnished the original impetus for the organization but there were present such additional factors as (a) the employer also prescribed the nature, structure, and functions of the organization; (b) the organization never developed any real form at all, such as a constitution or bylaws, dues or a treasury, never held any meetings and had no assets other than a contract bestowed by the employer; (c) representatives of management actually took part in the meetings or activities of the committee or attempted to influence its policies." Thus, in one case section 8(a) (2) was held violated in this sense under the following circumstances: The employer here notified an employee meeting that he did not intend to renew his contract with the incumbent union, suggesting that employee "committees" be formed which were to "follow through" on certain proposals regarding terms of employment proposed by the employer. Committee elections were attended by the employer's president who made membership suggestions. Supervisors voted at committee meetings and were elected as committee members. Elections were held on company property, employees being paid for time spent at meetings. The employer also assisted in the preparation of employee petitions designating the committee as their representative, posted notices of committee meetings, and furnished refreshments while meetings were held. The committee had no constitution, bylaws, dues, or funds, and did not seek a contract with the employer. In another case, the employer was likewise held to have unlawfully dominated a labor organization, the trial examiner having found that the employer caused the formation of the employee "Council" involved, fixed the areas in which it operated, and paid the expenses of the Council, which had no funds, by having councilmen perform their functions during working hours. In one case, an incumbent affiliated union was held dominated by the employer who dealt with its negotiating committee half of whose members the employer had appointed, and who entered hastily into a new contract when a rival union was about to enter the plant. The

---

[34] Lianco Container Corp., 173 NLRB No. 219 (1969), 70 LRRM 1047.

employer executed the contract over the protest of an employee-designated committee member, and also threatened reprisals against employees who favored a union other than the incumbent. While these events occurred more than 6 months before the charges were filed, and under section 10(b) of the Act could not be made the basis of an unfair labor practice finding, they could properly be considered, in the view of the majority of the Board panel here, insofar as they shed light on the employer's later conduct.

b. Assistance and Support

Section 8(a)(2) interference with labor organizations, other than complete domination, was again found in a number of cases where employers sought to foster or entrench a favored union by various kinds of conduct. Thus, one employer was held to have unlawfully assisted and facilitated the organizational drive of a union, which sought to oust the employees' incumbent bargaining representative, by shutting down the plants involved, terminating the incumbent union's contract and refusing to bargain with it, discontinuing payments in the incumbent's welfare and retirement fund, prematurely extending to the favored union exclusive recognition, and by furnishing it a mailing list of employees. In another case where unlawful assistance and support was found, the employer had similarly aided a union in displacing the employees' lawful representative by refusing to deal with the latter, by discharging its adherents, and by granting recognition to the favored rival union.

In one case, the employer was held to have unlawfully assisted a union by soliciting and procuring from employees and applicants for employment, during the hiring procedure, applications for union membership and signed authorizations for the checkoff of union dues.

Financial support of unions has consistently been held violative of the noninterference provision of section 8(a)(2), whether it took the form of direct payments to the assisted union, or payment and reimbursement of employees for time spent on the assisted union's business.

(1) Supervisor's Participation in Union Affairs

In several cases the Board had to concern itself with the question whether participation of supervisors in the intraunion affairs of an incumbent bargaining representative of which they are members may be imputed to the employer and may be regarded as violative of section 8(a)(2). In further clarifying the principles which govern employer responsibility in such situations, the Board distinguished between intraunion activities of supervisors who are members of the same union and bargaining unit as rank-and-file employees, and such activities of supervisors who are union members but are outside the bargaining unit.

Regarding intraunion activities of supervisors in the bargaining unit the Board applied the following rules:

1. Participation of member supervisors in intraunion activities will not be attributed to the employer and does not constitute evidence of either domination or assistance to the particular union, unless there is proof that the supervisors' participation was encouraged or authorized by the employer.

2. Unlawful assistance to the union will be found, however, where the employer acquiesced in the supervisors' voting at union elections and has been dealing with supervisors who represented the union as elected officers or members of negotiating committees.

On the other hand, regarding the participation in intraunion affairs of member supervisors who are outside the bargaining unit, it was made clear that—

[The Board] will apply the rule of *respondeat superior* to any active participation by them in union affairs to the same extent as [it applies] that rule to other areas of supervisory conduct . . . [and] that participation by supervisors, not in the bargaining unit, in the internal affairs of a union of rank-and-file employees constitutes unlawful interference with the administration of the union.

One final point should be kept in mind in assessing a possible violation of Section 8 (a) (2). An employer does not give unlawful assistance to a union when he states to employees his preference for one union over another. He can tell the workers that, in his opinion, a preferred union might serve them better and can even predict which union will better negotiate. Favoritism confined to speech is not unlawful; it is protected by the so-called "free speech" provision, Section 8 (c).

The general lessons of this discussion for the organizer should be clear: Avoid undue closeness with or dependence upon the employer and at the same time watch that the employer does not extend illegal assistance to a rival union.

Discrimination in Employment [Section 8 (a) (3)]

Section 8 (a) (3) is designed to protect employees or would-be employees against discrimination against them by an employer because of their union beliefs or protected union actions. When an employer engages in any discrimination with respect to "hire or tenure of employment to encourage or discourage membership" in a union he violates Section 8 (a) (3). The usual remedy is an order to hire or reinstate with back pay.

In most Section 8 (a) (3) cases the question of why the employer acted is crucial. In cases involving Section 8 (a) (1), motive is irrelevant. For instance, where an employer knew an employee was engaged in protected activity but also mistakenly, although in good faith, thought he was also guilty of misconduct, it was unlawful under Section 8 (a) (1) to fire the employee.[35] What counts is the effect on employees.[36] Not so in Section 8 (a) (3) cases. Here, as most experienced organizers know, all but the most stupid employers assert reasons for the discriminatory conduct that are pretext—mere cover so they can deny that they acted to discourage union membership. Witnesses, notes, dates, and times become vitally important in sustaining the burden of proof that the employer's motive was unlawful. Company knowledge of an employee's union activity is, of course, an essential element of proof of illegal motive in these cases. Such knowledge may, however, be inferred in proper cases, but the evidence must be pretty strong to support the inference.

If an employer shifts his position on the reasons for a discharge or demotion, it is good evidence that the real reason is unlawful, and, of course, equally good evidence is produced where witnesses prove that conflicting or incredible reasons were advanced by an employer for his acts. Where seniority is normally followed but there is a sudden deviation adversely affecting union adherents, the Board will find it hard to believe an employer's cries of innocence of motive. Careful attention should be paid to the remarks of supervisors and to the reasons for employer action given to other agencies, such as unemployment boards. The employer's discharge slip may not agree with his discharge letter or his oral statements.

The organizer is the person in the best possible position to coordinate and present all of this kind of evidence. Its importance cannot be overstressed. Many unions have won victories because they were able to vindicate the rights of employees who were unlawfully discriminated against by an employer.

Certain kinds of discrimination are so obvious that every experienced organizer knows them. For instance, it is clearly unlawful for an employer, in a campaign, to move an active union supporter to a less desirable job, or shift, for no legitimate reason and to tell him that "we both know the reason" or "you

---

[35] NLRB v. Burnup & Sims, Inc., 379 US 21 (1964), 57 LRRM 2385.
[36] NLRB v. Erie Resistor Corp., 373 US 221 (1963), 53 LRRM 2121.

know how to get your old job back." Similarly, where an employee who has recently been commended, promoted, or given a raise in salary becomes a leader in the union drive and is suddenly fired for no reason or an obviously false reason, there is unlawful discrimination. A temporary lockout to stop union organizing is another classic example. Another obvious violation is a refusal to hire a man because he is active in a union or a member of a union. If an employer, because of improper motives, makes it so rough on a prounion employee that he cannot reasonably stay on the job and is finally forced to quit, the Board will find that the employee was "constructively discharged" under 8 (a) (3) and is entitled to back pay and reinstatement.[37]

When an employer starts a pension, insurance, or other benefit plan and limits participation to those members of the bargaining unit who are not members of or represented by a union, he violates Section 8 (a) (1). When the union gets in and he refuses to permit represented employees to participate in his benefit plan, he violates 8 (a) (3).[38] Similarly, where an employer contracts out work *because* a union has been certified, the laid-off employees have been discriminated against under Section 8 (a) (3).[39]

Disciplining an employee for engaging in concerted activity protected by Section 7 is an 8 (a) (3) violation.[40] For example, an employer violates Section 8 (a) (3) when he refuses to reinstate employees who peacefully strike to protest the discharge of an employee or even of a minor supervisor.

An improper refusal to reinstate a striker who has made an unconditional offer to return to work is a Section 8 (a) (3) violation. The rules governing the rights of strikers to reinstatement seem to be in the process of changing in favor of employees. Unfair labor practice strikers, (persons who strike in protest of an employer's unfair labor practices or whose strike is prolonged by employer unfair labor practices) have an absolute right to rein-

---

[37] Keystone Floors, Inc., 130 NLRB 4 (1961), 47 LRRM 1234.

[38] Jim O'Donnell, Inc., 123 NLRB 1639 (1959), 44 LRRM 1182; *see also* Great Atlantic & Pacific Tea Co., 162 NLRB 1182 (1967), 64 LRRM 1157; *but see* Goodyear Tire & Rubber Co. v. NLRB, 413 F.2d 158 (CA 6, 1969), 71 LRRM 2977.

[39] Fine's Nearby Egg Corp., 132 NLRB 1585 (1961), 48 LRRM 1547.

[40] *See* Plastilite Corp., 153 NLRB 180 (1965), 59 LRRM 1401, enforced as modified 375 F.2d 343 (CA 8, 1967), 64 LRRM 2741.

statement, provided the strike was for a lawful purpose and was lawfully conducted. If the employer has hired replacements he will have to discharge them in order to put the returning strikers back to work.

Economic strikers (non-unfair-labor-practice strikers) have only a limited, but apparently expanding, right to reinstatement. If their jobs were not taken by "permanent replacements" while they were on strike, they are entitled to reinstatement. If their jobs were taken, and are occupied at the time of the offer to return, they are not entitled to reinstatement.[41] But what if the jobs, occupied at the time of the offer to return, soon become open? The Board has held, and the courts seem to be moving in the direction of holding, that the strikers must then be reinstated if (1) they have not obtained regular and substantially equivalent employment elsewhere and (2) the employer is unable to establish legitimate and substantial business reasons for not reinstating them.[42]

Three lockout cases ruled on in 1965 by the Supreme Court were all decided in favor of the employers and radically recast the law in that 8 (a) (3) area. One case holds that an employer lawfully may lock out his employees in support of his bargaining stance.[43] The second permits nonstruck employers who belong to a group bargaining jointly as one employer to respond defensively to selective or whipsaw union strategy, whereby only one of the group of employers is struck, by locking out employees and hiring temporary replacements.[44] The third case stands for the principle that an employer may go out of business altogether (but not partially or as a sham tactic) for any reason,[45] including resistance to unionization.

In the context of organizing new workers, however, the three decisions restate and emphasize certain basic principles. A

[41] MacKay Radio Corp., 5 NLRB 657 (1938), 2 LRRM 28.

[42] Laidlaw Corp., 171 NLRB No. 175 (1968), 68 LRRM 1252, enforced 414 F.2d 99 (CA 7, 1969), 71 LRRM 3054; *see also* the earlier Supreme Court decision in *NLRB v. Fleetwood Trailer Co.*, 389 US 375 (1967), 66 LRRM 2737 and a recent Board case, *Little Rock Automotive, Inc.*, 182 NLRB No. 98 (1970), 74 LRRM 1198.

[43] American Ship Building Co. v. NLRB, 380 US 300 (1965), 58 LRRM 2672. The requirement of impasse stated in *American Ship* has been eliminated in subsequent Board decisions. Darling & Co., 171 NLRB No. 95 (1968), 68 LRRM 1133.

[44] NLRB v. Brown, 380 US 278 (1965), 58 LRRM 2663.

[45] Textile Workers Union v. Darlington Mfg. Co., 380 US 263 (1965), 58 LRRM 2657.

fair reading of the Supreme Court's lockout decisions makes clear the following:

1. An employer still may not lock out during an organizing campaign as an antiunion move—that is, to defeat organization.[46]

2. Bosses still may not threaten to close up if a union gets into a plant.

3. A company may not close one facility to discourage unionism in another.[47]
The reason behind employer action remains of crucial importance.

Where there is a massive pattern of Section 8 (a) (1) and Section 8 (a) (3) activity by an employer, the Board may order an unusual remedy. Most organizers have some familiarity with the case of *J. P. Stevens & Co.* of North and South Carolina.[48] In 1966 the NLRB ordered an unusual remedy "to undo the effect of massive and deliberate unfair labor practices." Not only did the Board order 71 discharged workers restored to their jobs but, in a unanimous decision, it went far beyond its usual practice of ordering the employer to reinstate employees discriminatorily fired, to reimburse them for loss of earnings plus interest, and to post notices in the plants. The Board ordered a more sweeping remedy because of the facts of this case.

The Stevens Company, because of its widespread and persistent statutory violations in blocking the organization of its employees and because of an atmosphere of employee fear throughout the company's manufacturing operations, also was required to: (1) post the NLRB notice in all 43 of its North and South Carolina plants, not just the 20 in which it had committed unfair labor practices; (2) mail to each of its employees in the 43 plants copies of the notice; (3) have company officials read the notice during working time to assembled workers in the various departments of the North and South Carolina plants; and (4) give the Textile Workers union, upon request, reasonable access to plant bulletin boards for a period of

---

[46] *See* McGraw-Edison Co. v. NLRB, 419 F.2d 67 (CA 8, 1969) , 72 LRRM 2918.

[47] *See* Textile Workers Union v. Darlington Mfg. Co., above and the NLRB's supplemental order in that case, 165 NLRB No. 100 (1967) , 65 LRRM 1391, affirmed 397 F.2d 760 (CA 4, 1968), 68 LRRM 2356, cert. denied 393 US 1023 (1969), 70 LRRM 2225.

[48] 157 NLRB 869 (1966), 61 LRRM 1437, enforced in most respects 380 F.2d 292 (CA 2, 1967), 65 LRRM 2829, cert. denied 389 US 1005 (1967), 66 LRRM 2728.

one year. The Court of Appeals for the Second Circuit wholly enforced the first and second parts of the special order, modified the third part to have the notice read only in the 20 unfair-labor-practice plants, with the company having the option of having a Board agent rather than a company official read the notice, and refused to enforce that part of the order concerning access to company bulletin boards, because it had not been shown that the union lacked alternative ways to reach the employees with its organizational message.

Discussing the "flagrant unlawfulness of the Respondent's antiunion campaign," the Board said and the Court of Appeals agreed that the Stevens Company frustrated union organizing efforts by its wholesale illegal firings, spying upon employees' union activity, threatening reprisals to discourage union adherence, altering working conditions to thwart the union drive, barring employees from union activity, intimidating employees for giving statements to the NLRB, stripping employees of union insignia, and posting lists of union members in plants and then scratching the names of those persuaded to withdraw from membership.

The posting, the Board said, was clearly "an intimidatory tactic which was deliberately calculated to, and did coerce and restrain employees" in the exercise of their right, guaranteed under the labor relations law, to engage in self-organization activities.[49]

Discharge for Testifying [Section 8 (a) (4)]

Section 8 (a) (4) makes it unlawful for an employer to discharge or otherwise discriminate against an employee because the employee has filed a charge with the NLRB or has given testimony, as a witness, under the Act.[50]

Obviously, unlawful conduct under Section 8 (a) (4) includes demotion or discharge of an employee for failure to withdraw an unfair labor practice charge or failure to persuade others to

---

[49] See Decaturville Sportswear Co. v. NLRB, 406 F.2d 886 (CA 6, 1969), 70 LRRM 2472 for another case where special remedies for massive unfair labor practices were approved. See also NLRB v. Bush Hog, Inc., 405 F.2d 755 (CA 5, 1968), 70 LRRM 2070.

[50] See Hydroflo Valve and Mfg. Co., 158 NLRB 730 (1966), 62 LRRM 1203.

do so. Firing an employee for giving statements to a Board agent or testimony at a hearing is another clear violation of this part of the Act.

Finally, even though supervisors are not protected by the Act, the Board will, as a matter of public policy, insist that supervisors who are discriminated against because they were subpoenaed and gave testimony unfavorable to the employer be reinstated with back pay.[51]

Refusal to Bargain [Section 8 (a) (5)]

A full discussion of Section 8 (a) (5), which requires employers to bargain in good faith with unions representing a majority of their employees, would easily fill a good-sized volume. In this book, however, except for brief references to the bargaining violations that can and do occur after a union is recognized, the emphasis will be placed on Section 8 (a) (5) as it directly relates to unionization, and that subject is covered at length in Chapter V.

After a union has been recognized, many kinds of violations may be found as a result of certain employer conduct. Some of the classic kinds of violations are: (1) where an employer refused to give the union information necessary to fulfill its bargaining duty; (2) where he acts unilaterally in derogation of the union's representative status; (3) where he deals individually with employees to undermine the union; (4) where he subcontracts in a manner that adversely affects the unit without consultation with the union; (5) where he only "goes through the motions of bargaining"; and (6) where he refuses to discuss a subject included in the phrase "wages, hours, and other terms and conditions of employment."

Finally, there are the cases of the employer, who, in plain terms, refuses to recognize and bargain with a union even after the union has been victorious in an election, and of the employer who on some pretext, say after a union changes its name, refuses to bargain. And, of course, we have only touched lightly the area of violations of the duty to bargain after the union is established. The cases on this subject are legion.

---

[51] Pedersen v. NLRB, 234 F.2d 417 (CA 2, 1956), 38 LRRM 2227.

Conclusion

This chapter has generally surveyed the area of employer unfair labor practices with the single exception of Board-ordered recognition of unions, which is considered important enough to merit a special discussion in a later chapter.

Only the organizer on the scene can properly gauge the intensity and effect of unlawful conduct during the various stages of an organizing campaign. He is best situated to gather and present the facts in a way that will convince the Board. Certainly, in almost every instance, he will want to check the facts with his union superiors and, in most cases, with a labor lawyer before he acts. Proper timing and the accumulation and presentation of bare facts can make the difference between success and failure of a drive.

This chapter points out, generally, the kinds of conduct and statements which might or might not constitute unfair labor practices. Familiarity with this material is recommended before organizers categorically characterize any given employer behavior as permissible or illegal. Later, in Chapter IX, we discuss employer conduct which, whether or not it constitutes an unfair labor practice, can affect the conduct of elections sufficiently to cause the results to be overturned.

CHAPTER IV

UNION UNFAIR LABOR PRACTICES

The right to combine is absolute; but
the action of a combination must
necessarily be confined to such action
as is lawful, and should be confined to
such action as is reasonable.

Mr. Justice Brandeis, in
Mason's book, *Brandeis*,
150

Introduction

Organizers should know and avoid the kind of conduct that
might result in a finding of a union unfair labor practice. The
reasons for this are plain enough, but they bear repeating. First
and foremost, citizens, including union organizers, are expected
to obey the law. Moreover, there are practical reasons for not
behaving illegally. The commission of union unfair labor practices in the course of obtaining authorization cards can, of
course, render those cards meaningless. And a union that engages
in unfair practices and wins an election will, more often than
not, find the election set aside. Finally, when both sides are
tarred with the same unfair labor practice brush, the union has
lost a tremendous psychological and public relations advantage
over a law-breaker employer.

This chapter will treat those unfair labor practices that most
frequently occur in the context of an organizing campaign. Most
professional organizers are experienced enough to avoid the pit-
falls described here, but sometimes a reminder does no harm and
some good.

Restraint and Coercion of Employees [Section 8 (b) (1) (A)]

The law prohibits unions and their agents from "restraining or coercing" employees in the exercise of their rights to engage in, or *to refrain* from engaging in, union or concerted activity.

It is pretty plain to everyone that the main, but not sole, thrust of Section 8 (b) (1) (A) is aimed at violence and threats of violence—usually, but not necessarily—picket-line violence. The Board has found threats of violence to be implicit in certain conduct so that threats need not be orally expressed. Mass picketing and the blocking of entrances are forbidden by this section of the law.[1]

Violence and threats against supervisors have also been held to violate this section when employees were aware of such behavior, because it tends to restrain the workers in making choices under the law.[2] Peaceful picketing for recognition, however, even by a minority union, does not violate this section of the Act, although it may violate another section, 8 (b) (7).[3]

The Board holds that a union violates Section 8 (b) (1) (A) when its organizer tells an employee "the union is stronger than you. You cannot fight a union and win."[4] An organizer's remark during a drive that "there may be trouble later" if an employee should refuse to sign a card constitutes unlawful restraint and coercion.[5] And, of course, a threat to discipline or cause loss of work to an employee for filing a charge against the union is unlawful under this section.[6] Similarly, restraining employees from testifying against the union before the Board is unfair.[7]

The NLRB's 1957 Annual Report gives some idea of the scope of 8 (b) (1) (A):

To establish a violation of section 8(b)(1)(A), it must be shown that the conduct of the respondent union tends to restrain or coerce employees in respect to their statutory rights. It is sufficient that the

---

[1] *See* generally, for the best discussion of Section 8 (b)(1)(A), an old NLRB case, *Sunset Line and Twine Co.,* 79 NLRB 1487 (1948), 23 LRRM 1001.
[2] Twenty-third Annual Report of NLRB, 1958, p. 78.
[3] NLRB v. Teamsters Local 369 (Curtis Bros.), 362 US 274 (1960), 45 LRRM 2975.
[4] Randolph Corp., 89 NLRB 1490 (1950), 26 LRRM 1127.
[5] Fifteenth Annual Report of NLRB, 1950.
[6] Local 401, Boilermakers, 126 NLRB 832 (1960), 45 LRRM 1388; Bordas & Co., 125 NLRB 1335 (1959), 45 LRRM 1264.
[7] Personal Products Corp., 108 NLRB 743 (1954), 34 LRRM 1059.

conduct had a tendency to restrain or coerce. As often stated by the Board, "the Act does not require proof that coercive conduct has its desired effect."

In addition to manifestly coercive resorts to violence, or threats of violence, by union agents against employees because of their failure to give expected support, unlawful restraint and coercion was also found to have resulted from discriminatory employment practices under illegal agreements, and from causing discrimination in employment, as well as from attempts to cause such discrimination. It was pointed out again that "a union's attempt to cause a discriminatory discharge, even though unsuccessful and unaccompanied by threats of physical violence, may constitute an independent violation of Section 8(b)(1)(a)."

.   .   .   .

In one case, the Board sustained the trial examiner's finding that the respondent union unlawfully coerced employees who had engaged in rival union activities by refusing to represent them in processing their grievances. The trial examiner cited the earlier *Peerless Tool* case. There, the Board had made it clear that the duty of an exclusive bargaining agent to act as the genuine representative for all employees in the bargaining unit includes the duty to process their grievances impartially and without discrimination, and that discrimination against employees in the performance of this duty because of the employees' protected activities violates section 8(b)(1)(A).

One union was found to have engaged in coercive conduct by offering a discharged employee a cash payment and promising him employment in return for the withdrawal of unfair labor practice charges he had filed. The Board pointed out that inducement to withdraw charges coerces employees in the exercise of rights guaranteed by section 7, and, if engaged in by a union, violates section 8(b)(1)(A) just as it violates section 8(a)(1) if engaged in by an employer.

The cases where violations of sections 8(b)(1)(A) were found involved coercion against employees for such matters as activities on behalf of rival unions, a refusal to pay a fine imposed by the union's credit union, and a refusal to withdraw unfair labor practice charges.

To sum up, the Board generally finds violations of Section 8 (b) (1) (A) in the organizational context in cases involving violence, threats, and mass picketing in organizational strikes, cases involving deliberate deception of workers to secure union cards, and veiled threats to use the union's power to cause economic harm to those who refuse to cooperate with it.

Restraint and Coercion of Employers [Section 8 (b) (1) (B)]

Section 8 (b) (1) (B) declares that it is unlawful for unions "to restrain or coerce" an employer in the selection of his bargaining representatives. This section is of little importance to organizers since it usually comes into play only after a plant is organized and a union insists, sometimes to the extent of striking, that the company get rid of a particular employer representative such as a lawyer, labor-relations director, or supervisor.

Causing Discrimination [Section 8 (b) (2)]

This section is the union counterpart of Section 8 (a) (3), the employer discrimination section covered in the previous chapter.

The Board's 1963 Annual Report states as follows:

Section 8(b)(2) prohibits labor organizations from causing or attempting to cause, employers to discriminate against employees in violation of section 8(a)(3), or to discriminate against one to whom union membership has been denied or terminated for reasons other than failure to tender dues and initiation fees. Section 8(a)(3) outlaws discrimination in employment which encourages or discourages union membership, except insofar as it permits the making of union-security agreements under certain specified conditions. By virtue of section 8(f), union-security agreements covering employees in the building and construction industry are permitted under less restrictive conditions.

Most of the cases involve union attempts to have employees discharged for reasons other than failure to meet union-security requirements of an agreement, and they have little relevance to organizers except in those rare cases where the attempt is made by an incumbent union when another union is organizing.

Good-Faith Bargaining [Section 8 (b) (3)]

Section 8 (b) (3) requires unions to bargain in good faith. Since one of the main objectives of a union is to bargain, the section is rarely used. This section has little or no significance for organizers.

Most of the violations found under this section of the Act have been due to a union's failure, usually through negligence, to meet the notice requirements of Section 8 (d), whereby no strike may take place unless the employer has been given written word 60 days in advance and federal and state mediators have been notified in writing of the union's intention to terminate or modify a contract 30 days before a strike. Here again, this section comes into play *after* the union is organized, and usually after one or more contracts, although a union can violate this section by refusing to meet and bargain on a first or subsequent contract negotiation or by refusing to sign an agreement after having accepted its terms.

It should be noted that Section 8 (b) (3) as well as Sections 8 (b) (1) (A) and 8 (b) (2), in conjunction with the provisions providing for exclusive rights of representation (Section 9), gives rise to the union duty of fair representation.[8] While the problem of representation does not often face the organizer, the problem of forming the unit does. The Board has held that it "cannot validly render aid under Section 9 of the Act to a labor organization which discriminates racially when acting as a statutory bargaining representative."[9] The Board has ruled that unions which exclude employees from membership on racial grounds, or which classify or segregate members on racial grounds, may not obtain or retain certified status under the Labor Act. This prohibition against discrimination may be found either where it is expressly agreed upon or where it is only implied by the circumstances.[10] This same principle obviously applies during the working life of the agreement; *e.g.*, in the processing of grievances[11] and the maintenance of discriminatory seniority lists and segregated facilities.[12]

Finally, it is a refusal-to-bargain violation for a union to insist, to the point of impasse (that is, strike or breaking off negotiations), on contract terms that are illegal or about which the employer is not required to bargain because they deal with subjects not included in the statutory term "wages, hours and conditions of employment." It is lawful to insist on bargaining on "mandatory" subjects, but not "permissive" or illegal subjects.[13]

---

[8] *See* Syres v. Local 123, Oil Workers, 350 US 892 (1955), 37 LRRM 2068.

[9] Independent Metal Workers Union, Local 1 (Hughes Tool Co.), 147 NLRB 1573 (1964), 56 LRRM 1289.

[10] Local 12, Rubber Workers (David Buckner), 150 NLRB 312 (1964), 57 LRRM 1535, affirmed 368 F.2d 12 (CA 5, 1966), 63 LRRM 2395, cert. denied in 389 US 837 (1967), 66 LRRM 2306, US rehearing denied 389 US 1060 (1967).

[11] Independent Metal Workers Union, Local 1, above, note 9.

[12] Local 12, Rubber Workers, above, note 10.

[13] *See* NLRB v. Borg Warner, 356 US 342 (1958), 42 LRRM 2034.

Strikes and Boycotts [Section 8 (b) (4)]

Section 8 (b) (4) also is more relevant to situations other than organizing, so it will be treated briefly in this book by the following summary.

This section prohibits certain strikes, threats to strike and boycotts against an employer for the following unlawful objectives:

1. To force an employer or a self-employed person to join a union.

2. To force an employer to enter into a "hot-cargo agreement," that is, an agreement not to handle the goods of *another employer*.

3. To force an employer to cease dealing with or handling goods of another employer.

4. To force *another* employer to recognize an uncertified union.

5. To force any employer to recognize and bargain with the union if another union is certified.

6. To force the assignment of certain work to one union instead of to another (in a jurisdictional dispute), unless the union is entitled to the work by Board order.

Publicity and consumer picketing are exempted from the prohibition of Section 8 (b) (4) by the final proviso of the section. This means that a union may handbill, or warn it will,[14] or picket [15] the product of a company with whom it has a dispute in front of a store selling the product, so long as the action does not cause the stoppage of pick-ups or deliveries or cause the employees of the store to stop work.

Finally, nothing in 8 (b) (4) prevents workers from voluntarily honoring primary picket lines.

Initiation Fees [Section 8 (b) (5)]

This section forbids excessive or discriminatory initiation

---

[14] NLRB v. Servette, Inc., 377 US 46 (1964), 55 LRRM 2957.
[15] NLRB v. Fruit and Vegetable Packers, Local 760, 377 US 58 (1964), 55 LRRM 2961.

fees. For instance, where a union charged a higher fee to those who had refused to join before it made a union-shop agreement, there was a violation and the union was ordered to refund the difference.[16]

Featherbedding [Section 8 (b) (6)]

Section 8 (b) (6) outlaws certain kinds of featherbedding, but it is rarely used. Where a union causes or tries to cause an employer to pay for services neither done nor to be done, there is a violation of the Act and the Board will order the union to reimburse the employer and to cease and desist from the unlawful activity.

Organizational and Recognitional Picketing [Section 8 (b) (7)]

This section forbids certain organizational and recognitional picketing. In outline, a union may not picket for recognition in the following circumstances:

1. Where another union is lawfully recognized by the employer and an election petition is inappropriate (most commonly in a contract-bar situation) .

2. Where there has been a valid election conducted by the Board at the plant in the last year. In conjunction with Section 9 (c) (3) this means a new election is barred whether a union was or was not successful in obtaining certification at the prior election.

3. Where an election petition has not been filed within a reasonable period of time (not exceeding 30 days) , although informational picketing that does not cause a work stoppage would be permitted. Once the election petition is filed, the Board is required to hold an expedited election.

Where the employer has lawfully recognized a union and has entered into a collective-bargaining agreement that would constitute a contract bar were a petition for an election filed, another union is barred from picketing for organizational purposes or for purposes of gaining recognition by Section 8 (b) (7) (A) .[17]

---

[16] Local 153, UAW, 99 NLRB 1419 (1952), 30 LRRM 1169.
[17] Local 1298, Hod Carriers (Roman Stone Construction Co.), 153 NLRB 659 (1965), 59 LRRM 1430.

In the second of the above three circumstances, the Board has held that the 12-month wait after a previous election runs from the date of certification of the election results,[18] and the same case held that it makes no difference whether the picketing union took part in the election. Of course, if the election has not been properly conducted, there is no violation.[19]

Some of the most difficult cases are those involving "publicity" or "informational" picketing, for these are only partially regulated by Section 8 (b) (7) (C). The present state of the law is that if the *sole* purpose of the picketing is informational, *i.e.,* the motive is not to organize or gain recognition, then the entire Section 8(b)(7) does not apply and the picketing may go on indefinitely even if it causes the cessation of pick-ups and deliveries or the performnace of services. However, the union needs to be consistent in order to show that its objective is informational and not for purposes of recognition. The informational aspect can be manifested through picket signs such as the following:

> Houston Building and Construction Trades Council, AFL-CIO protests substandard wages and conditions being paid on this job by the [Employer]. Houston Building Trades Council does not intend by this picket line to induce or encourage the employees of any other employer to engage in a strike or a concerted refusal to work.

The Labor Board held that a union could lawfully picket a below-standard employer with this sign, where it had said in a letter to the picketed employer that it did not wish to write a contract and did not claim to represent a majority of the employees. This union previously had checked the wage scales of other employers and had picketed those not up to union standards. The *objective* of the union was solely informational; being informational, it was outside the scope of Section 8 (b) (7).[20] In this case the *effect* was to stop deliveries, but the effect was ruled to be *irrelevant* because of the manifested objective of the union.

There seems, however, to be a limit on what the Board will

---

[18] Retail Store Employees Union (Irvins, Inc.), 134 NLRB 686 (1961), 49 LRRM 1188.

[19] Department & Specialty Store Union (G. R. Kinney Co.), 136 NLRB 335 (1962), 49 LRRM 1771.

[20] Houston Building & Construction Trades Council (Claude Everett Construction Co.), 136 NLRB 321 (1962), 49 LRRM 1757.

regard as "standards" picketing outside the scope of 8 (b) (7) (C). In a recent case the Board found a violation despite an express disclaimer of a recognitional objective by the union where the "standards" sought by the picketing looked too much like a union contract. The union mailed to the employer copies of contracts it had with other employers in the area, with only the recognition and security clauses stricken out. Both the economic and noneconomic clauses of the contracts were left intact and thus appeared to be demands of the picketing. This, said the Board, exceeded the bounds of allowable standards picketing which is aimed at protecting union employees from cheap nonunion competition, and constituted an attempt to bargain for employees the union did not represent.[21]

The informational objective has to be more than pretext, or the Board must rule that a primary objective of the union is recognitional. For instance, despite the presence of picket signs and handbills containing disclaimers similar to the one quoted above, the union lost in one case where it failed to make any effort toward finding out what wages were actually being paid. The local union had been attempting to get the employer to sign a "Settlement Agreement" which incorporated almost all of the terms it had managed to negotiate with the area's employers and which would bind this employer to accept all future terms negotiated. In effect, the Board held, the union was seeking to place this employer in a multiemployer bargaining unit although his employees had never manifested a choice about the matter; this effort by the union violated Section 8 (b) (7).[22] A union's statement to an employer that it "would like to get [the employees] into our organization and give them job protection that all other crafts are getting in our line of work" and that it would like to sign a contract was fatal to a contention that the union was only seeking to inform the public.[23] Similarly, picketing a multiemployer construction site when the employer being called unfair is not present is also evidence that the "ob-

---

[21] Retail Clerks, Local 899 (State-Mart), 166 NLRB No. 92 (1967), 65 LRRM 1666, affirmed 404 F.2d 855 (CA 9, 1968), 70 LRRM 2220.

[22] Centralia Building and Construction Trades Council (Pacific Sign and Steel Building Co.), 155 NLRB 803 (1965), 60 LRRM 1430, affirmed 363 F.2d 699 (CA DC, 1966), 62 LRRM 2511.

[23] Operative Plasterers' Local 44 (Penny Construction Co., Inc.), 144 NLRB 1298 (1963), 54 LRRM 1237.

ject" of the picketing is more than the dissemination of information.[24]

If the picketing is not *solely* informational, but also has organization or recognition as a purpose, it comes within the scope of Section 8 (b) (7), but may still escape the 8 (b) (7) (C) filing requirement (reasonable period not exceeding 30 days) if the explicit condition of the 8 (b) (7) (C) proviso is met—the picketing must *not* have the effect of stopping pick-ups or deliveries of goods or the performance of other services.[25]

Finally, it should be pointed out that when picketing that comes within the section 8 (b) (7) (C) restriction is being conducted, the representation petition must be filed within the prescribed time period even if the picketing is being conducted by a majority union, or even if the employer has committed unfair labor practices and the union has filed charges. The single instance in which filing will be excused if the picketing falls within the scope of the section is where a meritorious 8 (a) (5) refusal-to-bargain charge is filed.[26]

Hot-Cargo Agreements [Section 8 (e)]

It is an unfair labor practice in most circumstances for a union and an employer to enter into a contract whereby they agree that the employer will not deal with another employer or certain unnamed other employers or will refuse to handle the products of others. It has been said that the policy behind the section is to prevent the automatic proliferation of disputes.[27] This is the so-called "hot-cargo" amendment added to the Act in 1959.

The purpose underlying Section 8 (e) is similar to that underlying Section 8 (b) (4) (B): to prohibit in many circumstances the use of one employer, with whom there is no dispute, to put pressure on another employer with whom there is a dispute.

---

[24] IBEW, Local 113 (ICG Electric), 142 NLRB 1418 (1963), 53 LRRM 1239.

[25] Hotel and Restaurant Employees Union, 130 NLRB 570 (1961), 47 LRRM 1321, supplemental decision and order 135 NLRB 1183 (1964), 49 LRRM 1648.

[26] Hod Carriers, Local 840 (C. A. Blinne Construction Co.), 135 NLRB 1153 (1962), 49 LRRM 1638.

[27] *See* Local 1976, Carpenters v. NLRB (Sand Door and Plywood Co.), 357 US 93 (1958), 42 LRRM 2243; Southern California District Council of Hod Carriers (Swimming Pool Gunite Contractors), 158 NLRB 303 (1966), 62 LRRM 1047.

But the wording of the section is such that, without limiting interpretation, it would bar contract clauses having as their intent and effect other than the proscribed purpose—most frequently, clauses seeking to protect employees in an existing unit from having work taken from them. As a result, when dealing with an 8 (e) charge the Board examines the intent and operation of the contract language under attack to determine whether it is truly violative of the statutory purpose.[28]

The test for lawfulness of the clause in question has been stated as

> whether the clauses "are germane to the economic integrity of the principal work unit" and seek "to protect and preserve the work and standards [the union] has bargained for" or instead "extend beyond the contracting employer and are aimed really at the union's differences with another employer." [29]

This general approach has yielded the following rules:

1. As an initial matter, a union has the right to picket for the inclusion of an absolute ban on all subcontracting, although this could be said to affect this employer's relationship with another.[30]

2. A conditional clause which limits the employer in his contracting out to employers whose employees "enjoy the same or greater wages and other benefits as provided in this agreement" is valid.[31] In short, the employer cannot undercut *this* agreement and threaten unit standards by hiring cheaper labor elsewhere.

3. A permissible variation is to prevent the employer from contracting out except on condition that the employer who receives the work "observe the wages, hours, and conditions of employment established by *labor unions having jurisdiction* over the type of services performed." [32] Again, this prevents union-busting by means of contracting out to lower priced labor.

[28] National Woodwork Manufacturers Assn. v. NLRB, 386 US 612 (1967), 64 LRRM 2801, US rehearing denied 387 US 926 (1967).
[29] Orange Belt District Council v. NLRB, 328 F.2d 534, 538 (CA DC, 1964), 55 LRRM 2293; *see also* National Woodwork Manufacturers Assn. v. NLRB, above, note 28.
[30] Meat & Highway Drivers, Local 710 v. NLRB, 335 F.2d 709 (CA DC, 1964), 56 LRRM 2570; Ohio Valley Carpenters District Council (Cardinal Industries, Inc.), 136 NLRB 977 (1962), 49 LRRM 1908; *see also* NLRB v. National Woodwork Manufacturers Assn., above, note 28.
[31] Meat & Highway Drivers, Local 710 v. NLRB, above, note 30.
[32] Teamsters Local 107, 159 NLRB 84 (1966), 62 LRRM 1224.

4. On the other hand, a clause which bars the employer from dealing with any other employer unless he has signed a *particular contract*,[33] or unless the employer has signed a contract with a particular local, is invalid.[34] The distinction between these two types of clauses is that a union-standards clause merely requires subcontractors to meet the standards of a particular unit before work may be taken from that unit and given to another, whereas a union-signatory clause forces other employers to bargain with a particular local union.

5. A contract clause that permits employees to refuse to cross a primary picket line, that is, a picket line in support of a strike that has been ratified or approved by a union that the picketed employer is required to recognize, is legal and is not a violation of Section 8 (e). But a clause which permits employees to refuse to cross secondary picket lines at a "neutral" employer's place of business is unlawful.[35] Also illegal is a clause which permits union members to refuse to work on any job on which work is being done below union standards.[36]

6. There is an exemption written into the Act allowing construction unions to negotiate so-called "hot cargo" agreements, but these have been narrowly construed by the courts. There is also an exemption affecting the garment and clothing industry which will not be discussed here.

This is a short exercise in what is a very complicated field. The lesson to be learned from it is that clauses which might affect other employers and unions must be carefully drafted. In any case, the negotiation of such a clause is, most often, not the job of the organizer; usually such an assignment falls to shop committees and servicing representatives or business agents after the organizational job is finished. This is the kind of delicate matter best referred to lawyers for technical advice.

---

[33] NLRB v. Joint Council of Teamsters No. 38, 338 F.2d 23 (CA 9, 1964), 57 LRRM 2422.

[34] Sheetmetal Workers Assn. (Johnson Service Co.), 156 NLRB 804 (1966), 61 LRRM 1153; *cf.* Meat and Highway Drivers, Local 710 v. NLRB, above, note 30.

[35] Local 695, Teamsters and Madison Employers Council, 152 NLRB 577 (1965), 59 LRRM 1131, enforced 361 F.2d 547 (CA DC, 1966), 62 LRRM 2135.

[36] NLRB v. Muskegon Bricklayers Union No. 5, 378 F.2d 859 (CA 6, 1967), 65 LRRM 2563.

Chapter V

RECOGNITION WITHOUT ELECTION—
VOLUNTARY AND BOARD ORDERED

> Out of its wide experience, the Board
> many times has expressed the view
> that the unlawful refusal of an em-
> ployer to bargain collectively with its
> employees' chosen representatives dis-
> rupts the employees' morale, deters
> their organizational activities and dis-
> courages their membership in un-
> ions. . . . One of the chief responsi-
> bilities of the Board is to direct such
> action as will dissipate the unwhole-
> some effects of violation of the Act.
>
> Mr. Justice Black in
> *Frank Bros.* v. *NLRB,*
> 321 US 702, 704 (1944)

Introduction

The first four chapters of the book dealt, in a sense, with
preliminary matters. This chapter, and subsequent ones, deal
with the actual attainment of recognition and bargaining rights.
Later on you will find chapters dealing with the problems involved when a union, in its attempt to obtain recognition, seeks
certification by the NLRB, through a Board-conducted election,
of its majority status. That is one way to gain bargaining rights,
but not the only way. Federal labor law *does* require that a
union represent a majority of employees in an appropriate unit
before it can be recognized as the exclusive bargaining agent,
but an election is not the only way in which a majority can be
demonstrated.

An employer lawfully may recognize a union that enjoys majority status, and he *must* recognize it when he has knowledge independent of the cards presented to him by the union that the union represents a majority of workers in a proper unit. Moreover, an employer may not, through unfair labor practices, destroy a union's majority status. And that is what this chapter is about.

Here we deal with recognition obtained by means other than NLRB-conducted elections—voluntary and Board-ordered recognition.

U. S. and Canadian Law Compared

The relevant Ontario, Canada, statute provides that a representation election *may* be dispensed with when the Ontario Labor Relations Board is satisfied that more than 55 percent of the employees are members of a petitioning trade union. When 55-percent membership is shown, the Board "may certify the trade union as bargaining agent without taking a representation vote," provided it is assured that the majority of the employees are members "and that the true wishes of the employees are not likely to be disclosed by a representation vote." [1] It is of interest in this chapter to compare that statute with our own law.

In the United States, *certification* on the basis of a card majority without an election *is* permissible under the Railway Labor Act. Such certification also was granted by the Labor Board under the Wagner Act, but Taft-Hartley precludes certification on cards. It provides that upon a showing of a representation question the Board *"shall"* hold an election, rather than permitting an election *"or any other suitable method"* of determining representation, as the Wagner Act had authorized. The legislative history of Taft-Hartley makes it clear that this change *was intended to preclude Board certification on cards.*[2] As this chapter will demonstrate, however, an "indirect certification" on cards is possible in some situations through Board bargaining orders.

The immediate-recognition or "indirect certification" rule was

---

[1] Revised Statutes of Ontario 1960, Chapter 202, Sec. 7.
[2] *See* H. Rep. 245 on H.R. 3020, p. 39; General Box Co., 82 NLRB 678 (1949), 23 LRRM 1589.

first enunciated in 1937 in the Board's decision in *Remington Rand, Inc.* There, the Board held that where a majority of the employees in an appropriate unit have designated a union as their representative by signing cards, the employer then has an immediate duty to bargain with that union unless he has a *good-faith doubt* of majority representation. The Board's decision was modified and enforced by the U.S. Court of Appeals at New York which held the employer's conduct to be a violation of Section 8 (5). The Supreme Court declined to review the case.[3] As we shall see, this rule has been substantially modified over the years.

It should be kept in mind that even if a union originally plans, as a tactical matter, to petition for an election, the material in this chapter is relevant before election time and, in certain circumstances, after an election. Of course, some unions decide, as a matter of policy, to seek Board certification in every instance. But even in those cases, because of the possible commission of unfair labor practices by the employer, the legal principles in this chapter might prove useful.

Voluntary Recognition

When a union has a majority of voluntarily signed authorization cards or membership cards in an appropriate unit, it has the right to request recognition from the employer. It should, in its recognition demand, offer to prove its majority. Commonly, an offer is made to submit the cards to an impartial third party for a cross-check of signed cards against payroll or W-4 signatures. Some unions offer to permit the employer himself to check the cards, although most do not for the obvious reason that there is at least an unspoken rule that the union will not show authorization cards to "the boss." If the parties want to shortcut the procedures of the Board it is perfectly lawful for them to agree to have a clergyman, an arbitrator, or any other mutually agreeable third party conduct an election. They may ask a state labor-relations agency or mediation board to supervise a vote where it might suit them or save them time or money. They might even agree to conduct their own election.

---

[3] Remington Rand Inc., 2 NLRB 626 (1937), 1 LRRM 88, enforced 94 F.2d 862 (CA 2, 1938), 1A LRRM 585, cert. denied 304 US 576 (1938), 2 LRRM 623.

If a union requesting recognition on the basis of a card majority provable by a third-party check receives a reply from the employer indicating that he might be willing to agree to submit the cards for determination of majority to a mutually agreeable third party, if the third party were permitted to inquire into the issues of whether the cards were gotten through coercion and whether the unit was appropriate, the union should at least discuss the possibilities of such a check. If it turns out that the employer has some reasonable grounds for doubts on these matters, he is entitled to raise them. An outright refusal to permit the third party to do more than check signatures in the face of such a request might preclude a later union claim that the employer refused the offer in order to gain time and to destroy the union's majority.

Once an employer agrees to a third-party card check and the impartial person declares the union's majority, the employer *must* bargain.[4] He cannot rely on a decertification petition filed by an employee, nor can he insist on an NLRB election; he *must* bargain for a reasonable period of time.[5, 6]

Voluntary recognition by an employer of a majority union is lawful in all respects. Since recognition and bargaining rights are the goals of every organizer, it would seem to make good sense to suggest the proposition to an employer in a particular campaign. Write the employer (or wire him) along the following lines:

Dear Sir:

This is to advise you that the majority of your employees in an appropriate bargaining unit at your *(name of plant)* plant in *(city or town)* have designated the *(union name)* as the exclusive representative of all such employees, for the purpose of collective bargaining in respect to rates of pay, wages, hours, and other terms and conditions of employment, to become effective immediately. The bargaining unit consists of *(describe unit)*.

We stand ready to prove our majority status by submitting signed authorization cards to a mutually selected impartial person.

The Union requests negotiations with you with respect to rates of

---

[4] Snow and Sons, 134 NLRB 709 (1961), 49 LRRM 1228, enforced 308 F.2d 687 (CA 9, 1962), 51 LRRM 2199.

[5] Universal Gear Service Corp., 157 NLRB 1169 (1966), 61 LRRM 1527.

[6] But apparently under some circumstances an employer will be allowed to repudiate an agreement to a card check if the check has not yet been held. *See* United Buckingham Freight Lines, 168 NLRB No. 90 (1967), 66 LRRM 1357.

pay, wages, hours, and other terms and conditions of employment. No other person or organization now represents a majority of such employees and you are hereby cautioned against entering into any contract, or any renewal of any of the provisions of any existing contract, or any collective bargaining or negotiating with any person or organization presuming to act as agent for, or in behalf of, any such employees.

We would appreciate a prompt reply.

> Very truly yours,
> *(Representative's name)*
> International Representative
> Union Name

If the employer agrees to recognize, or to a card check, the majority union is "in" and the organizer's job is finished. Usually, such agreement does not come and the organizer must plan his next steps.

Board-Ordered Recognition as Remedy for Unlawful Refusal to Bargain

The usual reaction of an employer to a demand for voluntary recognition is negative. Sometimes he will make no response whatsoever. More often he will refuse the request. Many employers couch their refusal in terms of doubt as to the union's claim of majority representation and insist upon an NLRB election.

In June, 1969 the Supreme Court issued its decision in the case of *NLRB v. Gissel Packing Company* [7] and seems to have, at least for the moment, clarified the rules with respect to the uses of authorization cards, an employer's right to reject a card majority and demand an election, and the authority of the Board to order an employer to recognize a union without holding an election or after an election has been lost.

This area of the law has undergone a series of confusing changes that increasingly in recent years have left judges and scholars divided as to the proper approach to the question of recognition without an election. Initially, under the doctrine of *Joy Silk Mills v. NLRB*,[8] a 1950 case, an employer was compelled to recognize a union on the basis of its showing a card

---

[7] NLRB v. Gissel Packing Co., Inc., 395 US 575 (1969), 71 LRRM 2481.
[8] 185 F.2d 732 (CA DC, 1950), 27 LRRM 2012.

majority unless he could come forth with evidence showing that he had basis for a "good faith" doubt as to the existence or validity of the claimed majority and was not simply stalling in order to gain time in which to take actions aimed at destroying the majority.

Later the burden of proof on the question of good-faith doubt of the majority was shifted from the employer to the Board's General Counsel. Instead of the employer having to show that he had a reasonable basis to doubt the union's majority, the General Counsel had to come forth with evidence to show that the employer did *not* have a good-faith doubt, that he was acting in bad faith in refusing the union's demand for recognition.[9] The shift in burden of proof reflected the Board's increasing preference for elections as a means for achieving recognition. The Board summarized its feelings as of 1966 in *Aaron Bros. Co.;* [10]

> While an employer's right to a Board election is not absolute, it has long been established Board policy that an employer may refuse to bargain and insist upon such an election as proof of a union's majority unless its refusal and insistence were not made with a good-faith doubt of the union's majority. An election by secret ballot is normally a more satisfactory means of determining employees' wishes, although authorization cards signed by a majority may also evidence their desires. Absent an affirmative showing of bad faith, an employer, presented with a majority card showing and a bargaining request, will not be held to have violated his bargaining obligation under the law simply because he refuses to rely upon cards, rather than an election, as the method for determining the Union's majority.
> Here, the Trial Examiner, in effect, found that good faith was missing because Respondent did not offer any evidence "warranting a conclusion that the Union's claim [of majority] was inaccurate or unsupportable." But where, as here, there is no prior bargaining relationship between the parties, as the Board recently held in *John P. Serpa, Inc.,* it is the General Counsel who must come forward with evidence and affirmatively establish the existence of such bad faith.

The present Board practice, approved of by the Supreme Court in the *Gissel* case, has enlarged one degree further the right of an employer to refuse to recognize a card-evidenced majority. Under the Board's new rules, an employer's good faith

---

[9] *See, e.g.,* The Board opinion in *John P. Serpa, Inc.,* 155 NLRB 99 (1965), 60 LRRM 1235, reversed 376 F.2d 186 (CA 9, 1967), 64 LRRM 2764.
[10] 158 NLRB 1077 (1966), 62 LRRM 1160.

doubt is largely irrelevant. When confronted by a recognition demand based on possession of cards allegedly signed by a majority of his employees, an employer need not grant recognition immediately. He may, unless he has knowledge independent of the cards that the union has a majority (gained, for example, by polling his employees), decline the union's request and insist on an election, either by requesting the union to file an election petition or by filing such a petition himself under Section 9 (c) (1) (B). In other words, under the Board's new view, employers now have a right to an election in virtually all situations. For instance, under current Board policy, even if a union presented the employer with cards signed by 80 percent of his employees, the employer could refuse to recognize the union until an election was held.

The Supreme Court did not have to decide the issue of whether a bargaining order was proper where there was no good-faith doubt of majority and there were no independent, substantive, unfair labor practices because of the facts in the *Gissel* cases. That question is still open in the Supreme Court.

Under what circumstances, then, will the Board issue a bargaining order without the holding of an election or after a union has lost an election? When an employer has committed independent (that is, independent of the refusal to bargain) and substantial unfair labor practices that interfere with the election processes and tend to preclude the holding of a fair election (or rerun election) the Board may issue such an order. If the Board finds that the possibility of erasing the effects of the past unfair labor practices and of ensuring a fair election (or a fair rerun) by the use of traditional remedies (*e.g.*, the posting of notices), though present, is slight, and that employee sentiment once expressed through cards would, on balance, be better protected by a bargaining order, then a bargaining order should issue.

But a bargaining order will not issue if the union obtained the authorization cards through misrepresentation or coercion or if the employer's unfair labor practices are "minor" or unrelated generally to the representation campaign.

The facts of the *Gissel* case itself, as stated in the Supreme

Court decision, illustrate the kinds of employer unfair labor practices that may result in a bargaining order:

> At the outset of the Union campaign, the Company vice president informed two employees, later discharged, that if they were caught talking to union men, "you God-damned things will go." Subsequently, the Union presented oral and written demands for recognition, claiming possession of authorization cards from 31 of the 47 employees in the appropriate unit. Rejecting the bargaining demand, the Company began to interrogate employees as to their union activities; to promise them better benefits than the Union could offer; and to warn them that if the "Union got in, (the vice president) would just take his money and let the union run the place," that the Union was not going to get in, and that it would have to "fight" the Company first. Further, when the Company learned of an impending Union meeting, it arranged, so the Board later found, to have an agent present to report the identity of the Union adherents. On the first day following the meeting, the vice president told the two employees referred to above that he knew they had gone to the meeting and that their work hours were henceforth reduced to half a day. Three hours later, the two employees were discharged.[11]

Such conduct, of course, constituted independent and substantial 8 (a) (1) and 8 (a) (3) violations. Because the Board was still applying its *old standard* and therefore had not made a finding as to whether the employer conduct destroyed or so limited the possibility of holding a fair election that it was preferable to rely on the previously presented cards, the Court sent the case back to the Board for further findings.

The wisdom that can be gleaned from the *Gissel* decision coupled with present Board practice can be summarized as follows:

1. The duty to bargain can arise without a Board election under the Act; authorization cards are reliable enough to provide an alternate route to majority status in certain situations.

2. An employer who does not commit unfair labor practices, or who commits unfair labor practices that do not sufficiently interfere with the election processes, may refuse to recognize a union that presents him with a majority of cards and may insist on an election to determine majority status, so long as he has no independent knowledge of the union's majority.[12]

3. An employer who refuses to recognize a union which presents him with a majority of cards, *and which actually has a*

---

[11] NLRB v. Gissel Packing Co., above, note 7.
[12] *See* Seymour Transfer, Inc., 179 NLRB No. 5 (1969), 72 LRRM 1306.

majority at the time of presentation and demand for recognition, and who commits independent and substantial unfair labor practices that tend to undermine majority strength and interfere with the election processes and tend to preclude the holding of a fair election will be ordered to recognize and bargain with the union without an election being held or after the union has lost an election.[13]

A note on bargaining orders following lost elections: From 1950, when *Joy Silk Mills* was decided, until 1954, the rule was that a union retained its right to file refusal-to-bargain charges despite its participation in an election. In 1954, however, the NLRB ruled in *Aiello Dairy Farms*[14] that a union had to *choose* at the outset whether it would seek to gain bargaining rights through refusal-to-bargain charges or through an election petition. Under *Aiello,* by the filing of a representation petition, the union waived any right to file a refusal-to-bargain charge later.

In 1964 the Board overruled *Aiello,* in the *Bernel Foam Products Co.* case.[15] Under the rule of *Bernel,* the Board finds that a union's decision to proceed with an election does not preclude it from thereafter filing and obtaining Board action on a refusal-to-bargain charge based on the employer's refusal to recognize the union prior to the election. Under this ruling the union actually may get two shots at the establishment of bargaining rights. First it may request recognition and, if the employer refuses, it may proceed with the election. If it loses the election it may then file unfair labor practice charges *along with objections to the election.* If the unfair labor practice charges are successful, the Board order has the same effect as a certification, for it directs the employer to bargain with the union as the representative of his employees.

A later case [16] made clear a requirement implied in *Bernel.* It is not sufficient in seeking to use the *Bernel* rule merely to file the 8 (a) (5) (refusal to bargain) charge. There must

---

[13] For cases illustrating the Board's approach since *Gissel, see, e.g., All-Tronics, Inc.,* 179 NLRB No. 19 (1969), 72 LRRM 1281 and *Garland Knitting Mills,* 178 NLRB No. 62 (1969), 72 LRRM 1112.
[14] 110 NLRB 1365 (1954), 35 LRRM 1235.
[15] 146 NLRB 1277 (1964), 56 LRRM 1039.
[16] Irving Air Chute, 149 NLRB 627 (1964), 57 LRRM 1330, affirmed 350 F.2d 176 (CA 2, 1965), 59 LRRM 3052.

be also a timely (within five working days) filing of valid objections to the conduct of an election.

The *Bernel* decision underscores the importance of proper authorization cards which can in no way be construed as limited to use as mere interest-showing documents in support of an election petition.   (See Chapter II.)   It similarly emphasizes the importance of a recognition request and the employer's response thereto.

A bargaining order may issue against an employer where an election lost by the union is set aside *on the basis of objections filed by the employer*.   This could happen where the outcome of an election depends on challenged ballots, both sides file objections, and the employer's objections are found to be meritorious. If the Board then also finds unlawful preelection conduct on the employer's part, which it reasons was calculated to destroy the union's majority, the employer could be ordered to bargain.[17]   No organizer should, however, rely on an employer's objections. He should file his own.

It must constantly be kept in mind by any organizer who might later decide to use *Bernel Foam* and *Gissel* doctrines that there are difficult items of proof in these cases. There must be proof of majority status at the time of the recognition demand—which means, of course, valid, dated authorization cards, obtained as general authorization and not solely as interest-showing for an election, and without unlawful threats or promises.

A recent case [18] alerts unions to a new pitfall: If a union has a razor-thin majority, and a number of employees sufficient to affect that majority ask for return of their authorization cards, it no longer has a majority. The physical possession of union authorization cards by the union was not enough in this case. The NLRB held that the union lacked majority status on the date the company received the recognition request, since two employees had *tried* to retrieve cards they had previously signed. The two employees had signed the cards when they were in a hurry to clock in. Later they decided they really didn't know what they had signed and asked for the return of the cards. Even though the cards were never returned, the employees' attempt

---

[17] Photobell Co., 158 NLRB 738 (1966), 62 LRRM 1091.
[18] TMT Trailer Ferry, 152 NLRB 1495 (1965), 59 LRRM 1353.

to get them back was all that was needed to deprive the union of majority status.

The recognition request must be plain and simple so that an employer cannot later prove he was confused by it. Finally, careful records of incidents and employer conduct that might possibly constitute other unfair labor practices must be maintained.

Bargaining Order to Remedy Flagrant Violations

Finally, there is a type of case in which there has been no recognition or bargaining request and no 8 (a) (5) (refusal to bargain) charge, but where an employer's massive violations of other sections of the Act, such as 8 (a) (1) and 8 (a) (3), have destroyed the union's majority and made it practically impossible for the union to win an election. In these cases, of course, the union must still be able to prove that it had a majority of employees in an appropriate unit before the employer destroyed it.

Northwest Engineering Co.[19] illustrates the kind of situation which the Board ordinarily remedies with a bargaining order. In this case a union with a card majority of better than 60 percent filed objections and unfair labor practice charges (8 (a) (1)) after losing an election. The employer, in a period of two weeks before the election, engaged in the following activity: timed an announcement of increased insurance benefits so as to undermine the union; instituted direct negotiations with employees over grievances; permitted an extraordinary amount of overtime work; threatened economic reprisals if the union won; and promised additional benefits if the employees would repudiate the union. Moreover, while the union's election objections were pending, the employer unilaterally improved employee benefits.

There were two Board decisions in this case. In its first decision,[20] the Board found that the employer had violated Section 8 (a) (1) and had engaged in conduct which interfered with the election. It set aside the election and ordered the em-

---

[19] 158 NLRB 624 (1966), 62 LRRM 1089, enforced 376 F.2d 770 (CA DC, 1967), 64 LRRM 2650.

[20] Northwest Engineering Co., 148 NLRB 1136 (1964), 57 LRRM 1116, affirmed 376 F.2d 770 (CA DC, 1967), 64 LRRM 2650.

ployer to cease and desist from his unlawful activities. Then the union asked the Board to reconsider its decision and order the employer to bargain. The Board did so, saying:

> In the exercise of its remedial powers, the Board is required to re-store a situation which calls for redress as nearly as possible to that which would have obtained, but for the unfair labor practices in-volved. Applying this principle, the Board has in the past ordered an employer to bargain with a union where the employer's unfair labor practices caused the dissipation of a union's majority, even in the absence of a finding or an allegation that the employer refused to bargain with the union in violation of Section 8(a)(5) of the Act. We deem such a remedy appropriate in the present case.

> The record shows, and we have found, that prior to the unfair labor practices here involved, the Union represented a majority of Re-spondent's employees. If, in these circumstances, the Union had retained its majority status and had requested bargaining, it would manifestly be Respondent's duty to bargain with the Union as the representative of its employees. However, as previously stated, Re-spondent embarked upon a course of action, involving serious viola-tions of the Act, which resulted in the dissipation of the Union's majority and the destruction of the conditions for a fair election in which the Union could have demonstrated that majority. To require the Union to submit to another election under these circumstances would be to permit Respondent to profit from its own unlawful conduct at the expense of the Union and the majority of Respond-ent's employees. Accordingly, we find that only an order requiring Respondent to bargain with the Union can restore as nearly as pos-sible the situation which would have obtained but for Respondent's unfair labor practices and thereby effectuate the policies of the Act.

The Supreme Court approved of this remedy when, in affirm-ing the Board and the First Circuit in *Sinclair Co.* v. *NLRB,*[21] one of the cases decided together with *Gissel,* it noted with ap-proval the Board's finding that the employer's threats of reprisal were so coercive that, *even in the absence of a Section 8 (a) (5) violation,* a bargaining order would have been necessary to re-pair the unlawful effect of those threats.[22] In cases where an 8 (a) (5) charge has been filed, if the other unfair labor prac-tices are found to be of sufficient magnitude, a bargaining order will be appropriate regardless of the legality of the em-

---

[21] 395 US 575 (1969), 71 LRRM 2481.

[22] Earlier appeals courts cases upholding the NLRB's power to issue bargaining orders to remedy 8(a)(1) violations include: *NLRB* v. *Delight Bakery,* 353 F.2d 344 (CA 6, 1965), 60 LRRM 2501; *D. H. Holmes* v. *NLRB,* 179 F.2d 876 (CA 5, 1950), 25 LRRM 2408; *NLRB* v. *Flomatic,* 347 F.2d 74 (CA 2, 1965), 59 LRRM 2535; *NLRB* v. *Priced-Less Discount Foods,* 405 F.2d 67 (CA 6, 1968), 70 LRRM 2007.

ployer's refusal to bargain.[23] Such a determination seems to have become popular with the Board since *Gissel* as it creates alternative positions with which to face court review.[24]

It hardly needs saying that this route to recognition is not a matter of tactics. An organizer does not just decide to operate this way. If, however, the employer *forces* the union to seek a bargaining order through his conduct, the organizer should know enough to seek that remedy from the Board.

Conclusion

Some organizers have expressed the opinion that *Joy Silk, Bernel,* and cases similar to *Northwest* are "not too important" because it is better and even quicker to seek an election. This is a short-sighted view. It overlooks the substantial deterrent effect of these bargaining-order cases on the employer's conduct. Plainly, if the only consequence of an employer's questionable behavior is another election, or perhaps a series of elections, there is little incentive for him to obey the law or the Board's rules as to election conduct. When, however, the possible result is a bargaining order, it is reasonable to assume that the employer will take more care to stay within the letter and spirit of the law.

Moreover, despite the unwillingness of a majority of Board members to fashion new remedies for blatant, prolonged refusals to bargain, some courts have shown an interest and unions will continue to push for remedies that will increase the employer's risk in refusing to bargain.[25]

There is no doubt that this line of cases has helped to promote collective bargaining by its effect on employer behavior in campaigns, as well as in direct bargaining orders.

---

[23] *See, e.g.,* NLRB v. Quick Shop Markets, Inc., 416 F.2d 601 (CA 7, 1969), 72 LRRM 2451.

[24] *See* All-Tronics, Inc. and Garland Knitting Mills, above, note 12; *see also* G.P.D., Inc., 179 NLRB No. 31 (1969), 72 LRRM 1294 and Welcome-American Fertilizers Co., 179 NLRB No. 37 (1969), 72 LRRM 1295.

[25] *Compare* Ex-Cell-O Corp., 185 NLRB No. 20 (1970), 74 LRRM 1740, with IUE v. NLRB (Tiidee Products, Inc.), 426 F.2d 1243 (CA DC, 1970), 73 LRRM 2870, and Food Store Employees v. NLRB (Heck's, Inc.), — F.2d — (CA DC, 1970), 74 LRRM 2109.

CHAPTER VI

NLRB REPRESENTATION CASE PROCEDURE

> Administration is more than a
> means of regulation; administration
> is regulation.
>
> Mr. Justice Frankfurter in
> *San Diego Bldg. Trades
> Council* v. *Garmon,* 359
> US 236, 243 (1959)

The Petition

An organizer starts a representation case before the NLRB by filing four copies of a petition for certification on forms supplied by the Board. The petition should be filed with the Regional Director for the region in which the bargaining unit is sought. The petition contains a statement by the person signing it that, under penalties of the Criminal Code, the contents are true to the best of his knowledge and belief. (See Appendix D.)

The petition contains a description of the collective bargaining unit sought or in being, the nature of the employer's business (factory, store, and so forth), the approximate number of employees in the unit, and the names of all interested unions which may claim to represent employees.

Where a union petitions for certification (or an employee petitions for decertification), the interest showing—usually authorization cards—should be supplied to the Board not later than 48 hours after the petition is filed, and in no event later than the last day when a petition can be timely filed. Never rely only on an employer's petition (RM) —file your own petition with an interest showing so that you can exercise control over your own part of the case.

The most important part of the petition is the description of the unit involved, item 5 on the Board's form. Identification of the proper unit should be made as soon as possible. (For comprehensive discussion of some of the more common unit problems see Chapter VII.) If a lawyer or experienced professional organizer is not available, the fledging organizer should seek the aid of a Board agent to fill in the "Included" and "Excluded" categories because this is complicated business and could be crucial to the campaign.

Item 7a of the Board's form *seems* to require that the union have previously sought recognition from the employer, but this is not so. Obviously, it cannot be so for unions are permitted to petition with an interest showing of 30 percent, and that is not enough to back up a recognition request. Use of the Board's representation and election process is itself a bid for recognition. Of course, if the union has majority status and has indeed sought recognition, it should say so in 7a; otherwise leave this item blank.

The Investigation

When a petition is filed in a regional office of the NLRB it is "docketed" (officially listed and given a case number) and assigned to a Board staff member for investigation. The examiner or attorney assigned to the case makes the following five basic inquiries in the investigation:

1. Does the employer meet the Board's jurisdictional standards, *i.e.*, do his operations "affect interstate commerce" and are they large enough to meet the Board's economic "yardstick" requirements?

2. Is there a bona fide or real question concerning representation within the meaning of the statute?

3. What unit shall be deemed appropriate for collective bargaining in this case?

4. Would an election reflect the free choice of the employees concerned and, thereby, effectuate the policies of the Act?

5. If a union files a petition for certification, or an individual seeks a decertification election, is the required interest showing made? (Employers' petitions need not be supported by interest showing.)

Withdrawal or Dismissal Before Hearing

A petitioner in the early stages of an investigation may make a request to withdraw the petition without prejudice. (See Appendix D.) Normally, a petition is withdrawn because the union decides, on its own, that: (1) it requires additional time; (2) the unit sought is inappropriate; (3) a contract bar exists; (4) the union has an insufficient interest showing; or (5) it cannot win a Board election.

The regional director may decide that the petition should be withdrawn or dismissed because it is for an improper unit, because a written contract would, under Board rules, bar an election, or because there is a deficiency of interest; and he may request a withdrawal. Failing to receive the requested withdrawal, the regional director may dismiss the petition. If this happens, the petitioner has 10 days to appeal to the national office of the Board in Washington, which will either affirm the dismissal or direct the regional director to do something else, such as hold a hearing or check interest again.

AFL-CIO Unions

Because of the AFL-CIO's constitutional prohibition of raiding and its internal procedures for dealing with interunion disputes, the NLRB always notifies the AFL-CIO when an affilated union petitions it and another affiliated union is involved in the case. In these cases the Board will not act for two weeks, so as to give the Federation a chance to do something on its own. If a union not affiliated with the AFL-CIO is involved, the Board waits only one week. If one AFL-CIO union petitions where another is certified or has had a contract for more than a year, the Board notifies the AFL-CIO and withholds further action for a month. If the Federation has not resolved the problem during the waiting period, the petition is processed like any other. (See Chapter I, interunion agreements.)

Agreed-Upon Elections

Although since the passage of the Taft-Hartley Act a formal hearing before an election is ordered is compulsory (except in certain picketing cases discussed later) if the parties want it, the Board provides two types of voluntary routes for employers and unions who wish to agree on an election without a formal hearing. These two kinds of arrangements are called "consent election agreements" and "stipulations for certification." (See Appendix D.) In most uncomplicated cases, where it appears appropriate to hold an election, Board agents will attempt to obtain a consent-election agreement, under which all issues that may later arise, such as objections to the election and challenges, may be finally determined by the regional director; or, secondarily, they will try to get a stipulation for certification under which the Board in Washington determines all contested issues, usually after a previous recommendation by the regional director.

It is fair to say, and history and statistics support the assertion, that many employers insist upon a full hearing even where there are relatively simple, uncomplicated issues; and it is a reasonable assumption that this insistence is based on a desire to stall the election until enthusiasm for the union has waned. Unquestionably, employers have, in the past, added *months* to the representation process by insisting upon hearings and using perfectly legal delaying tactics. It is a little more difficult to do that now, although not impossible. Some companies still find it possible to stall for months, but since the Board has delegated "R" case authority to its regional directors, most uncomplicated decisions come out in three to six weeks. Usually, because the regional director is eager to work out a voluntary election agreement, he will permit an employer "to bargain out" the same amount of time as he would have had in a contested case.

Consent-election agreements and stipulations for certification have become more common, mostly because employers lose little or no time by signing them. In both cases the parties agree, subject to regional-director approval, on the essentials: the appropriate unit, time and place of the vote, and the payroll period for determining eligibility. There is often an informal conference dealing with observers, check of the payroll, and the mechanics of the election. This is the proper time to settle such questions as: the number and identity of union and company observers; the physical setup and location of the voting booths; the time of voting; the method of releasing employees from work for voting; and, if possible, problems as to possible challenged votes. Unions and companies that wait until balloting time to meet those problems often regret it.

Summary of Agreed-Upon NLRB Elections

As we have said, there are two kinds of voluntary elections that unions and employers can agree upon. A stipulated-election agreement is one in which the regional director reports the results of his investigation of any challenges or objections to the conduct of the election to the parties and sends a recommendation to the Board. In the stipulated-election procedure, the Board in Washington can make the final decisions. The consent-election procedure, on the other hand, involves an agreement between the union and the employer *to be bound* by the decision of the regional director as to any objections to the election and any challenges. There is *no appeal* to the Board in a *consent election*. The question for organizers looking for elections is which kind of voluntary route should they try to go.

It is impossible to formulate a general rule, to be followed in each instance, as to whether organizers should seek stipulated or consent elections. Some of the considerations are as follows:

1. If the election is being held in a region where the regional director is believed to lean toward management, obviously the union should either go to hearing on the election or insist upon a stipulated election because a consent election would bind it to that regional director's views.

2. If an employer insists on either a stipulated or a consent election and the alternative is the delay resulting from a full hearing, it may be to the union's advantage to take the one the

employer insists on even though it would prefer the other voluntary route because of the conservation of time.

3. If the union knows that a certain employer is likely to
engage in borderline or illegal tactics during the campaign, it
may be better to go to full hearing if the employer will not
agree to a stipulated election.

There are other variables which will have to be taken into
account before the organizer makes the decision on a case-by-case
basis.

Formal Hearings

If the regional office is unable to get the parties to agree to an
informal adjustment of the representation question, a formal
hearing is scheduled. The notice of hearing along with a copy
of the petition is served on all interested parties.

The Board's Statements of Procedure [Section 101.20 (c)]
describe the formal hearing as follows:

> The hearing, usually open to the public, is held before a hearing
> officer who normally is an attorney or field examiner attached to the
> regional office but may be another qualified official. The hearing,
> which is nonadversary in character, is part of the investigation in
> which the primary interest of the Board's agent is to insure that the
> record contains as full a statement of the pertinent facts as may be
> necessary for determination of the case. The parties are afforded full
> opportunity to present their respective positions and to produce the
> significant facts in support of their contentions. In most cases a
> substantial number of the relevant facts are undisputed and stipu
> lated. The parties are permitted to argue orally on the record before
> the hearing officer.

A full transcript is made at the hearing. The parties and the
hearing officers may call witnesses by subpoena and question
them. Witness fees and mileage must be paid by the party at
whose instance the witness appears. The parties and the hearing
officer have the power to introduce written and oral evidence.
Witnesses are sworn, but the strict rules of evidence governing
court trials do not apply. Objections to the rulings of the hearing
officer or the conduct of the hearing may be made in writing or
orally.

If a witness refuses to answer a proper question, the hearing
officer may strike all of his testimony. The hearing officer may

exclude any person for misconduct at the hearing, and even more stringent action may be taken against lawyers who misbehave.

There are certain matters that a good hearing officer will not permit to be litigated at all in a representation hearing. The showing of interest of a union, for instance, is an administrative matter and should not be gone into at the hearing. No testimony introduced to prove the commission of an unfair labor practice should be allowed. Motions to dismiss petitions should not be ruled on by the hearing officer but should be referred to the regional director.

Experience counsels precaution on formal "R" case hearings. Often it is best for unions to be wary, and they should not accept at face value bland predictions by either Board agents or employers that there will not be major issues at a hearing. This is especially true where the union has no legal representative and the employer has a skilled, experienced lawyer. Sometimes an employer will try to "load" a unit with people who should be excluded. Stipulations are often sought on the basis of one-sided testimony or mere statements of the employer. Consequently, where the unit is large and the employer is strongly antiunion and represented by experienced lawyers, the union should consider it almost a necessity to have its own legal counsel at the hearing. Finally, if, during a hearing, an unforeseen major issue arises, the union should give consideration to seeking a postponement in order to get evidence and to have the benefit of legal counsel. In practice, the Board seldom refuses an adjournment request by an unrepresented party for the purpose of securing legal advice or meeting surprise evidence.

After the Hearing

After the hearing closes, the hearing officer reports to the regional director, summarizing issues and evidence, but refraining from making any recommendation. The regional director also gets the entire record made in the case.

Parties may automatically file briefs with the regional director within seven days of the close of the hearing, and the hearing officer may permit more time, not to exceed 14 days. Sometimes, in rare cases, the regional director may permit additional time for filing briefs and, in even more unusual cases, he may listen to oral argument from the parties.

After a complete review of the entire case, the regional director will issue a decision directing an election or dismissing the petition, unless he thinks the case important or difficult enough for direct transmittal to the Board in Washington. In more than 95 percent of the cases the regional directors make the decisions themselves.

Board Review

A party adversely affected by any decision issued by a regional director in a representation case may file within 10 days thereof a request for review by the Board. Pursuant to Section 102.67 (c) of the Rules and Regulations, the Board will grant such a request only upon one or more of the following grounds:

(1) That a substantial question of law or policy is raised because of (a) the absence of, or (b) a departure from, officially reported Board precedent.

(2) That the regional director's decision on a substantial factual issue is clearly erroneous on the record and such error prejudicially affects the rights of a party.

(3) That the conduct of the hearing or any ruling made in connection with the proceeding has resulted in prejudicial error.

(4) That there are compelling reasons for reconsideration of an important Board rule or policy.

To save time, the regional office of the Board will often seek a waiver of the right to file for review and, if successful, will schedule the election as soon as it can. If no waiver is obtained, the Board will schedule the election far enough in advance to permit a Board ruling on a request to review. If there is a request to review, any other party may file a statement opposing review. Both the request for review and the opposition to it must be "self-contained" so that the Board can decide the case without further filings. In both cases, eight copies must be filed with the Board in Washington (carbons are not permitted) and there must be a copy served on all other parties. The practical result in almost every representation case is that the Board is the "supreme court" because ordinarily there is no review of Board election decisions by the courts.

The Election

Board agents conduct NLRB elections. In the vast majority of instances, the elections are conducted on the employer's premises where the employees involved are located and, most frequently, employees vote during working hours. The election is by secret ballot and each party is entitled to an observer who must be a nonsupervisory employee of the employer, in the absence of a written agreement of the parties to the contrary.

Unions may not insist on using professional organizers as observers, just as employers may not insist on naming supervisory or management persons to observe. Sometimes, in a multilingual plant, for instance, the Board will permit each party to have more than one observer. The best observer is one who really knows the people and therefore can best challenge those thought to be ineligible to vote. It also bears saying that the union observer should be a *popular* person with his fellow workers because he is the last person connected with the union whom the voters will see before balloting.

Timing of the Election

The regional director will choose a day for the election, and set hours for the balloting, that will afford an opportunity for substantially all employees, on all shifts, to vote.

If the employer's business is seasonal in nature and there are wide fluctuations in employment depending on whether it is in-season or off-season, the election will be set for a date when peak employment is expected so that the maximum number of eligible employees have an opportunity to express their wishes.[1] Occasionally this rule will result in a delay of many months in holding the election. But if the projected seasonal increase in employment is speculative, and the employer has a substantial complement of year-round employees, the Board may order that an election be held immediately rather than at the anticipated peak season.[2]

Another situation in which the Board may refuse to order an immediate election is where there is an "expanding unit." Such a

---

[1] Nephi Processing Plant, Inc., 107 NLRB 647 (1953), 33 LRRM 1211; Brooksville Citrus Growers, 112 NLRB 707 (1955), 36 LRRM 1076.
[2] Mark Farmer, Inc., 184 NLRB No. 93 (1970), 74 LRRM 1597.

case normally occurs where an employer is opening a new facility or expanding an existing one. The Board will order an election when the employee complement is "representative and substantial" in relation to the anticipated permanent work force. The Board has declined to set a hard and fast formula to determine when the "representative and substantial" standard is met and has said

> The size of the employee complement at the time of the hearing, the nature of the industry, the time expected to elapse before a full, or substantially larger, complement of employees is on hand, and other variables all militate against a rigid formula, and dictate the Board's approach. The Board must often balance what are sometimes conflicting *desiderata*, the insurance of maximum employee participation in the selection of a bargaining agent, and permitting employees who wish to be represented as immediate representation as possible. Thus it would unduly frustrate existing employees' choice to delay selection of a bargaining representative for months or years until the very last employee is on board. Conversely, it would be pointless to hold an election for very few employees, when in a relatively short period the employee complement is expected to multiply many times.[3]

In the case in which the Board made these comments it ordered an election where 40 of a projected 140 employees were already in the unit, and it appeared that over 50 per cent of anticipated future job classifications were represented by these employees.

Where a unit has contracted in size from previous employment levels, an election will be ordered if there are no present plans to increase production and employment to their previous levels in th near future.[4]

Voting Eligibility

Briefly, and in general, employees eligible to vote are those in the unit who were employed in the payroll period selected for the eligibility date and who are also employed on the date of the election. An important exception is made in the construction industry where the Board permits balloting by any employee on the company payroll at least 30 days during the previous year, or any employee on the payroll at least 45 days in the

---

[3] Clement-Blythe Companies, 182 NLRB No. 74 (1970), 74 LRRM 1132.
[4] E.I. duPont de Nemours & Co., 112 NLRB 434 (1955), 36 LRRM 1016.

previous two years, provided that he has had some employment with the company in the last year.[5]

Employees on temporary layoff, or absent because of vacation or sickness are considered employed and therefore may vote if they present themselves. (If there is a large number of such persons it may be possible to arrange for mail ballots.) If the election takes place during a strike, as a general rule both strikers and permanent replacements are eligible to vote. There are, however, times when a striker will not be allowed to vote, as, for example, when he has taken a permanent job elsewhere.[6]

Challenges to Voters

The Board agents and the parties may, for good cause, challenge persons who present themselves at the polls to vote. The Rules and Regulations of the National Labor Relations Board (Section 102.69) state:

> Any party and Board agents may challenge, for good cause, the eligibility of any person to participate in the election. The ballots of such challenged persons shall be impounded.

We take this to mean that as long as an election observer advances a good-faith reason for the nonparticipation of a voter and asserts a challenge, the Board agent *may not* deny him the exercise of the privilege granted by the Board's rules. Good-faith reasons for challenge would include the following:

1. Allegations that the person challenged is a supervisor.

2. Claims that he or she is no longer employed by the employer.

3. Claims that the attempted voter falls within an excluded class or group according to the unit description.

4. Claims that the person was not (or was improperly) on the payroll at the crucial date.

There are, of course, other bases for challenges, but the above-listed ones are the most common. We do not view the function

---

[5] Daniel Construction Co., 133 NLRB 264 (1961), 48 LRRM 1636; Daniel Construction Co., 167 NLRB No. 159 (1967), 66 LRRM 1220.

[6] W. Wilton Wood, Inc., 127 NLRB 1675 (1960), 46 LRRM 1241; Pacific Tile & Porcelain Co., 137 NLRB 1358 (1962), 50 LRRM 1394.

of the Board agent as that of deciding whether the challenged voter is, in fact, eligible; his job is merely to impound the ballot for later decision, provided there are good reasons advanced for the challenge. Accordingly, election observers might well be instructed *not* to sign a statement that the Board properly conducted the election if the Board agent *refused* to permit a good-faith challenge (even though signing such a statement waives nothing).

As an afterthought, we add that arbitrary instructions issued by a Labor Board agent to the effect that observers may challenge only a certain percentage or number of prospective voters generally should be ignored.

One more word needs to be said about challenges. Often the Board, in a preelection conference or at a hearing, will attempt to obtain agreement on eligibility among the parties. An *oral* agreement by an organizer that he is satisfied as to the eligibility of those on a list after such a conference will *not* prevent a challenge based on later or more accurate information, although, of course, even oral agreements as to eligibility should be made with great care.[7]

Where the union and the employer sign a *written* eligibility agreement, the agreement will, however, control. Challenges will not be heard, unless the challenges involve persons, such as supervisors, guards, professionals, or confidential employees, who must be excluded according to the Act or NLRB policy.[8] Consequently, organizers should be *very* careful about signing eligibility agreements or initialling eligibility lists.

In *Cruis Along Boats, Inc.,*[9] the Board affirmed its rule that the parties are held to certain preelection eligibility agreements. Nevertheless, the parties might be allowed to challenge certain voters during the election. In *Cruis Along Boats,* all 11 challenged voters had been included in a previous stipulation by the parties. The regional director certified the question to the Board. The Board held that *the parties were bound by the stipulation "in the absence of some showing by the Petitioner*

---

[7] NLRB v. Hood Corp., 346 F.2d 1020 (CA 9, 1965), 59 LRRM 2418; Lloyd A. Fry Roofing Co., 118 NLRB 312 (1957), 40 LRRM 1223.
[8] Norris Thermador Corp., 119 NLRB 1301 (1958), 41 LRRM 1283; accord Fisher-New Center Co., 184 NLRB No. 92 (1970), 74 LRRM 1609.
[9] 128 NLRB 1019 (1960), 46 LRRM 1419.

that the contentions advanced to repudiate the stipulation were newly discovered or not available at the time of the original hearing." So where there has been fraud by the employer or significant, newly discovered evidence, even a written agreement or a stipulation at a formal hearing may be upset.

Upon the completion of voting, ballots ordinarily are counted immediately by the Board agent with the assistance of representatives of the parties. At the conclusion of the count a tally of ballots normally is served upon the parties. Full opportunity is supposed to have existed, before the voter deposited his ballot into the ballot box, to challenge the ballot if the voter's eligibility was questioned. The secrecy of such challenged ballots is maintained.

Within five days of the service of the tally of ballots upon the parties, objections may be filed (original and 3 copies to the Board, one copy to each party) to the conduct of the election or conduct affecting the results of the election, together with a short statement of the reasons for the objections. Such objections—and challenged ballots where they are determinative of the results of the election—are investigated by an agent of the regional director. The issues are resolved on the basis of an administrative investigation or, if it appears to the regional director that substantial and material factual issues exist which can be resolved best after a hearing, on the basis of a hearing before a hearing officer designated by the regional director. Thereafter, the objections or challenges are resolved by the director in a formal supplemental decision or report. At the conclusion of the case, a certification reflecting the results of the election is issued and copies are served upon the parties.

Runoff Elections

It should be kept in mind that certification of a union as the exclusive bargaining representative of employees depends upon proof that the union represents a majority. *In a tie vote, the union loses* and there is no rerun.

If, however, there are two or more unions on the ballot and no single union has a majority but more votes are cast for union representation than for "no union," the Board will conduct another or runoff election. The eligible voters will be those originally eligible who are still in an eligible category as of the date of the runoff election. No one who was not eligible to vote in the original election can be eligible to vote in the runoff election. In the new election the choice is between the two highest choices in the first election. One such choice may be "no union."

Where Union Is Picketing for Recognition

Where a representation petition is filed involving an employer named in a picketing [8 (b) (7)] charge, it is handled expeditiously if there is a probability that the picketing is for recognition and the petition is filed within a "reasonable time" not exceeding 30 days from the start of the picketing.

In these cases, the Board will investigate to see if the unit is proper and if an election would effectuate the policies of the Act. On the basis of that investigation, the regional director may, without a hearing, order an election or dismiss the petition. Parties aggrieved by his action may seek special permission from the Board to appeal to it. On the other hand, if the regional director believes that a hearing is required, he may order one, at which briefs and delays normally are not allowed. Parties may, with the regional director's consent, resolve their differences in an informal consent procedure in these cases.

If the regional director decides to order an election, the Section 8 (b) (7) charge will be dismissed, unless it is withdrawn. Should the representation petition be withdrawn or dismissed, the processing of the picketing charge continues.

Mailing Lists

On February 6, 1966, the NLRB handed down an important, almost landmark, decision broadening the rights of unions in NLRB election campaigns. In an opinion announced in *Excelsior Underwear, Inc.,*[10] the Board ruled that employers will be required to make available to unions lists of the names and addresses of all eligible voters in election campaigns. This ruling has come to be known as the *Excelsior* rule.

---

[10] 156 NLRB 1236 (1966), 61 LRRM 1217.

The specific language of the Board's ruling is as follows:

> [W]ithin 7 days after the Regional Director has approved a consent-election agreement entered into by the parties pursuant to Section 102.62 of the National Labor Relations Board Rules and Regulations or after the Regional Director or the Board has directed an election pursuant to Section 102.67, 102.69, or 102.85 thereof, the employer must file with the Regional Director an election eligibility list, containing the names and addresses of all the eligible voters. The Regional Director, in turn, shall make this information available to all parties in the case. (Emphasis added)

Excelsior and Mailing Lists

The Board decided in *Excelsior* that unions are entitled to the names and addresses of employees. An employer must, *within seven days* of signing a consent- or stipulated-election agreement or of the direction of an election, supply the Board with a list of names and addresses of all employees. *The Board will make the list available to the union.* Failure to make the list available will be ground for setting an election aside *when proper objections are filed.* An employer may not condition the supplying of the list on a poll as to whether the employees wish to have their names and addresses given to the union or devise other alternatives to supplying the list.[11]

Unions were disappointed that the Board, though it granted the request for mailing lists, denied pleas for open access to the employees on the employer's premises. Indeed, the Board even refused, at this time, to grant unions any automatic right of reply to employer captive-audience speeches.

The Board made it clear that it would wait for the effects of its new mailing-list rule to be felt before it considered any changes in rules with respect to union campaigning on employer premises. The Board said:[12]

> These arguments were, of course, made at a time when we had not yet decided *Excelsior Underwear, Inc.,* 156 NLRB No. 111. Thus, the Unions' allegations as to the effect of employer campaigning on company premises were necessarily predicated on the assumption that a union engaged in efforts to communicate with employees prior

---

[11] Montgomery Ward & Co., 160 NLRB 1188 (1966), 63 LRRM 1107; Union Bleachery, 11-RC-2398 (1966), 63 LRRM 1208; British Auto Parts, Inc., 160 NLRB 239 (1966), 62 LRRM 1591.

[12] General Electric Co., 162 NLRB 912 (1967), 64 LRRM 1104.

to a Board election might not even know the names or addresses of
some of those employees. That assumption, as a result of our decision in *Excelsior,* is no longer valid. Henceforth, whenever an election is directed by the National Labor Relations Board or a Regional
Director, (except for Section 8(b)(7)(C) expedited election, see *Excelsior, supra* . . .) and whenever the parties consent to an election,
all parties to the election will have available to them, within a very
few days, the names and addresses of all eligible voters.

In light of the increased opportunities for employees' access to communications which should flow from *Excelsior,* but with which we
have, as yet, no experience, and because we are not persuaded on the
basis of our current experience that other fundamental changes in
Board policy are necessary to make possible that free and reasoned
choice for or against unionization which the National Labor Relations Act contemplates and which it is our function to insure, we
prefer to defer any reconsideration of current Board doctrine in the
area of plant access until after the effects of *Excelsior* become known.
Accordingly, we shall deny the request for review in *McCullough.*
In *General Electric,* we reject Petitioner's exception to the Regional
Director's recommendations with respect to Objection No. 5 and
shall certify the result of the election.

The issue of union access to workers on company property as
a general election rule is not dead. It is dormant for the time
being. Further consideration of this matter obviously will depend
on how employers use their captive audiences and the results
unions get with the mailing lists.

Suggestions to Organizers Based on Excelsior

1. Organizing campaigns will now need a different type of
planning geared to the availability of employee address lists
after direction of election or employer consent. This planning
should consider extensive house calls, phone contacts, and home
mailing campaigns in addition to other organizing methods.
This should not be a "one-man show" but should be a cooperative effort mobilizing as many key in-plant people as
possible.

2. All mailings should contain materials designed on a *positive
basis.* Unions must realize that they are approaching the worker
and his family in their home and community environment
rather than in that of the factory. They should talk about
what the union can accomplish in terms of security for the family
breadwinner and economic benefits and protections for the

family group. Name calling or attacks upon the employer should be carefully avoided. Mailings should be cleared with organizing directors prior to mailing.

3. These lists must be kept locked in a safe place at all times and never shown or given to any outsiders. Misuse of such lists could jeopardize the communications gain made in the *Excelsior* decision.

4. When an election is won, preserve the list. It can come in handy later.

5. If an election is lost, again *preserve* the mailing list. It may be invaluable for a later campaign.

Remember, the techniques made possible by the availability of the mailing lists are not a substitute for a regular campaign or traditional methods but, rather, an aid and adjunct to them.

Getting the list—Organizers should *not* rely on the NLRB automatically making the list available, even though it will do so. Tell the NLRB regional director or his agent that you want the list *as soon as it is received* from the employer. If you are located near the NLRB office, it would be wise to pick up the list. The sooner you have it, the better you can use it to inform those in the unit.

Timing—If a payroll eligibility date is selected which is later than the consent-election agreement, or the ordered election date, the employer may wait until seven days from that date. So, to get the list as soon as possible, seek to have as the payroll eligibility date the one prior to the date of the election order or consent agreement. If the organizers want to make two weeks' use of the list, they should try to set the election date *three weeks ahead of the agreement date because the employer has a week in which to supply the Board with the list.*

Extensions of time in supplying the list—We assume that the union will oppose *all* employer requests to extend the seven-day limit in which the list is to be furnished. Extensions are not likely to be granted except in very unusual situations.

No right of waiver—You should know that, as of now, the Board will not permit a union to waive its right to the mailing lists. Moreover, it is not likely to do so in the future. There are excellent policy reasons for this rule. After all, the purpose of the *Excelsior* mailing-list rule is not to help unions. It is to permit employees to be better informed, so the fact that a union may wish to waive the right to get a concession from the employer or speed the election should not be wholly determinative. And, of course, where there are two or more unions, the one that had most of the names and addresses could waive and embarrass the others into waiving, or else accuse the others of delaying the election by insisting on the list. Finally, if the right of waiver existed, employers probably would insist on a waiver in most cases as consideration for agreeing to a prompt election, so that the mailing-list rule would have less and less value.

Refusal to supply lists—In the case of *Wyman-Gordon* v. *NLRB*,[13] decided in April 1969, the United States Supreme Court passed on a number of questions concerning the legality of the *Excelsior* rule which had split the lower courts. Most importantly the Court held that the substance of the rule—that employers be required to supply name and address lists prior to an election—was proper. The Court said that, although in simply announcing the new rule in the *Excelsior* case the Board had acted improperly, it could, on a case by case basis, order employers to supply the lists. Thus in the *Wyman-Gordon* case itself, because the regional director had ordered the employer to supply the list as part of his Direction of Election, the employer was obligated to do so.

If an employer, after being ordered to supply the list, refuses to do so, the Board has two options. It can either go ahead and hold the election and then set it aside upon objection if the union loses, or it can use its *subpoena* power to force the employer to produce the list. Following the *Wyman-Gordon* decision it seems unlikely that many employers will refuse to supply the lists.

Errors in list—Check the mailing list as soon as possible and complain promptly to the NLRB if it is inaccurate. If an employer *intends* to defraud the union with a bogus list, he is buying a lot of trouble. Honest but substantial errors in the list, say 10 to 15 percent, may also invalidate an election.[14]

---

[13] 394 US 759 (1969), 70 LRRM 3345.
[14] *See* Pacific Gamble Robinson Co., 180 NLRB No. 84 (1970), 73 LRRM 1049.

In one case where an employer gave the NLRB a "substantially inaccurate" list for transmission to the union and used a corrected list for its own mailings, without supplying the new list to the Board and the union, the election was set aside.[15] Nor will an employer's claim that the union already has the information relieve him of the obligation to supply the list.[16]

Objections—Failure to supply a list is a good ground for setting aside a lost election, but proper objections must be filed within five working days after the results are announced.

NLRB Election-Information Program

In 1967, the Board took an important step toward better administration of the Act in elections. The NLRB press release described the new election procedures as follows:

> The Board project seeks not only to alert workers to their rights, but also to warn unions and management against conduct impeding fair and free elections. The Agency, which conducts about 8,000 elections a year with a 90 percent rate of voter participation, is seeking to avoid post-election objections by stimulating fair play in the election process and forewarning interested parties against prohibited conduct.
>
> The three-part effort includes leaflets explaining the election process; plant bulletin board notices reminding employees, employers and labor organizations of mutual rights and responsibilities; and election notices which, in addition to giving the time and place of the balloting and displaying a sample ballot as in the past, now include a reminder of the right of workers to vote free of improper pressures.
>
> The leaflets will be available at NLRB headquarters in Washington and the 31 Regional Offices for distribution to interested working men and women. The first bulletin board notice to employees will be issued when a petition is filed with the Board seeking an election to determine whether employees want to be represented by a union. If an election is ordered or agreed to, the second bulletin board notice of election will be issued. (In more than 75 percent of the cases, employers and labor organizations consent to the holding of NLRB elections.)
>
> Emphasized in all three documents is the workers' right under Federal law to self-organization, to bargain collectively through representatives of their own choosing or to refrain from any or all such

---

[15] Titche-Goettinger Co., not reported (1967).

[16] *See, e.g.,* Murphy Bonded Warehouse, Inc., 180 NLRB No. 29 (1969), 72 LRRM 1609.

activities. All parties to the election are urged to
in "maintaining basic principles of a fair electi
law." They are specifically warned against:

Making threats of loss of jobs or loss of benefits by
of carrying out such a threat

Firing employees or causing them to be fired in order to encourage
or discourage union activity

Making promises of promotions, pay raises, or other benefits, to
influence an employee vote, by a party capable of carrying out
any such promise

Making threats of physical force or violence to employees to influence their vote in the election

Making misstatements of important facts where another party does
not have a fair chance to reply

Making campaign speeches to assembled groups of employees on
company time within the 24-hour period before the election.

Inciting racial or religious prejudice by inflammatory appeals.

Conclusion

Any organizer worthy of the name must have some basic
familiarity with the Board's representation-case procedure, for in
most cases this is the generally accepted method of winning an
enforceable right to recognition.

While one need not have legal training to handle successfully
most of the problems that arise under this procedure, in a few
cases legal representation is an absolute necessity. Where there
is, for instance, a complicated issue as to the composition of the
appropriate unit or the eligibility of a significant number of
workers, or even just a very large unit, the organizer would be
well advised to consult a lawyer. Normally, in these instances,
employers retain counsel.

CHAPTER VII

BARGAINING UNITS

Experience is of all teachers the most
dependable, and . . . experience also
is a continuous process.

Mr. Justice Sutherland in
Funk v. *United States,*
290 US 371, 381 (1933)

Introduction

The bargaining unit is that group of employees which is represented by the union in collective bargaining. The union has exclusive bargaining rights for those employees within the unit; it has no bargaining rights, per se, for those employees outside the bargaining unit. The bargaining unit concept is of critical importance in organizing.

The definition of the "appropriate bargaining unit" may have a great effect on the success or failure of an organizing campaign, and will influence the type of campaign that is conducted. In order to determine whether a petitioning union has a sufficient showing of interest there must, at the every least, be a presumption that the unit in which the interest showing is tested is a proper unit. If a union with an apparent majority seeks recognition in a plainly inappropriate unit, an employer may lawfully refuse to bargain. If there is to be a representation election the Board will hold it only in an appropriate unit.

Although there is, naturally, little talk of it in either the parties' arguments or in the Board's decisions, what is most basically at stake in contested bargaining unit determinations is the likelihood of election victory. The union will normally urge the appropriateness of a unit in which it feels it has a good chance to win a majority. The employer will often approach the question of appropriateness with an eye toward defining a unit in which the union cannot achieve a majority.

In the absence of agreement between the parties the NLRB determines the appropriate bargaining unit. The Labor Board's power to define the bargaining unit comes from Section 9 of the Act which directs that the Board "shall decide . . . the unit appropriate for the purposes of collective bargaining." The Supreme Court has ruled that such determinations will not be overturned unless they are "lacking in a rational basis." [1] Very few unit determinations are so unreasonable as to be overturned by the courts. Although the Act has been amended since that time to include a number of minor considerations to be used by the Board when it acts, such as the special situations involving plant guards and professional employees, its unit-determination power and authority remain very broad. In most cases, NLRB representational decisions are not directly reviewable by the courts.

The Board is not required to find the *most* appropriate unit. Often, employers try to enlarge the scope of the unit to the point where the organizing union cannot hope to win an election or, in some cases, even make the required showing of interest. But the Board has solidly established the proposition that a union need not seek an election in the *most comprehensive* unit possible but can, instead, have one in *any* appropriate unit; that is, one that constitutes a homogeneous, identifiable, and distinct grouping of employees. As the Board said in *Federal Electric Corp.*:[2]

> Section 9(b) of the Act directs the Board to make appropriate unit determinations which will 'assure to employees the fullest freedom in exercising rights guaranteed by the Act,' i.e., the rights of self organization and collective bargaining. In effectuating this mandate, the Board has emphasized that the Act does not compel labor organizations to seek representation in the most comprehensive grouping of employees unless such grouping constitutes the only appropriate unit,

---

[1] NLRB v. Hearst Publications, 322 US 111 (1944), 14 LRRM 614.
[2] 157 NLRB 1130 (1966), 61 LRRM 1500.

and again in *Bagdad Copper Co.*:[3]

> Recently, the Board, in order to effectuate this mandate [of Section
> 9(b)], re-emphasized its view that the Act does not compel labor orga-
> nizations to seek representation in the most comprehensive grouping
> of employees unless such grouping constitutes the *only* appropriate
> unit.

The Board's special emphasis on the rule that the unit can be
any appropriate one, instead of the most comprehensive grouping, has been expressed on numerous occasions.[4]

In *Continental Baking*[5] the Board set forth its general criteria for making unit determinations:

> First and foremost is the principle that *mutuality of interest* in
> wages, hours, and working conditions is the prime determinant of
> whether a given group of employees constitutes an appropriate unit.
> In deciding whether the requisite mutuality exists, the Board looks
> to such factors as to the *duties, skills,* and *working conditions* of the
> employees involved, and especially to any *existing bargaining history.*
> In relevant cases, the Board also considers the extent of organization,
> and the desires of employees where one of two units may be equally
> appropriate. Where the employees of more than one plant of an
> employer are involved, such factors as the *extent of integration* be-
> tween plants, *centralization* of management and supervision, em-
> ployee *interchange,* and the *geographical location* of the several
> plants are also considered. (Emphasis added)

Most of the rest of this chapter will be devoted to an examination of the Board's elaboration of these general criteria for application to various situations. But before moving on to particular types of unit problems, we should say a few words about
several matters of general importance in the area of unit determination.

Agreement by Parties on Scope of Bargaining Unit

The Board encourages unions and employers to reach agreement on the appropriate unit for bargaining. The Board has
said that it "has a 'well established policy of honoring conces-
sions made in the interest of expeditious handling of represen-

---

[3] 144 NLRB 1496 (1963), 54 LRRM 1264.

[4] *See, e.g.,* P. Ballentine & Sons, 141 NLRB 1103 (1963), 52 LRRM 1453; F. W.
Woolworth Co., 144 NLRB 307 (1963), 54 LRRM 1043; Dixie Bell Mills, Inc., 139
NLRB 629 (1962), 51 LRRM 1344; Sav-On Drugs, Inc., 138 NLRB 1032 (1962), 51
LRRM 1152; Quaker City Life Ins. Co., 134 NLRB 960 (1961), 49 LRRM 1281.

[5] 99 NLRB 777 (1952), 30 LRRM 1119.

tation cases,' even though there may be some question of the ultimate propriety of including certain employees in the unit were the matter litigated." [6] Where such an agreement is reached, it will normally be approved by the regional director and form the basis for a Stipulation for Certification and consent election.[7]

Once there is a stipulation, "the Board is bound by the parties' stipulation of the unit, unless that unit is inappropriate as a matter of law. Only where the parties' stipulation is ambiguous may the Board turn to consider the usual factors governing the 'appropriate' unit in determining whether employees fall within or without the unit." [8] Normally the Board's role after a stipulation is confined to "merely interpreting the language used by the parties to define and limit the unit." [9]

The lesson for organizers should be clear: It is often desirable to stipulate so that a quick election will be held. But once you have stipulated to the inclusion or exclusion of certain employees you will normally be bound by your agreement.

Another kind of agreement about bargaining units should be briefly noted. If a union has agreed not to seek to represent certain employees during the term of a contract which it has with an employer covering other employees, it will be bound by that agreement, and a representation petition filed during the contract term will be dismissed.[10]

Accretions

An accretion is the addition to an established bargaining unit of employees who have not previously been a part of that unit. A true accretion will be recognized by the Board without the holding of an election. An accretion exists where it can be shown that the employees sought to be included really are a part of the already existing unit rather than a distinct group that should belong to a separate unit or be given the choice of joining or not joining the unit.

---

[6] Stop 127, Inc., 172 NLRB No. 41 (1968), 68 LRRM 1318.
[7] See NLRB Rules and Regulations Sec. 102.62(b).
[8] Electrical Workers v. NLRB, 418 F.2d 1191 (CA DC, 1969), 71 LRRM 2991.
[9] NLRB v. J. J. Collins' Sons, 332 F.2d 523 (CA 7, 1964), 56 LRRM 2375.
[10] Briggs Indiana Corp., 63 NLRB 1270 (1945), 17 LRRM 46; Allis-Chalmers Mfg. Co., 179 NLRB No. 1 (1969), 72 LRRM 1241.

Typically, accretion questions arise where an employer creates new job classifications, or expands the scope of his operations, or merges with another company, or buys or builds a new plant. Obviously, it will be to the advantage of a union representing an established unit to argue that the "new" employees are an accretion to that unit. In this way it will get representational rights without the difficulty of an election. On the other hand, if there are two or more unions representing units of employees of a particular employer, there may be a conflict about which unit the "new" employees should be added to. And if there is an outside union which would like to represent these employees it will argue that there is no accretion at all and that there must be an election.

If the jobs sought to be added to the unit were in existence at the time of the original certification, and were not included in the unit or in subsequent bargaining, normally the Board will hold that there can be no accretion.[11] The same rule applies as to plants that were in existence at the time of the original certification.

In determining whether there is an accretion the Board tries to discern whether there is a community of interest between the "new" employees and those in the existing unit. The factors that it evaluates are similar to those used in other unit-determination situations.[12] They include:

1. Is there common supervision of the new employees and unit employees?

2. Are the new jobs of the same kind as the unit jobs? Are the required skills similar?

3. Is the new operation functionally integrated with the old operation?

4. Do the new employees work in close physical proximity to the old employees [or is the new plant close to the old plant (s)]?

---

[11] Crucible Steel Casting, 162 NLRB 1513 (1967), 64 LRRM 1211.

[12] *See, e.g.,* Lee Way Motor Freight, Inc., 138 NLRB 937 (1962), 51 LRRM 1170; Local 620 AIW v. NLRB, 375 F.2d 707 (CA 6, 1967), 64 LRRM 2828; General Iron Works Co., 150 NLRB 190 (1964) , 58 LRRM 1068. One note of caution should be mentioned. If an employer extends recognition for new employees to a union on an accretion theory, and the Board later finds that no true accretion existed, both the employer and the union will be held guilty of unfair labor practices. Sheraton-Kauai Corp. v. NLRB, 429 F.2d 1352 (CA 9, 1970), 74 LRRM 2933; *contra* NLRB v. Appleton Electric, 296 F.2d 202 (CA 7, 1961) , 49 LRRM 2103.

5. Is there much interchange between employees in the unit jobs and the new jobs? Were any unit employees transferred to the new jobs?

6. Is there any history of bargaining for the new employees with the unit employees?

7. Do the new employees have equivalent wages, hours, fringe benefits and working conditions to the unit employees?

8. Is the new operation part of the same company administrative unit as the old operation?

Although accretion questions arise, and may be determined, in several ways perhaps the easiest, and now the most common, is through a unit-clarification (UC) petition filed with the Board. Either an employer or a union may file such a petition.

Self-Determination Elections

Although in most disputed cases the Board decides the appropriate unit, sometimes the Board will order a special kind of election in which employees are given a choice of which unit (if any) they want to be a part of. As we shall see, such a procedure is required by the Act before professional employees can be included in a unit with non-professionals. It is also utilized by the Board occasionally where other identifiably distinct groups, such as craftsmen, technicians, or members of a department might appropriately be included in any of several units or in no unit.[13] Recently the Board has directed self-determination elections to determine whether employees wished to continue separate representation (by the same union) or to be represented by that union in a multiplant unit.[14]

---

[13] *See, e.g.,* National Cash Register Co., 168 NLRB No. 130 (1967), 67 LRRM 1041. *See also Libbey-Owens-Ford Glass Co.,* 169 NLRB No. 2 (1968), 67 LRRM 1096, where the Board directed self-determination elections among the employer's employees in two single-plant units represented separately by the same union to determine whether they wished to be represented as part of a multiplant unit together with the eight other plants of the employer then represented by the same union in the multiplant unit.

[14] Libbey-Owens-Ford Glass Co., *above,* note 13, NLRB enjoined (DC DC, 1968), 67 LRRM 2712, reversed 403 F.2d 916 (CA DC, 1968), 68 LRRM 2447, cert. denied 393 US 1016 (1969), 70 LRRM 2225.

Identifying the Employer: Related Employers,
Joint Employers, and Contract Employees

Sometimes situations arise where it is necessary to determine who the employer is before it can be decided what an appropriate bargaining unit is. One such situation arises where there are a number of related business enterprises, often constituted as separate corporations, and the union seeks a single bargaining unit including employees of the related businesses. If sufficient interrelation among the several enterprises can be shown, such as common ownership and management, integrated operations, and common physical location, the Board will hold that the several entities constitute a single employer and is likely to find a bargaining unit encompassing employees of the several units appropriate.[15]

In recent years a very common type of case in this area has involved a large department or discount store, one or more of whose departments is operated by an outside company under an operating agreement. The question of who the employer is often comes up when a union seeks a unit including all of the selling employees in the store, and the store claims that the outside company, rather than it, is the employer of those employees working in the contracted-for department. The Board's approach is to look at the operating agreement and the practice to see how much control of the department's operation is retained by the store. If it finds that significant control is retained over the mode of operation of the department, and especially over the terms and conditions of employment of the department's employees, the Board will find that the store and the outside operator are "joint employers" and, if it is otherwise appropriate, the department's employees will be included in the same unit with other store employees.[16]

Another type of case where identifying the employer becomes important is where a company uses "contract employees"—employees supplied by an agency to perform work that is usually a regular part of the company's operations. It appears that the Board will examine the same kind of evidence in these cases

---

[15] *See* Okeh Caterers, 179 NLRB No. 84 (1969), 72 LRRM 1405.
[16] *See, e.g.,* Thriftown, Inc., 161 NLRB 603 (1966), 63 LRRM 1298; K-Mart Division of S. S. Kresge Co., 161 NLRB 1127 (1966), 63 LRRM 1385; and Jewel Tea Co., 162 NLRB 508 (1966), 64 LRRM 1054.

as in the contract-department cases. It will examine how much control each company exercises over the employees. In holding in the *Manpower* case [17] that the company using the labor and the agency were joint employers the Board found that the company tested the employees to determine if they were qualified and could reject unqualified employees, gave the employees safety instructions and a safety manual, established the work schedules and made work assignments, and generally supervised the employees in their work. This was sufficient evidence of control even though the agency hired and fired the employees, determined their rates of pay, and made for them the contributions and deductions required by law.

Multi-Employer Unit

Bargaining on a multi-employer basis has been increasing in recent years. Some think that advantages are offered to both the union and the employer. Sometimes greater knowledge and experience are brought to the bargaining table, uniformity in wages and working conditions is achieved among otherwise competing employers, and certain problems, such as automation, are handled better than at the single-employer level. Although Congress, at one time, considered making such units illegal, it is clear that such units are valid under the law.[18]

The question of whether an employer is to be considered as part of a multi-employer unit is to be determined from his intention,[19] and this intention may be manifested by actively participating in the *current* negotiations of a joint group, [20] or by participating in such a group for a substantial period of time.[21] For a finding of a multi-employer unit there is no necessity that the unit be certified initially on such a basis by the Board. Continuing to bargain in a multi-employer group precludes the individual employer from withdrawing from the group, unless reasonable notice has been given before negotiations have begun or unless special circumstances arise during the course of collective bargaining.[22] The same rules apply to

[17] Manpower, Inc., 164 NLRB No. 37 (1967), 65 LRRM 1059.
[18] NLRB v. Teamsters Local 449, 353 US 87 (1957), 39 LRRM 2603.
[19] The Kroger Co., 148 NLRB 569 (1964), 57 LRRM 1021.
[20] United Productions of America, 111 NLRB 390 (1955), 35 LRRM 1490.
[21] Quality Limestone Products, Inc., 143 NLRB 589 (1963), 53 LRRM 1357.
[22] *Ibid.*

unions that wish to bargain together as a single unit or that wish to bargain with a multi-employer group.[23]

Whether or not there is a multi-employer unit can be very important in organizing. For example, in *Des Moines Packing Co.*[24] the Board was confronted with the following situation: The United Packinghouse Workers had organized two separate companies, the Des Moines Packing Co. and the Bookey Packing Co. The two companies chose to bargain together. Negotiating teams for both the union and management sides came from both companies. The contracts were virtually identical, the differences resulting from the slightly different type of operation at each company.

After the last contract was signed, an independent union was organized at the Des Moines Co. and sought recognition from the employer. The employer filed a petition with the Board in order to find out who represented the employees. The Board held here that past bargaining history was important. The employer had taken no steps toward withdrawing from the multi-employer unit, nor did it want to bargain separately. The bargaining had been an effective form of representation in the past, so the Board refused to permit an election in the one plant because it found there was a single unit spreading across both companies. If there had been individual bargaining in the two plants, there is no doubt that the independent union would have gotten an election, but because the Board found the single plant to be an inappropriate unit, no election was held.

Where there is no past history, or the history is vague, the Board will consider such criteria as mutual interests of employees, amount of interchange of employees, extent of organization, centralization of management, desires of employees and geography. These factors are often the same as those considered by the Board in deciding whether single-plant or multiplant units of a single employer should be classified as appropriate units. Because one employer so often has multiple plants, that situation will be explored more deeply.

---

[23] Evening News Assn., 154 NLRB 1494 (1965), 60 LRRM 1149, affirmed 372 F.2d 569 (CA 6, 1967), 64 LRRM 2403; Publishers Assn. of New York City v. NLRB, 364 F.2d 293 (CA 2, 1966), 62 LRRM 2722.
[24] 106 NLRB 206 (1953), 32 LRRM 1432.

One Employer—Multi- or Single-Location Unit

Many employers have an organizational structure which features plants or stores spread over a wide geographical area. The Board considers a number of factors before deciding whether an "appropriate bargaining unit" is composed of a single plant or whether all the plants of a single employer constitute a single unit.

One of the most significant factors, as in multi-employer units, is the extent to which there is a prior bargaining history.[25] Its presence and character can be crucial. If there has been prior bargaining as a multiplant unit, the Board possibly will consider this a determining factor leading it to conclude that a multiplant unit is the appropriate one. The Board's theory is that the purpose of organizing is to achieve a system of collective bargaining; once that object is achieved, it is not easily changed by later organizing efforts. Conversely, the absence of a prior bargaining history as a multiplant unit may lead the Board to find a single unit proper. In *Sav-On Drugs, Inc.*,[26] the Board considered the lack of prior multistore bargaining history as a point in favor of considering a single store to be "appropriate," although the employer had other stores in the area.

The physical proximity of plants to one another is a second point of consideration. In the case of *Bear River Lumber Co.*[27] the fact that the two plants, a sawmill and a planing mill, were only two and a half miles apart was found significant by the Board. Stores in the *Sav-On Drugs* case were confined to the New York metropolitan area; however, as a factual matter, they were spread fairly widely over the area. The distances between stores varied from 5 to 63 miles. The Board found that they were too far apart to coordinate their bargaining efforts.[28]

The question of the "appropriate" unit turns in part on the relations among the employees in different locations as well as the nature of their supervision. In the *Bear River Lumber Co.*

---

[25] For three different opinions on the problems of combining several individual units into a single multiplant unit *see PPG Industries*, 180 NLRB No. 58 (1969), 73 LRRM 1001.

[26] Sav-On Drugs, Inc., *above*, note 4.

[27] 150 NLRB 1295 (1965), 58 LRRM 1261.

[28] *See also* McCoy Co., 151 NLRB 383 (1965), 58 LRRM 1442.

situation the Board found that a significant number of employees *were transferred* or *used interchangeably* between the two operations, and that indicated a common operation. Further, the president of Bear River personally *directed the work of both groups*. We can contrast this with *Parsons Investment Co.*[29] where the Board found that two units of maintenance employees were appropriate, although the two office buildings were commonly owned and were separated only by an alley. The board held that the chief consideration was that supervision was separately exercised within each of the buildings. Each supervisor did his own hiring, firing, and promoting. Furthermore, in contrast to *Bear River,* where the president ordered all of the materials used, the supervisor for each building ordered his own.

Another factor which the Board considers is the formation of labor policy. If there is centralized administration of labor policy, the Board is more likely to determine that a multiplant unit is appropriate. However, this can be outweighed by other considerations. In the *McCoy Co.* case, the employer had a centrally administered labor policy with regard to wages, pensions, and insurance. All employees hired had to be approved by the central office. These were important considerations in favor of a multiplant unit, the Board found, but not important enough to outweigh the otherwise local nature of supervision in general, the great distance between stores, the lack of transfer of employees from one branch to another, and the general lack of bargaining history covering a multiplant operation.

Another factor is the extent of union organization. The Act was amended [Section 9 (c) (5)] to prevent this factor from controlling. However, the Board is not precluded from considering it as a factor.[30] This consideration has been in controversy lately in connection with the organizational efforts among insurance agents. If the union is unable to get representation on a statewide basis but can make collective bargaining meaningful within some smaller geographical unit, such as a metropolitan area, or at a single office, as in the *Metropolitan* case cited above, it may convince the Board of the propriety of the smaller unit. For in that case, the union had attempted to organize on a

29 152 NLRB 192 (1965), 59 LRRM 1027.
30 Metropolitan Life Insurance Co., 147 NLRB 688 (1964), 56 LRRM 1342.

state-wide basis but had been unable to do so. After considering
the geographical area and the degree of supervision as well as
the generally independent character of insurance agents, the
Board held that a unit confined to the one office in the city
of Holyoke, Massachusetts, constituted an appropriate unit. Apparently, in line with the policy of the Act, the Board reasoned
that collective bargaining is desirable, and, therefore, unionization should not be impeded. While a larger unit, such as one
covering the entire state, might be better, it would seem that
this smaller unit, like half a loaf, was considered better than
none.

The Board has recently said that a single-location unit in a
retail chain is presumptively appropriate, *i.e.,* that such a unit
will be found appropriate unless countervailing factors are present.[31] Yet hard-and-fast rules do not come easily.[32] Perhaps the
best way to say it is that the Board looks at each particular case
and decides which factors seem the most important. There was
a time, for instance, when the Board established retail bargaining units solely on the basis of the employer's administrative
organization. This policy was changed in the *Sav-On Drugs*
case, above; and now the Board applies the same tests to
retail stores as to all other industries. A good example is *Big
Y Supermarket*.[33] Here the Board weighed the employer's centralized administrative organization against other important factors such as the independent authority of store managers in labor
matters, the absence of employee interchange, and the absence of
past bargaining in a larger unit and found each store to be
an appropriate bargaining unit.

The pattern of unionization within the employer's organization
may also be considered. In *Joseph E. Seagram & Sons, Inc.,*[34]
the Board had to decide how much weight to give to the fact
that the *production* employees in 15 Seagram plants were represented by a single union as a single unit, in the light of a
petition by a union requesting the Board to find that a unit
composed of the guards at four of the plants was appropriate.

---

[31] Haag Drug Co., Inc., 169 NLRB No. 111 (1968), 67 LRRM 1289.
[32] *Compare The Pep Boys,* 172 NLRB No. 23 (1968), 68 LRRM 1308, where the
Board dismissed a petition for a single-store unit because a combination of factors
was sufficient to "overcome the presumption."
[33] 161 NLRB 1263 (1966), 63 LRRM 1412.
[34] 101 NLRB 101 (1952), 31 LRRM 1022.

The fact that all the production employees were covered in one unit, "although persuasive, should not *invariably* control the bargaining pattern for every other group of unorganized employees," the Board said. It certified the unit composed of guards from the four plants.

Occasionally the Board has recognized that either a single or a multilocation unit would be appropriate and has left the choice up to the involved employees by ordering a self-determination election.[35]

Cases sometimes arise where a union petitions for neither a single-location nor a company-wide unit but rather for a grouping of plants or stores in a particular geographic area. Such a "regional" unit may be appropriate if sufficient economic and geographic integration and community of interest of the workers in the region can be shown.[36]

Some have said that the Board has created confusion by throwing out a lot of factors, no single one of which it considers determinative in *arriving at its judgment* as to whether a particular unit is, or is not, "appropriate." But this process of judgment is no different from the one people normally use every day. For example, in driving a car we often make a decision whether to pass the car ahead. That decision is based on a number of considerations—how fast both cars are going, how much of a hurry we're in, the type of pavement, the weather, how alert we are, and how fast our car can go. To say that we pass the car ahead without thinking is obviously wrong. It is not a mechanical decision. We arrive at a judgment about passing much as the Board does about the appropriate unit. The only difference between the two kinds of decisions is that the Board, in creating a unit which can engage in meaningful collective bargaining, is required to sit down and write out its reasons, while in day-to-day personal decisions there normally is no such requirement.

To summarize, it would seem that the Board must examine evidence on the following points before it decides the scope of a bargaining unit:

---

[35] *See, e.g.*, Hilton-Burns Hotel Co., 167 NLRB No. 29 (1967), 66 LRRM 1033.

[36] *See, e.g.*, Drug Fair, 180 NLRB No. 94 (1969), 73 LRRM 1065. *See*, for an example of an impermissible regional unit, *Local 1325, Retail Clerks* v. *NLRB*, 414 F.2d 1194 (CA DC, 1969), 71 LRRM 2721.

1. Does the unit asked for have a prior history of collective bargaining? If so, the Board will rely heavily on it.

2. Are the plants located in close physical proximity to one another? If so, the Board might tend to favor a company-wide unit in the interest of coordinated bargaining.

3. Are the plants run as one operation, with employees of one being used interchangeably with employees of the other? This can incline the Board to find that the company-wide or multiplant unit is favored because the employees of the various plants have a common interest and common contacts. (Remember, mutuality of interest is always *very* important.)

4. Are the plants supervised by the same persons, and do they have the same scale of wages and other benefits? If so, the Board will favor a company-wide unit on the ground that the company is functionally integrated in its operation.

5. Are the labor policies of the various plants coordinated by one central office so that all the hiring, firing, promotion, and labor-relations matters are handled on a centralized basis? If so, the Board is likely to favor a company-wide unit, for the company has indicated by its actions that it sees its labor policy as an integrated whole.

6. What is the extent of organization in this plant and in this industry? The scope of organizing may be important, but never controlling.

7. What is the pattern of organization within the structure of the employer's operations among other kinds of employees in other unions? A bargaining history among other types of company employees can be important.

Production-and-Maintenance Units

The industrial unit that is usually sought, and normally granted, in a newly organized plant is a production-and-maintenance unit. Such a unit is described, for purposes of the Representation Petition, in language such as the following:

Included

All production and maintenance employees at the Employer's Madison, Wisconsin plant.

Excluded

All other employees of the employer, including office clericals, guards, and supervisors as defined in the National Labor Relations Act.[37]

Where there is no history of collective bargaining, and where there is no objection made to the joining of production and maintenance workers in a single unit, the request will be granted.[38] As a matter or fact, production-and-maintenance units are generally favored in industrial plants.

If there have been historically two units, represented by two different unions, the Board will be reluctant to upset these bargaining arrangements and merge the two units into one unless both units vote for inclusion in such a combination. In *Federal Yeast Corp.*[39] the bargaining history revealed that production and maintenance employees had bargained with the employer separately for 12 to 15 years prior to the petitioner's appearance. In view of this evidence of two separate units, the Board allowed each unit to vote separately with the understanding that should both vote for inclusion in a single unit, the Board would honor the request. It stated:

In accordance with our usual practice and in recognition of the normal community of interest between production and maintenance workers, absent the bargaining history at the Employer's plant, we would find the overall unit appropriate. However, the Board is reluctant to disturb existing . . . units, established by collective bargaining.

Where the situation is the reverse, however, and the historical unit consists of a single unit of production and maintenance employees, the Board will *not* permit a severance.[40] In the normal case, the Board will hold that the community of interest present initially, and intensified through a history of collective bargaining, will preclude such severance.

Where this bargaining history is absent, the Board will turn to

---

[37] The reasons for these exclusions will be made clear in later sections of this chapter.
[38] *See* A. O. Smith Corp., 111 NLRB 200 (1955), 35 LRRM 1444.
[39] 100 NLRB 826 (1952), 30 LRRM 1353.
[40] Cincinnati Division, Davison Chemical Co., 110 NLRB 85 (1954), 34 LRRM 1606.

a consideration of a number of factors before deciding whether to designate the two groups as one unit or two.[41]

1. *Degree of integration of the two units*—Where transfers had been made over a period of time between two units and promotions were made from the maintenance unit into the production unit as a matter of course, the Board held that there was, in substance, a common interest and therefore a single unit.[42]

2. *Degree of integration in employer's operations*—The problem here is one of interchange of employees between different types of jobs. In *Ben Pearson's Inc.,*[43] employees were constantly shifted between the two production divisions in response to shifts in consumer demand, and between the maintenance and production sections, so the Board found that the appropriate unit was one of all production and maintenance employee—a single "P & M" unit.

3. *Degree of centralization*—This point depends on how the employer has run his plant in the past. If the employer, as in *Ben Pearson's,* has had such things as a single labor-relations supervisor, a payroll based upon manufacturing divisions rather than a separation of maintenance from production employees, and only one set of such facilities as parking lots or locker rooms, the Board is again likely to find that the two groups should be treated as one. Conversely, if the employer maintained separate operations, the Board may be led to certify each operation separately, assuming no objection from any party. The range of factors varies, but the greatest single one is the presence or absence of collective bargaining history.[44]

Where two unions are involved in organizing a plant, and one seeks an inclusive production-and-maintenance unit, while the other seeks a true departmental or craft unit, which consists of only part of the production or maintenance employees, the Board will usually direct a self-determination election which will

---

[41] *See* American Cyanamid, 131 NLRB 909 (1961), 48 LRRM 1152. A recent case where a maintenance unit was found to be inappropriate is *Monsanto Co.,* 183 NLRB No. 53 (1970), 74 LRRM 1300.

[42] McKamie Gas Cleaning Co., 80 NLRB 1447 (1948), 23 LRRM 1244.

[43] 133 NLRB 636 (1961), 48 LRRM 1708.

[44] *See* Warner Lambert Pharmaceutical Co., 131 NLRB 1441 (1961), 48 LRRM 1279.

allow the departmental or craft employees to decide which unit they wish to be in.

The Board, it should be clear at this point, prefers a combined unit of production and maintenance employees to separate units. However, whatever its practice in this regard, it will not certify a *segment* of an unorganized maintenance or production unit except for certain craft or craft-type situations. For example, four departments of nine in a plant devoted to general plant maintenance, arbitrarily gathered together, do not make up an appropriate unit. [45]

Residual Units

Before leaving production and maintenance it would be well to give some consideration to "residual" units. A residual unit will consist of that group of employees, generally varied in skills, which is left over after a unit containing fewer than all employees has been found to be appropriate. The usefulness and appropriateness of the residual unit arise out of the exclusion of employees from the first unit and their consequent unrepresented status. The residual unit concept provides these employees with an opportunity for representation in a readily available unit.

The Board may find *both* the residual and an overall unit to be appropriate units and give the residual employees an option. In *J. R. Simplot Co.*, [46] the production and maintenance employees were represented by Union A, and the residual unit was sought by Union B. The Board directed an election in each unit, allowing the two units to merge if a majority of the employees of both groups voted for a single union, either A or B, but allowing separate units if the employees of the two units chose to be represented by the different unions.

It can be seen that the question of self-determination here is very similar to the question of whether truly distinct production and maintenance departments are to be represented separately or together. If there is a close business relationship (*e.g.*, centralized management) between the unit already formed and the

---

[45] *See* International Harvester Co., 103 NLRB 1268 (1953), 31 LRRM 1624.
[46] 130 NLRB 1283 (1961), 47 LRRM 1481.

proposed residual one, the Board will deny a separate certification to the residual unit.

Although the Board has said in some cases that a residual unit must cover all of the unrepresented employees, not just a segment,[47] proper units may be found among residual or fringe groups (those sought to be added to an existing unit) which do not include *all* residual employees. [48] It depends on the facts of the particular case—the number of unrepresented employees, interchange, mutual interest, the administrative setup of the employer, and other factors. Illustrative is the case of *The Martin-Marietta Corp.* [49] There the Board reversed its regional director and ordered an election among all technicians at the secondary standards laboratory of the Systems Test and Support Department at the Denver facilities of the employer. It said that eligible employees should vote to be included in a production-and-maintenance unit represented by the UAW or to remain unrepresented.

The director had dismissed the petition for the limited unit of technicians, concluding that they had an overriding community of interest with other, unrepresented technicians. The Board, however, after noting the substantial degree of integration of the duties of technicians in the secondary standards laboratory with the duties of production and maintenance employees, wrote:

> We further conclude, contrary to the Regional Director, that these technicians, because of their specialized functions and their separate supervision and location, are an identifiable group with distinct interests and that they constitute an appropriate voting group apart from other unrepresented technicians.

Craft and Special Departmental Units

The relevant statutory material is contained in Section 9 (b) :

> The Board shall decide in each case whether, in order to assure to employees the fullest freedom in exercising the rights guaranteed by this Act, the unit appropriate for the purposes of collective bargaining shall be the employer unit, craft unit, plant unit, or subdivision thereof: *Provided,* that the Board shall not . . . (2) decide

---

[47] Los Angeles Statler Hilton Hotel, 129 NLRB 1349 (1961), 47 LRRM 1194.
[48] Jacobs Mfg. Co., 99 NLRB 482 (1952), 30 LRRM 1087.
[49] 162 NLRB 319 (1966), 64 LRRM 1007.

that any craft unit is inappropriate for such purposes on the ground that a different unit has been established by a prior Board determination, unless a majority of the employees in the proposed craft unit vote against separate representation . . .

The NLRB, on December 30, 1966, announced major policy changes with respect to election petitions for craft and special departmental employee representation in industrial plants.[50] The effect of the changes was to make it much *more difficult to sever a craft unit* in an industrial plant—except in lumber, wet milling, steel, and aluminum, where special industry insulation was eliminated, and in unorganized plants. Chances for craft-severance elections in long-organized plants have greatly diminished. [51]

Until these decisions came down, severance was *automatic* in industries other than the four insulated ones, provided three tests were met: (1) The scope of the unit sought was proper; [52] (2) the employees involved constituted a true craft or departmental group; and (3) the union trying to carve out the unit was one that traditionally had represented and concerned itself with the problems of the kind of employees involved. [53] Now, severance is no longer mechanical and automatic, and the arbitrary distinctions between industries are abolished. *American Potash* [54] is overruled and *National Tube Co.* [55] has been greatly revised.

In the lead *Mallinckrodt Chemical* case,[56] the Board, by a four-to-one majority, indicated some of the factors it would take into consideration in deciding whether to carve out craft units from plant structures. These areas of inquiry determine whether severance should be permitted, although other relevant circumstances probably will receive Board attention in future cases. The point is that now the Board decides these matters on a

---

[50] Mallinckrodt Chemical Works, 162 NLRB 387 (1966), 64 LRRM 1011; Holmberg, Inc., 162 NLRB 407 (1966), 64 LRRM 1025; E.I. DuPont & Co., 162 NLRB 413 (1966), 64 LRRM 1021.

[51] *See, e.g.,* Rayonier, 170 NLRB No. 96 (1968), 67 LRRM 1474.

[52] G.M. Cadillac Division, 120 NLRB 1215 (1958), 42 LRRM 1143.

[53] American Potash & Chemical Corp., 107 NLRB 1418 (1954), 33 LRRM 1380, overruled 162 NLRB 387 at 391 (1966), 64 LRRM 1011 at 1013.

[54] *Ibid.*

[55] 76 NLRB 1199 (1948), 21 LRRM 1292, overruled 162 NLRB 387 at 392 (1966), 64 LRRM 1011 at 1013.

[56] Mallinckrodt Chemical Works, *above,* note 50.

case-by-case basis, relying on material and relevant criteria rather than the mechanistic approach of the past.

The Cases Themselves

Before discussing the rationale of the Board and the import
of these decisions in more detail, it it is helpful to see just
what happened in the three cases. The Board's press release offers
a good summary:

A rundown on today's three decisions follows:

1) *Mallingckrodt Chemical Works, Uranium Division,* Waldon
   Springs, Missouri, is a plant which purifies uranium ore, manufactures uranium metal under a cost plus fixed fee contract with
   the Atomic Energy Commission. It is the only plant of its kind
   contracting with AEC where the full production process is employed to extract uranium from adulterated ores and convert
   it into finished solid metal for AEC and Department of Defense
   use.

   The plant has 560 employees. Of these a group of 280 production and maintenance employees are represented by the
   Independent Union of Atomic Workers. Among these workers
   are 12 instrument mechanics. Local 1 of the International
   Brotherhood of Electrical Workers (IBEW) sought to sever them
   from the overall unit represented by the Union of Atomic
   Workers.

   In dismissing IBEW's petition, the Board majority decided
   that it should not permit disruption of the production and
   maintenance unit by permitting the requested severance since
   (1) the plant's production process *is highly integrated,* with *work*
   of the instrument mechanics being *"intimately" related to the
   production process* as is the work of other employees in the
   production and maintenance unit, (2) the instrument mechanics
   have been represented *as part of the production and maintenance unit for 25 years,* and the record does not show that their
   interests have been neglected by their bargaining agent *(rather,
   their pay rates are comparable with those of skilled electricians
   at the plant who are represented by the IBEW),* (3) *they have
   their own seniority system for transfers, layoffs, and recalls,* and
   (4) *IBEW has not traditionally represented instrument mechanics.*

   While the instrument mechanics may be an "identifiable"
   group of skilled journeymen mechanics who might otherwise be

permitted to sever from a broader bargaining unit, the Board
majority concluded that the IBEW petition should be dismissed
because "it appears that the separate community of interests
which these employees enjoy by reason of their skills and training has been largely submerged in the broader community of
interests which they share with other employees by reason of
*long and uninterrupted association in the existing bargaining
unit, the high degree of integration of the employer's production processes, and the intimate connection of the work of these
employees with the actual uranium-making process itself.*"

(2) *Holmberg, Inc.,* Brooklyn, N. Y., manufactures metal stamp
products. At Holmberg Local 1614 of the International Brotherhood of Electrical Workers (IBEW) represents a production and
maintenance unit of 75 employees, including 25 tool and die
workers. A petition was filed by the Tool-Die and Moldmakers
Guild, Independent, to sever the tool and die workers from the
overall unit.

In dismissing the petition, the Board majority found that the
tool and die makers have a significant *overlapping of duties*
with other employees in the unit, and they perform as an *"integral part of the production process."* The Board majority said
that the record of the case has not shown that the grouping of
the tool and die workers with other employees in the bargaining
unit has proved unworkable, that the IBEW is not equipped to
represent the tool and die workers, or that the interests of those
workers have been ignored by the IBEW. To the contrary, the
majority said, *the record shows that tool and die makers are the
highest paid in the plant,* and that *their promotion is governed
by special provisions in the contract between IBEW and the employer.* The majority concluded that "our evaluation of all
relevant factors, including the *24-year bargaining history,* leads
us to find that the overall interests to be served through maintaining the stability of the existing bargaining unit outweigh
such special interests as the tool and die makers may have in
setting themselves apart as a separate bargaining unit."

(3) *E. I. DuPont de Nemours and Company, May Plant,* Camden,
South Carolina, is the manufacturer of the acrylic fibre, "orlon."
At this 7-day, 24-hour operational plant, Local 382 of the International Brotherhood of Electrical Workers IBEW) petitioned
for an election in a separate unit of 40 electricians out of a production and maintenance force of 950 employees. *None of the
plant's employees presently are represented by a union.*

In unanimously ordering that an election be held among the
electricians on the basis of the IBEW petition, the Board in its

main opinion, joined in by four members, decided that *although the plant's production process is integrated and electricians are required to coordinate their operations with those of production employees, these circumstances do not bar separate representation of the electricians.*

Noting first that *there is no history of bargaining at the plant,* the Board majority also stated that the record in the case shows that although some of the electricians' work is coordinated with that of production workers, the actual work is done solely by electricians, and this work is done under direction solely of electrical supervisors. While some other employees may do some of the less skilled work of electricians, they do so infrequently, the Board majority said. It is pointed out that the electricians are required to have the recognized skills of craftsmen, and to be considered such they must go through a three-year training program requiring on-the-job training and experience, as well as classroom instruction. (Emphasis supplied, throughout)

Factors Isolated by the Board

1. *Bargaining history* at the employer's facilities is shown by analysis to be the *most* significant consideration. The Board must balance industrial stability against the right to bargain separately. In view of the public policy of the Act, the Board's term "industrial stability" must refer to situations where collective bargaining exists. The emphasis here would be on "whether the existing patterns of bargaining" had, over the years, produced stability and "whether such stability would be disrupted by destruction of the existing pattern of representation."

Obviously, the *length of time* a bargaining relationship has existed is of great significance. Important also will be the *quality* of the relationship, that is, whether there is a pattern of relative industrial peace or one of continual, explosive, undisciplined hostility. In this connection, it should be noted that in the two cases in which severance was denied, there were bargaining histories of 25 and 24 years and in the case in which a craft unit was found permissible, there was *no* bargaining history, as the plant was unorganized. This factor, bargaining history, cannot be overstressed.

2. The second consideration is whether the proposed unit is "*a distinct and homogeneous group of skilled journeymen* crafts-

men performing . . . on a nonrepetitive basis or of employees constituting a *functionally distinct department, working* in trades or occupations for which a tradition of separate representation exists."

The Board has tightened up the "true craft or departmental group" test of *American Potash*. In a footnote, the Board noted that its disagreement with previous policy was not limited to the "overriding importance" assigned to that factor, "but also to the loose definition of a true craft or traditional department" used in past cases. This means, of course, that it will be harder to sever departments and odd groups, as well as "near crafts" or mixed trades. In the *Holmberg* case,[57] for instance, one factor heavily relied on was that the tool-room group did not meet the new, more stringent test.

3. The third consideration is the *extent to which employees have maintained a separate identity* while being included in a broader bargaining unit, their participation in the bargaining for the existing broad unit, and previous opportunities they may have had for separate representation. This catch-all consideration is new in Board law. It deals with the quality of representation and the failure over the years to try to break away. In *Mallinckrodt* the Board notes that the skilled group was well represented, was highly paid, and enjoyed separate seniority.

4. The Board announced that it would also look at the *history and pattern of collective bargaining in the industry* involved. This is a criterion left over from *National Tube* reasoning.

5. The degree of *integration* of the employer's production process, including the dependence of production processes on the work of the group in the proposed unit, is also a factor.

This is another *National Tube* residual test kept alive by the Board. In *Mallinckrodt,* the Board notes that the uranium operations of the employer are fully as "integrated" as wet milling, steel, aluminum, and lumber. "The instrument mechanic's work . . . is intimately related to the production process itself."

---

[57] Holmberg, Inc., *above,* note 50.

6. Still another factor is the *qualifications of the union seeking to carve out a separate unit*—including the union's experience in representing like employees. This is a restatement of the *American Potash* rule that the union must be one that has traditionally devoted itself to the special problems of the craft.

The Board, in *Mallinckrodt,* stated in a footnote that it no longer would require "traditional" representation as an absolute, as it did in the *Potash* line of cases; but note that in *Mallinckrodt* itself, the Board found that the IBEW *fell short* of qualifying under this test, thus implying that while experience in representing employees of the type in question is no longer a necessity, but only a factor, it remains an important factor.

In considering the law of craft and departmental units it is useful to keep in mind two different situations: (1) where there has been no prior history of union representation or collective bargaining, and (2) where there has been such a history and the representation petition seeks to change the existing pattern.

The Board has always looked less favorably upon attempts to establish craft or departmental units after a more inclusive unit has been in existence than upon such attempts during the initial organizational period. This attitude was reaffirmed after the addition of Section 9 (b) (2) in 1947 when the Board held that section to permit consideration of prior history so long as it was not the sole ground for preventing the creation of a craft unit.[58] The *Mallinckrodt* criteria, in placing heavy reliance on past bargaining history, obviously implied a continuation of past Board policy, and this has since been made explicit:[59]

> Thus, while we find the Mallinckrodt tests useful in our determination of the appropriateness of the unit requested here, we will not apply the same measure in dealing with whether an appropriate craft unit should initially be established.

On balance, these decisions will work to the benefit of industrial unions in organized plants with substantial bargaining history.[60] At the same time they destroy the unrealistic, favored

[58] National Tube, *above,* note 55.

[59] Fremont Hotel, Inc., 168 NLRB No. 23 (1967), 66 LRRM 1250; *see also* Fulton Cotton Mills, 175 NLRB No. 17 (1969), 70 LRRM 1484.

[60] *See* Lear-Siegler, Inc., 170 NLRB No. 114 (1968), 67 LRRM 1522, for a typical, well articulated decision denying severance.

position of four industries. It also seems, however, that most old-line, A F of L craft unions will not be adversely affected. Interunion no-raiding pacts, both official and de facto, have minimized the importance of craft raids on organized shops, and craft unions, of all kinds, are permitted more latitude in unorganized shops.

One word of caution is needed. It is not correct to assume that no craft severance will be permitted in organized plants. Situations do arise where the Board, on the basis of the factors in these cases and other as yet unarticulated factors, will find a severance proper. [61]

Office and Plant Clericals

Clerical employees generally fall into two separate groups, plant clericals and office clericals. While it is easy to classify them on paper, in practice it is sometimes more difficult. Despite the difficulty of the task, organizers often need to decide whether certain employees are office or plant clericals because their inclusion or exclusion in a particular unit probably depends on which they turn out to be.

The Board generally speaks of "community of interest" in distinguishing between the two kinds of clericals, just as it uses that phrase to determine unit placement, but that standard is too general to furnish guidance to laymen. To understand what the Board means, one should know the factors it considers in deciding whether or not one group of employees has a "community of interest" with another. There are three key factors: *job function, work location,* and *the terms and conditions of employment.*

For comparison purposes we can analyze these factors in terms of office and plant clericals side by side.

Job Function

Plant Clericals	Office Clericals
1. Work usually related to the production operations rather than administrative ones.	1.Duties usually entirely clerical but may include a little nonclerical work.[62]

---

[61] *See, e.g.,* Buddy L. Corp., 167 NLRB No. 113 (1968), 66 LRRM 1150.
[62] Archie's Motor Freight, 130 NLRB 1627 (1961), 47 LRRM 1568.

2. Inventory clerks and checkers are usually plant clericals.

2. Office clericals are usually concerned with executive, commercial, or administrative work rather than production or shipping.[63]

3. Typical duties are record keeping and accumulating information.[64]

3. Typical jobs are in accounting, sales, and payroll.[65]

Work Location

Plant Clericals

1. Usually common location with production employees.[66]

2. May even be an office in the plant or a desk in a garage.[68]

Office Clericals

1. Usually located away from production and maintenance employees in a "regular" office area.[67]

2. May even be in a separate building[69] or outside plant gates.[70]

3. Location may, however, be simply a matter of convenience rather than a real factor in distinguishing between kinds of clericals.[71]

Terms and Conditions of Employment

Plant Clericals

Usually share working conditions with physical employees. The following are typical indications:
1. Punch a time clock.[72]

2. Work on a shift basis.[74]

3. Method of pay.[76]

Office Clericals

The following factors might help to distinguish an office clerical from a plant clerical:
1. Hours of work, whether a time clock is punched.[73]

2. Paid by salary rather than hourly rated.[75]

3. Under clerical supervision.[77]

---

[63] Purolator Products, 73 NLRB 1075 (1947), 20 LRRM 1093; Baltimore Gas & Electric Co., 138 NLRB 270 (1962), 51 LRRM 1012.
[64] Meramec Mining Co., 134 NLRB 1675 (1961), 49 LRRM 1386; Mixermobile Mfg., 119 NLRB 1617 (1958), 41 LRRM 1358.
[65] Greenbrier Dairy Products, 100 NLRB 432 (1952), 30 LRRM 1304.
[66] Air Reduction Co., Inc., 127 NLRB 410 (1960), 46 LRRM 1039.
[67] May Department Stores Co., 153 NLRB 341 (1965), 59 LRRM 1483.
[68] Greenbrier Dairy Products, above, note 65.
[69] Vulcanized Rubber & Plastics Co., 129 NLRB 1256 (1961), 47 LRRM 1175.
[70] International Smelting & Refining Co., 106 NLRB 223 (1953), 32 LRRM 1436.
[71] Dupont, 107 NLRB 734 (1954), 33 LRRM 1249.
[72] Badenhausen Corp., 113 NLRB 867 (1955), 36 LRRM 1430.
[73] International Smelting & Refining Co., above, note 70.
[74] Badenhausen Corp., above, note 72.
[75] Avco Corp., 131 NLRB 921 (1961), 48 LRRM 1170.
[76] The Joclin Mfg. Co., 144 NLRB 778 (1963), 54 LRRM 1128.
[77] International Smelting & Refining Co., above, note 70.

4. Under production supervision.[78]
5. Rarely associate with administrative or office clerical employees.[80]
6. Likely to be covered by same fringe benefits as production employees.[81]

4. Amount of contact with production employees.[79]

Unit Placement of Clericals

There are many factors which can bear on the issue of whether a particular group of employees has a sufficient "community of interest" with another, so that they may be included in a single unit. The most common factors are these:

1. Contact with other employees.[82]

2. Interchange with the other employees.[83]

3. Supervision.[84]

4. Bargaining history.[85]

5. Similarity of working conditions.[86]

6. Type of industry.[87]

7. Whether any union seeks to represent separately a portion of the proposed unit.[88]

8. Desires of the parties.[89]

9. Similarity of skills and job functions.[90]

10. Organization of the plant.[91]

---

[78] Meramec Mining Co., *above,* note 64.
[79] Air Reduction Co., *above,* note 66.
[80] Mixermobile Mfg., *above,* note 64.
[81] Girton Mfg. Co., Inc., 129 NLRB 656 (1960), 47 LRRM 1027.
[82] The Budd Co., 136 NLRB 1153 (1962), 49 LRRM 1956.
[83] Armstrong Rubber Co., 144 NLRB 1115 (1963), 54 LRRM 1197.
[84] *Ibid.*
[85] Sheffield Corp., 134 NLRB 1101 (1961), 49 LRRM 1265; International Smelting & Refining Co., *above,* note 70.
[86] Sheffield Corp., *above,* note 85.
[87] *Ibid.*
[88] *Ibid.*
[89] *Ibid.*
[90] General Electric, 147 NLRB 558 (1964), 56 LRRM 1250; Sheffield Corp., *above,* note 85.
[91] Sheffield Corp., *above,* note 85.

11. Location in the plant.[92]

12. Number of employees involved.[93]

13. Whether labor relations are separately supervised.[94]

14. Similarity of education and training.[95]

15. Similarities in amount of pay, method of pay, and fringe benefits.[96]

16. Area practice.[97]

17. Similarity in schedule of hours.[98]

18. Degree of integration and cooperation.[99]

19. Social activities carried on in common.[100]

20. Closeness of work to that of employees not in the unit.[101]

Plant Clericals—In view of the similarity of interests and working conditions, the Board customarily includes plant clerical employees in production-and-maintenance units unless the parties have agreed to exclude them as class.[102] Where the petitioning union already represents the production and maintenance employees, the Board will direct an election among the plant clericals offering them the option of being added to the existing unit or remaining unrepresented.[103] A separate unit of plant clericals is appropriate where the employees would otherwise go unrepresented. [104] There is another line of cases which seems to indicate that plant clericals may constitute an

---

[92] The Budd Co., *above*, note 82.

[93] Charles Bruning Co., Inc., 126 NLRB 140 (1960), 45 LRRM 1287.

[94] Mack Trucks, Inc., 116 NLRB 1576 (1956), 39 LRRM 1048.

[95] Armstrong Rubber Co., *above*, note 83; Albuquerque Division, ACF Industries, Inc., 145 NLRB 403 (1963), 54 LRRM 1393.

[96] *Ibid;* The Budd Co., *above*, note 82; Boston Consolidated Gas Co., 107 NLRB 1565 (1954), 33 LRRM 1442; Jay Kay Metal Specialties Corp., 129 NLRB 31 (1960), 46 LRRM 1480.

[97] Columbus Plaza Motor Hotel, 148 NLRB 1053 (1964), 57 LRRM 1119.

[98] Rudolph Wurlitzer Co., 117 NLRB 6 (1956), 39 LRRM 1140.

[99] Boston Consolidated Gas Co., *above*, note 96.

[100] *Ibid.*

[101] Donovan Construction Co., 105 NLRB 204 (1953), 32 LRRM 1338.

[102] Divco-Wayne Corp., 122 NLRB 162 (1958), 43 LRRM 1089; Avco Corp., *above*, note 75; Yale & Towne Mfg. Co., 112 NLRB 1268 (1955), 36 LRRM 1184; Baden-hausen Corp., *above*, note 72.

[103] Robbins & Myers, Inc., 144 NLRB 295 (1963), 54 LRRM 1047; General Electric Co., 107 NLRB 70 (1953), 33 LRRM 1058; ACF Industries, Inc., 115 NLRB 1106 (1956), 37 LRRM 1498; Vulcanized Rubber & Plastics Co., *above*, note 69.

[104] Minneapolis Moline Co., 85 NLRB 597 (1949), 24 LRRM 1443.

appropriate separate unit even where they do not qualify as a residual unit.[105] Board policy usually precludes the establishment of a separate unit of plant clerical employees where the petitioning union currently represents the production-and-maintenance unit.[106] However, where the plant clericals have not in the past been included in the production-and-maintenance unit and where the parties agree that they should be established as a separate unit, the Board may permit the same union to represent them separately.[107]

Office and plant clericals may not be joined in a single unit in the absence of the agreement of the parties,[108] but a combined unit of office and plant clericals is appropriate where the parties agree and the interests of the two groups are not substantially different.[109] The Board will permit the inclusion of technical employees in a unit with plant clericals, regardless of whether any of the parties object, where a balancing of the factors points to a community of interest.[110]

Office Clericals—Office clerical employees will most often constitute a separate appropriate unit because of the lack of a community of interest with other groups of employees.[111] Where a group of an employer's office clericals share similar interests, a unit including only a segment of the group will not do.[112] Thus, depending on the facts, the proper unit may be a department, a division, a plant, several plants, or the entire company. Where the question is whether two groups of office clerical employees in different parts of a company's operation can appropriately be joined in a single unit, the test is whether a community of interest exists.[113] The Board will permit the inclusion

---

[105] Mixermobile Mfg., *above*, note 64; Donovan Construction Co., *above*, note 101; Republic Steel Corp., 131 NLRB 864 (1961), 48 LRRM 1171; Swift & Co., 131 NLRB 1143 (1961), 48 LRRM 1219; *see also* Yale & Towne Mfg. Co., *above*, note 102; and Armstrong Rubber Co., *above*, note 95.

[106] Robbins & Myers, Inc., *above*, note 103; Vulcanized Rubber & Plastics Co., *above*, note 69.

[107] Swift & Co., *above*, note 105; Republic Steel Corp., *above*, note 105.

[108] Robbins & Myers, Inc., *above*, note 103; Armstrong Rubber Co., *above*, note 95; Rudolph Wurlitzer Co., *above*, note 98.

[109] Eljer Co., 108 NLRB 1417 (1954), 34 LRRM 1226; The Budd Co., *above*, note 82.

[110] The Budd Co., *above*, note 82; Sheffield Corp., *above*, note 85; Monarch Machine Tool Co., 158 NLRB 104 (1966), 62 LRRM 1007.

[111] Meramec Mining Co., *above*, note 64; Long-Lewis Hardware Co., 134 NLRB 1554 (1961), 49 LRRM 1375.

[112] Kroger Co., 116 NLRB 1842 (1956), 39 LRRM 1112; Schieffelin & Co., 129 NLRB 956 (1960), 47 LRRM 1105; Bank of America, 174 NLRB No. 21 (1969), 70 LRRM 1097.

[113] Mack Trucks, Inc., *above*, note 94.

of technical employees in a unit of office clericals where a balancing of the factors points to a community of interest.[114]

The Board has developed several per se, or automatic, rules on unit exclusions. Notice, however, that each of these rules is founded on the notion that in a particular situation no community of interest exists. It is possible, therefore, that at some time an attack could be mounted against these rules in cases where a true community of interest could be shown. It is Board policy, in the case of a manufacturing operation, not to include in a single unit office clerical employees and production and maintenance employees if one of the parties objects, even if there has been a history of bargaining.[115] Even where the parties have agreed to combine them in a single unit, the Board may, in the absence of bargaining history, find the unit inappropriate.[116] Where there is *both* agreement of the parties and a history of bargaining, the unit will probably be held appropriate.[117] In the case of a public utility, where a high degree of integration exists, the Board will find a unit combining office clerical employees with factory employees appropriate.[118] In retail store units, because of the integrated nature of the operations, office clerical employees *will* be joined with selling employees if there is not a contrary bargaining history and no union seeks to represent them separately.[119] In wholesale establishments, office clericals are excluded from the overall unit if any party objects to their inclusion.[120] It should be noted that, where office clerical employees are excluded from a unit of employees who do nonclerical work, the union that is the bargaining agent for the production and maintenance employees is also qualified to represent the clerical employees in a separate unit.[121]

---

[114] The Budd Co., *above*, note 82.
[115] Schieffelin & Co., *above*, note 112; General Electric Co., *above*, note 103.
[116] John H. Harland Co., 127 NLRB 588 (1960), 46 LRRM 1060.
[117] *Ibid.*
[118] Boston Consolidated Gas Co., *above*, note 96; East Ohio Gas Co., 94 NLRB 61 (1951), 28 LRRM 1023.
[119] Interstate Supply Co., 117 NLRB 1062 (1957), 39 LRRM 1380; Charles Bruning Co., *above*, note 93.
[120] Interstate Supply Co., *above*, note 119; Newark Electronics Co., 131 NLRB 553 (1961), 48 LRRM 1117.
[121] Birmingham Electric Co., 89 NLRB 1342 (1950), 26 LRRM 1109.

Technical Employees

The Board has defined "technical" employees as that group "in between" professional and ordinary employees. It has stated:

> . . . [T]echnical employees, because of their distinctive training and experience and functions, are viewed as having different interests from other employees. Generally, those held to be technical employees are employees who do not meet the strict requirements of the term "professional employee" as defined in the Act but whose work is of a technical nature involving the use of independent judgment and requiring the exercise of specialized training usually acquired in colleges or technical schools or through special courses. . . . . [T]here are inherent differences in the interests, background, and functions between the technical workers and other employees. *Litton Industries of Maryland, Inc.*, 125 NLRB 722 at 724, 725 (1959).

Although the *Litton* case was overruled in part by *Sheffield Corp.*,[122] this definition remains valid and will still be applied.[123]

Parts of the above definition have been applied in a number of cases. Specialized training is cited in several instances, [124] failure to meet the definition of "professional employee" in others,[125] and the use of individual judgment in still others.[126]

Surveyors and their associates [127] are typical technical employees. Surveyors require training in a "specialized scientific knowledge," and they "exercise discretion in the application of that knowledge." The Board noted in *Meramec* that they measure the mineshafts and make surveys; often, with the help of their shaftsmen, they make maps and detail drawings; and they work under the overall supervision of a mining engineer. On these facts the Board held them to be technical employees. Other examples might include electronic technicians, requiring a high school education plus two years' additional training, who do research and development of electronic instruments,[128] or lab engineers in a pump engineering department who have

---

[122] Sheffield Corp., *above*, note 85.
[123] Dewey Portland Cement Co., 137 NLRB 944 (1962), 50 LRRM 1302.
[124] Sheffield Corp., *above*, note 85; E.F. Drew & Co., Inc., 133 NLRB 155 (1961), 48 LRRM 1615.
[125] Design Service Co., Inc., 148 NLRB 1050 (1964), 57 LRRM 1115; Hazelton Laboratories, Inc., 136 NLRB 1609 (1962), 50 LRRM 1063.
[126] Victor Mfg. & Gasket Co., 133 NLRB 1283 (1961), 49 LRRM 1031.
[127] *See, e.g.*, Meramec Mining Co., *above*, note 64.
[128] Sheffield Corp., *above*, note 85.

some advanced training and experience and perform tests on experimental and production models of pumps, measure stresses and pressures, verify engineering data, and generally evaluate the working parts.[129] Highly skilled aerospace technicians are good examples of technicals.[130] A quality control engineer and an apprentice quality control employee are technicals where they are salaried and have different interests from regular hourly employees.[131]

Many of the characteristics outlined above in other connections, and used to define other groups as separate units, are applicable here also. As the Board stated in *Robbins & Myers:* [132]

> Characteristic of all the categories in the technical group is their close *association with professional engineers* with whom they share *common supervision* . . . work the same *hours* and are at the same general *location.* None of the technicals interchange with production or clerical workers. They have little or *no contact with production* or plant clerical workers and only slight contact with certain office clericals . . . While they are on a *salaried* payroll along with plant and office clericals and receive similar benefits, all non-production workers are similarly treated including managerial and professional employees. We conclude that the technical employees . . . have an identifiable community of interest . . . [and] find a separate unit of technicals appropriate. (Emphasis added)

Prior to *Sheffield,*[133] the Board granted an *automatic* separation of technical employees from a unit composed of production and maintenance personnel where the employer or the union so requested, although there might have been a *community of interest* between the two groups and the technical employees could have been *adequately represented.* In the *Sheffield* opinion the Board announced that it would not adhere to this policy in the future, stating in part:

> In order, therefore, to give effective weight to such *community of interest,* we shall no longer utilize an automatic placement formula, but shall, instead, make a pragmatic judgment in each case, based upon an analysis of the following factors, among others: *desires* of the parties, *history* of bargaining, similarity of *skills* and job functions, common *supervision, contact* and/or *interchange* with other employees, similarity of *working conditions,* type of industry, orga-

---

[129] *See* Robbins & Myers, Inc., *above,* note 103.
[130] Bell Aerosystems Corp., 131 NLRB 130 (1961), 48 LRRM 1002.
[131] Drexel Furniture Co., 116 NLRB 1434 (1956), 39 LRRM 1009.
[132] Robbins & Myers, Inc., *above,* note 103.
[133] Sheffield Corp., *above,* note 85.

nization of plant, whether the technical employees work in separately controlled areas, and whether any union *seeks to represent technical* employees separately. Of course where the parties are in agreement . . . [we shall] give *considerable weight to the desires of the parties.* (Emphasis added)

The *Sheffield* case is a good illustration of how the Board deliberates in a concrete situation.[134]

1. In *Sheffield* the Board dealt with the problem of three electronic technicians and two electro-mechanical technicians who *worked with* production and maintenance employees and were involved with the research, development, and construction of electronic instruments. All the employees, production and technical, in the department were *supervised* by the departmental foreman and all were located within the same *general area.* All were *hourly paid* and had the same vacation and holiday *benefits.* The Board held that these technicals should be included in the production unit.

2. In the same case, the Board considered another group of technical employees. This group worked in *separate engineering* departments or laboratories, generally with professional engineers, in the area of developing new ideas and products. They were under *separate supervision* and were located in *areas different* from those in which production and maintenance employees were found. These technicals were salaried employees who received a bonus for overtime in contrast to the production employees' hourly rate. The Board ruled in favor of defining this group of employees as a separate unit not having the requisite community of interest to be included with production employees in a single unit.

The Board, here, as in other areas, will dismiss a petition covering only a segment of the employees in the appropriate unit. In *Ingalls Shipbuilding Corp.,*[135] the Board dismissed a petition covering only a few rate setters, holding that an appropriate petition would have covered many other employees doing technical work whose jobs were substantially similar.[136] And as in other kinds of unit cases, the Board may find that it

---

[134] Other examples include American Cyanamid Co., 172 NLRB No. 241 (1968), 69 LRRM 1161 and Wayne Pump Division, 170 NLRB No. 191 (1968), 68 LRRM 1009.

[135] 137 NLRB 576 (1962), 50 LRRM 1209.

[136] *See also* Avco Corp., 173 NLRB No. 185 (1968), 70 LRRM 1030.

would be appropriate either to add technicians to an existing unit or to allow formation of a separate unit. In this event a self-determination election will be ordered.[137]

A footnote should perhaps be added as to the unique status of timekeepers. They have, depending on the rates of pay, hours worked, and other circumstances, been classified as plant clericals and therefore with the production unit;[138] or as office clericals;[139] or have been allowed to form their own units in conjunction with a special unit of other plant clericals, such as checkers.[140] The difference in results for both the unions and the employees in cases like these turns on FACTS. Inevitably the party that can show the most *comprehensive picture* of such factors as what the employees do, where they work, who does the supervising, how they are paid, *i.e.*, the party that can present the most concretely detailed case as to why a particular unit is or is not appropriate—is the winner. All such cases are close. It goes without saying that this is a difficult task for an organizer, because only the employer has complete access to the facts and usually he presents the factual picture in the way that will best advance his position.

Professionals

The problems of professional employees differ in some measure from those generally found in other units. Professionals are generally small in number and presumably face the prospect of being "swamped" by the needs of the majority if they are placed within a unit dominated by nonprofessionals. Further, the professional is expected to maintain "professional standards," usually not a consideration of the production worker.

In order to protect the professional and safeguard his interests, the Wagner Act was amended in 1947 to include the following provision as part of Section 9(b)(1):

. . . [T]he Board shall decide . . . the unit appropriate for the purposes of collective bargaining . . . the Board shall not . . . decide that any unit is appropriate for such purposes if such unit

---

[137] *See, e.g.,* The Martin-Marietta Corp., *above,* note 49.
[138] American Beryllium Co., 142 NLRB 457 (1963), 53 LRRM 1057.
[139] Mead-Atlanta Paper Co., 123 NLRB 306 (1959), 54 LRRM 1423.
[140] Steamship Trade Assn. of Baltimore, 155 NLRB 232 (1965), 60 LRRM 1257; Hampton Roads Maritime Assn., 178 NLRB No. 44 (1969), 72 LRRM 1061.

includes both professional employees and employees who are not professional employees, unless a majority of such professional employees vote for inclusion in such unit.

The Act furnishes a definition of the professional employee in Section 2 (12) :

(a) any employee engaged in work (i) predominantly intellectual and varied in character as opposed to routine mental, manual, mechanical, or physical work; (ii) involving the consistent exercise of discretion and judgment in its performance; (iii) of such a character that the output produced or the result accomplished cannot be standardized; (iv) requiring knowledge of an advanced type in a field of service or learning customarily acquired by a prolonged course of specialized intellectual instruction and study in an institution of higher learning . . . as distinguished from a general academic education or from an apprenticeship or from training in the performance of routine mental, manual or physical processes.

A supplementary provision covers those persons who have completed their advanced specialized courses but have not completed some further "related work under the supervision of a professional person." This provision would cover such people as hospital interns.

Two essential characteristics of professional work are advanced training and the exercise of discretion. In *Ryan Aeronautical Co.*,[141] the Board held that electronics engineers having college degrees, plus advanced work in electronics, were professionals. Their work required advanced knowledge, applied in the design of aircraft and navigation instruments. The same case holds that a group of people, most of whom are college graduates, is *presumed* to be professional.

It should be noted, however, that it is the job done and not the degree that counts. A person with a degree who might otherwise be called a professional may not be one under this test; similarly, a man without a degree may be held to be a professional. For example, the Board held in *Ryan* that one employee who had had only three years of mechanical engineering in college but 14 years experience in the field was a professional. His job involved the design, analysis, and investigation of problems in electromechanics. We can contrast this case with *Starrett Brothers & Eken, Inc.*,[142] where the Board held

[141] 132 NLRB 1160 (1961), 48 LRRM 1502.
[142] 77 NLRB 276 (1948), 22 LRRM 1003.

that mechanical engineers with degrees were not professionals within the meaning of the Act. These engineers did routine tasks, recording the amount of pipe covering and inspecting the installation of sanitary sewers, storm sewers, and similar projects performed by the contractor. Their work did not involve the requisite amount of discretion to qualify them as professional people.

Although some outside guides may be used by the Board, the question is to be determined in the light of the purposes of the Labor Act. For example, in *Starrett Bros.*, the Board referred to, but did not find binding, the description of work found in the *Dictionary of Occupational Titles,* published by the U.S. Department of Labor. Each case, as indicated above, must be judged independently on the basis of the type of work done by the employee.

As we have seen above, the label "professional" is not necessarily confined to persons with a degree. However, the fact that a person may not be a professional person *himself* does not necessarily mean that he will be precluded from joining a professional unit. Technical employees may become part of a professional unit if there is a close community of interests existing between the two groups. For example, the Board held in *Reynolds Electrical & Eng. Co.*,[143] that a medical unit of first-aid men, whose medical knowledge generally consisted of training by the armed forces as medical corpsmen or hospital orderlies, would be proper as a technical unit. The men there had specialized knowledge but had no degrees and were not registered. Similarly, the Board found that the x-ray technician and laboratory technician were technical employees, not professionals. On the other hand, it held that the resident physician and the pharmacist, both licensed, were professionals, as were the two registered nurses. The Board then held that because of the close community of interest manifested by the various parties in their daily contact, their type of work, and the degree of their isolation from other units, placement of the two groups in one unit was warranted. However, the professionals were allowed to vote for inclusion in or exclusion from such a unit.[144]

It is now settled that the Board *must* give professional em-

---

[143] 133 NLRB 113 (1961), 48 LRRM 1603.
[144] *See also* Yale & Towne Mfg. Co., 135 NLRB 926 (1962), 49 LRRM 1600.

ployees the right to decide whether they want to be in a unit with other employees.[145] The usual method is to provide three ballot choices: no union, production (or other nonprofessional-type) unit, and pure professional unit. It is lawful for an employer and a union to make a contract covering professional and nonprofessional employees, but the Board may not include them together in a unit unless the professionals vote for this arrangement.

A unit may be composed of two different types of professional employees if they have the requisite community of interest. Where tools are interchanged, tasks are related, and the same area of the plant is used by two different groups of professionals, the Board may hold that the two groups should constitute a single, appropriate bargaining unit.[146] Conversely, where the two groups are relatively unrelated, they will not be joined. In *Standard Oil Co.*,[147] the Board would not join two professional groups, nurses and engineers, where it was shown that employees in the two groups had different training, duties, and education. Further, they were under separate supervision, worked in separate areas, and had no contact with each other, at least on a professional level. The Board held that it was *not required* to hold a representation election on the issue of whether the two professional groups wished to be placed in the same unit. This is in sharp contrast with the Act's requirement that every joinder of *nonprofessionals* with professionals requires such a vote.[148] The Act requires a vote only when professionals are *included* with nonprofessionals, not when they are *excluded*. Here the Board excluded professional employees from a bargaining unit in which they had previously participated without permitting them to vote on the matter.

Although professional employees must be separately considered, there is no legal barrier erected against representation by a union accepting nonprofessionals.[149]

On the other hand, professionals in a mixed unit may request a severance from the nonprofessionals. This, the Board

---

[145] Leedom v. Kyne, 358 US 184 (1958), 43 LRRM 2222.
[146] *See* Ryan Aeronautical Co., *above*, note 140.
[147] 107 NLRB 1524 (1954), 33 LRRM 1424.
[148] Leedom v. Kyne, *above*, note 144; *see also* Standard Oil of Indiana, 80 NLRB 1275 (1948), 23 LRRM 1229.
[149] *See, e.g.*, Reynolds Electrical & Engineering Co., *above*, note 142.

holds, is implied by Section 9 (b) (1). The professionals, in effect, may not be kept in a mixed unit against their will.[150] The proper route to achieve this result must be, the Board holds, through a representation proceeding rather than one for decertification. A second union necessarily must be in the picture. Decertification implies that the entire unit will be decertified. There is no policy in the Act, express or implied, which requires the Board to decertify part of an existing unit or an entire existing unit and disrupt established relationships in order to satisfy the wishes of a small group of professionals.[151]

Truck Drivers

At one time truck drivers were automatically severed from a larger unit whenever a union sought such severance, but that is no longer true.[152] Similarly, truck drivers are not *automatically* included in a production-and-maintenance unit when no union seeks to represent them separately, a principle established in *E. H. Koester Bakery Co.*[153] In these two kinds of situations the Board will consider whether the drivers have special interests of their own and whether they make up a functionally distinct group. Bargaining history is important, as are the integration of the operation, the interchange of employees, and the similarity of working conditions.

Time-Study Personnel, Inspectors, Checkers

Many employers consider time-study employees an arm of management, but unless these workers are employed in a supervisory capacity they are eligible for union representation. As a rule, where they act as a kind of industrial engineer, setting standards and timing workers, they are considered technical employees,[154] although under certain conditions they may be held plant clericals and included in a production-and-maintenance unit.

---

[150] *See, e.g., S.S. White Dental Mfg. Co.*, 109 NLRB 1117 (1954), 34 LRRM 1519, allowing severance despite a history of collective bargaining.
[151] *See* Westinghouse Electric Corp., 115 NLRB 530 (1956), 37 LRRM 1341.
[152] Kalamazoo Paper Box Corp., 136 NLRB 134 (1962), 49 LRRM 1715.
[153] 136 NLRB 1006 (1962), 49 LRRM 1925.
[154] Swift & Co., 129 NLRB 1391 (1961), 47 LRRM 1195.

Inspectors and checkers, unless they reach the standards of technical employees—as, for instance, quality-control engineers —are generally included in production-and-maintenance groups since they are, ordinarily, considered plant clericals.

Miscellaneous Exclusions and Inclusions

There are often sharp differences between employers and unions as to whether certain persons should be included in bargaining units and/or be considered eligible to vote in NLRB elections. This discussion of bargaining units would be incomplete if there were not brief mention of some of the more common exclusion-inclusion problems, to alert those involved in organizing. Arguments over inclusions and exclusions typically concern the eligibility of employees described as "confidential," "managerial," "supervisory," "temporary," or "seasonal", laid-off or discharged employees, trainees, and foremen.

Supervisors

Supervisors are excluded from bargaining units because they are not employees under the Act.[155] The Act defines a supervisor as:[156]

> any individual having authority, in the interest of the employer, to hire, transfer, suspend, lay off, recall, promote, discharge, assign, reward, or discipline other employees, or responsibly to direct them, or to adjust their grievances, or effectively to recommend such action, if in connection with the foregoing the exercise of such authority is not of a merely routine or clerical nature, but requires the use of independent judgment.

As the definition makes clear it is not enough to look at a job title to determine whether one is a supervisor; we must look to the job duties. Although the statement of the general rules seems clear enough, actual cases are often difficult, and the line between employees and supervisors in a given situation may be finely drawn. Leadmen who make a few cents more an hour than other workers are the most common problem. Generally, leadmen who act only as "straw bosses" are not supervisors.[157]

---

[155] Section 2(3).
[156] Section 2(11).
[157] *See* Schott Metal Products, 129 NLRB 1233 (1961), 47 LRRM 1164; U.S. Gypsum Co., 118 NLRB 20 (1957), 40 LRRM 1120.

It should be remembered that the *exercise* of supervisory authority is not essential—the mere *existence* of the power is sufficient for the Board to find supervisory status.

The following are the most common questions the Board has asked in a host of cases dealing with the identification of supervisors:

1. Does the man in question hire or really participate in a meaningful way in the hiring process?

2. Does he deal significantly with promotions, incentives, pay, or transfers?

3. Is he paid considerably more than other employees?

4. Does he attend management meetings?

5. Does he decide who shall be demoted, laid off, or fired?

6. Does he handle grievances on the management side?

7. Does he decide to whom and how work shall be assigned and distributed?

8. Does he have the power to excuse or punish tardiness or absence?

9. Can he issue warnings?

10. Does he spend most of his time watching or teaching others, rather than on manual work?

11. Does he wear different clothing from other workers and have special privileges such as exemption from clock-punching, or even salaried status?

12. What is the ratio of supervisors to employees in the department or plant?

13. Is the man in question referred to, regarded as and generally thought of as a "boss"?

14. Does he act as if he thinks of himself as a "boss"?

15. Does he do the same kind of work as admitted supervisors?

Managerial Employees

This exclusion was created by Board rule rather than by statute. Then Judge, now Chief Justice, Burger has identified the tests for managerial employees this way:

> [T]here seem . . . to be two tests. The first is whether, even if they do not supervise other workers, their position with the employer presents a potential conflict of interest between the employer and the workers, e.g., employment interviewers who have authority in hiring. This strand of the managerial employee test is often phrased in a more conclusory manner, *i.e.*, that the employee is closely related to or aligned with the management; such a determination, however, also seems to turn on the possibility of a conflict of interest arising . . .
>
> The Board also excludes from the protection of the Act, as managerial employees, 'those who formulate, determine, and effectuate an employers' policies,' and those who have discretion in the performance of their jobs, but not if the discretion must conform to an employer's established policy.[158]

As with other inclusion and exclusion determinations, it is the substance of the job that is important, and artificial titles and distinctions, such as being on "the management payroll" are not controlling.

Confidential Employees

This exclusion is very limited and applies to persons who are plainly employees under the Act but who should be excluded from a unit for good policy reasons. In almost every case the excluded confidential is either a secretary or clerk to a high-up company person. To exclude an employee as "confidential" it must be shown that the person in question determines, formulates, and effectuates management policies *in the field of labor relations* or aids someone who does.[159] Employees will not be excluded merely because they have access to information the employer considers to be confidential, such as personnel and payroll records.[160]

---

[158] Retail Clerks v. NLRB, 366 F.2d 642 (CA DC, 1966), 62 LRRM 2837, cert. denied 386 US 1017 (1967), 65 LRRM 2059. But the Board has recently held that managerial employees, whom the Board excludes from bargaining units, will not be denied unfair-labor-practice protection unless they are not "employees" within the statutory definition. North Ark. Elec. Coop., 185 NLRB No. 83 (1970), 75 LRRM 1068.

[159] B.F. Goodrich Co., 115 NLRB 722 (1956), 37 LRRM 1383; Quaker City Life Ins. Co., *above*, note 4.

[160] Goldblatt Bros., Inc., 118 NLRB 643 (1957), 40 LRRM 1233.

Temporary, Seasonal, and Part-Time Employees

The test of eligibility for one said to be a temporary, seasonal, or part-time employee usually boils down to the likelihood of continued or regular employment which would justify participation in the selection of a bargaining representative. The more remote his chances for recall or permanency, or the more irregular his work record, the less connection he has with the unit. The test is whether he has sufficient interest in the job to be allowed "a say."

As a rule, temporary employees, such as students working during a summer vacation, do not have a sufficient "stake" in the employment and will not be allowed to vote in a representation election.[161] Regular part-time employees, on the other hand, will normally be allowed to vote if they work along with or otherwise have a community of interest with full-time employees.[162]

Seasonal employees will be allowed to participate in an election if they have a "sufficient community of interest with the year-round employees and possess a substantial enough interest in employment conditions to warrant their inclusion . . ." [163] In determining whether this test is met the Board looks at such factors as: the length and regularity of the season; whether the seasonal employees are drawn from the same labor market each year; whether the company gives hiring preference to employees who have worked for it in previous seasons; whether the regular and seasonal employees work together on the same kind of work and under the same supervision; whether seasonal employees have an opportunity to become permanent; and the percentage of seasonal employees who return from one season to the next.

Laid-off or Discharged Employees

The question the Board seeks to answer in deciding whether to permit laid-off employees to vote is whether such employees have a reasonable expectation of recall in the foreseeable

---

[161] *See, e.g.,* Richman Brothers Co., 157 NLRB 1666 (1966), 61 LRRM 1570, affirmed 387 F.2d 809 (CA 7, 1967), 67 LRRM 2051.

[162] *See, e.g.,* Shannon & Luchs, 166 NLRB No. 123 (1967), 65 LRRM 1702.

[163] California Vegetable Concentrates, Inc., 137 NLRB 1779 (1962), 50 LRRM 1510.

future. This question must, however, be answered in the light of all the relevant facts and not simply on the basis of what an employer says. Sometimes where there is a dispute over the eligibility of laid-off employees, they are permitted to vote challenged ballots and the issue is not resolved unless the votes are determinative.[164]

In one UAW case, the employer testified that certain laid-off employees had *no* chance of recall and the NLRB regional director ruled that the challenged votes should not be counted, but the Board reversed on the basis of union evidence which proved that the foreman who laid off the girls had told them they would be back soon, the employer had told the unemployment-compensation commission that the girls were temporarily laid off, and similar seasonal layoffs had always been recalled.[165]

Discharged employees are another story. Those discharged for cause are ineligible, but those who are the subject of charges alleging a discriminatory discharge vote subject to challenge and, if their votes become crucial, counting must await the outcome of the unfair-labor-practice proceedings.[166]

Trainees

Trainees who might become supervisors or might fill management positions may be eligible to vote. The Board's tests seem to be: (1) the kind of work they are doing at the time of the contest; (2) whether they work under the same conditions and for the same pay as other employees; (3) whether special training is required; (4) whether there is an eventual guarantee of a top management job; and (5) the length of the training period.

Guards, Firemen, and Certain Janitors

Under Section 9 (b) of the Act, the Board may not include *guards* in a unit with other employees. If the duties of a fire-

---

[164] *See, e.g.,* Snap-Out Binding and Folding, Inc., 160 NLRB 161 (1966), 62 LRRM 1397.

[165] Unfortunately, the Board did not print this decision, *North Hill Products* (1964).

[166] Hunt Heater Corp., 113 NLRB 167 (1955), 36 LRRM 1277.

man, watchman, or janitor include any significant part of a *guard's* duties, such as responsibility for property and more than occasional watchman-type responsibilities, the employee may not be included in a production-and-maintenance unit. Inclusion or exclusion in a particular case will depend on facts. Sometimes where there is a fire-fighting force and a plant-guard force, the issue can be very close.[167]

---

[167] *See* North American Aviation, 161 NLRB 297 (1966), 63 LRRM 1235.

CHAPTER VIII

OTHER UNIONS

[U]nity of organization is necessary to
make the contest of labor effectual,
and . . . societies of laborers lawfully
may employ in their preparation the
means which they might use in the
final contest.

Mr. Justice Holmes in
Vegelahn v. *Gunter,*
167 Mass. 92, 108 (1896)

Introduction

In this chapter we discuss some of the many problems en-
countered when an organizer attempts to organize into his union
workers who work in a shop where there is already a collective-
bargaining relationship involving another union.

Election-Bar and Certification-Bar Doctrines

Section 9 (c) (3) of the Act provides, in part, that:

No election shall be directed in any bargaining unit or any subdivision within which, in the preceding twelve-month period, a
valid election shall have been held.

This provision thus creates a one year election bar. Regardless
of the outcome of an election—win, lose, or draw—the Board
cannot hold another election for 12 months. Of course, if the
election was invalid, for example, it was improperly conducted by
the Board, or conduct by one party or the other necessitates
setting it aside, then another election can be held without

waiting the year's period. The Board has held that a valid election conducted by a state agency will act as a bar in addition to NLRB conducted elections.[1] Although a second election will not be held until a full year has passed, a petition may be filed as early as 60 days ahead of the first election's anniversary date.[2]

While 9 (c) (3) bars the holding of a second election in a year in the same unit or in a subdivision of a unit in which an election has been conducted, the Board holds that the converse situation will not act as a bar—*i.e.,* that an election in a smaller unit will not bar an election in a more comprehensive unit later in the same year. Thus an election conducted in a craft or departmental unit does not bar a subsequent election in a larger overall unit [3] and an election in a single-plant unit will not bar an election in a multiplant unit in the same year.[4]

Related to the election-bar rule is the Board's certification-bar doctrine, according to which, in the absence of unusual circumstances, the Board will not direct an election where it has issued a certification covering the same unit in the preceding 12 months.[5] When a certification is in effect, a full 12-month period must pass *before any petition can be filed.*[6]

Contract-Bar Doctrine

The NLRB has designed a rather intricate set of rules, conveniently lumped together under the name of *the contract-bar doctrine* which, unlike the election-bar doctrine, is not derived from an explicit statutory mandate. The reasons the Board has formulated its contract-bar rules are to promote stability in industrial relations and to encourage the execution and proper administration of bona fide collective-bargaining contracts. More and more rules have been included in the growing body of law concerned with contract bar as the Board has pursued the delicate objective of balancing the public interest in stability with the

---

[1] Olin Matheison Chemical Corp., 115 NLRB 1501 (1956), 38 LRRM 1099.

[2] Vickers, Inc., 124 NLRB 1051 (1959), 44 LRRM 1585.

[3] Thiokol Chemical Corp., 123 NLRB 888 (1959), 44 LRRM 1011; Pacific Maritime Assn., 110 NLRB 1647 at 1651 (1954), 35 LRRM 1299.

[4] Vacuum Cooling Company, 105 NLRB 794 (1953), 32 LRRM 1361; Leslie Metal Arts Co., Inc., 167 NLRB No. 96 (1967), 66 LRRM 1134.

[5] Centr-O-Cast & Engineering Co., 100 NLRB 1507 (1952), 30 LRRM 1478; Ray Brooks v. NLRB, 348 US 96 (1954), 35 LRRM 2158.

[6] Rockwell Valves, Inc., 115 NLRB 236 (1956), 37 LRRM 1271.

equally important public interest in freedom of choice for workers.

Generally, for a contract to bar an election (decertification, employer petition, or another union's petition) the Board requires that it be: written; properly executed, ratified and binding; of reasonable duration; and contain terms and conditions consistent with the law.

Before we make a more detailed analysis of the varieties of problems and rules concerned with how, when, and under what conditions a contract will bar an election, a word of caution must be said. *The wise organizer who has a contract-bar problem that seems at all complicated had better see a good lawyer.* This kind of highly technical, constantly changing detail is not even taught in many law schools. The subject does not lend itself well to "do-it-yourself" techniques.

Because, however, of the importance of the contract-bar rules, it is essential to discuss some of the more important of these rules in readily understood language.

Rule I

To bar an election a contract must be signed and, if by its terms ratification is required, ratified.

All parties must have executed the contract *before* the filing of the petition for the contract to bar an election.[7] However, if there has been a genuine signing by authorized representatives of both parties, such as a written proposal and an acceptance which are both signed, the contract will bar even if not done up as a formal document.

Rule II

The Board usually holds the date of execution to be the latest date available, if it has choices.

For instance, where a contract didn't bind the parties until approved and signed by an international official, it could not bar until the international had signed it.[8] The actual date of

---

[7] Appalachian Shale Products, 121 NLRB 1160 (1958), 42 LRRM 1506.
[8] Charles Leonard, Inc., 131 NLRB 1104 (1961), 48 LRRM 1202.

signing was held by the Board to be the execution date where a contract was signed after a petition had been filed and made retroactively effective (to before the petition date).[9] Where a contract was written and dated before a petition was filed but was not fully signed until after the filing, the later date controlled.[10] A contract actually executed in time to bar a petition nevertheless cannot bar if the contract, by its written terms, does not become effective until a date after a petition is filed. Finally, oral evidence at odds with the dates on a written contract cannot vary the express written date.

Rule III

Generally, a petition filed the day a contract is executed is barred by the contract if the employer has not been informed at the time of execution that a petition has been filed.[11]

Rule IV

A petition filed more than 90 days before the expiration date of a contract is untimely because it is premature; and one filed during the 60 days immediately preceding the expiration date is untimely because that 60-day period is "insulated" against rival petitions so that the contracting parties can negotiate a new agreement.

This means that there is *only* a 30-day open period—between the ninetieth and the sixtieth day prior to contract expiration—during which a petition is timely, unless, of course, the contracting parties fail to make a new agreement by the expiration date, in which case all bets are off.[12]

Rule V

To bar a petition, the contract must clearly cover the employees sought in the petition.

A contract covering only *some* of the employees in an appro-

---

[9] Nissen Baking Corp., 131 NLRB 589 (1961), 48 LRRM 1098.

[10] Printing Industry of Delaware, 131 NLRB 1100 (1961), 48 LRRM 1196.

[11] DeLuxe Metal Furniture Company, 121 NLRB 995 (1958), 42 LRRM 1470; Rappahannock Sportswear Co., 163 NLRB 703 (1967), 64 LRRM 1417.

[12] *See* Leonard Wholesale Meats, Inc., 136 NLRB 1000 (1962), 49 LRRM 1901.

priate unit will not bar;[13] and a "members only" contract cannot bar.[14]

Rule VI

A contract that is racially discriminatory on its face will not bar an election.[15]

Rule VII

A contract will bar for only three years. Contracts for longer periods will bar for the first three years only.[16]
A contract for an indefinite period will not act as a bar.

Rule VIII

A contract containing a checkoff or union-security clause that is unlawful on its face will not operate to bar an election.

The Board in *Paragon Products Corp.*[17] set up the following rules to determine whether contracts with certain union-security clauses could bar:

> . . . [O]nly those contracts containing a union-security provision which is clearly unlawful on its face, or which has been found to be unlawful in an unfair labor practice proceeding, may not bar a representation petition. A clearly unlawful union-security provision for this purpose is one which by its express terms clearly and unequivocally goes beyond the limited form of union-security permitted by Section 8(a)(3) of the Act, and is therefore incapable of a lawful interpretation. Such unlawful provisions include
>
> (1) those which expressly and unambiguously require the employer to give preference to union members in hiring, in laying off, for purpose of seniority;
>
> (2) those which specifically withhold from incumbent [nonunion employees] and/or new employees the statutory 30-day grace period;
>
> (3) those which expressly require as a condition of continued em-

---

[13] Pure Seal Dairy Co., 135 NLRB 76 (1962), 49 LRRM 1434; Sound Contractors Assn., 162 NLRB 364 (1966), 64 LRRM 1009.
[14] Appalachian Shale Products, *above*, note 7.
[15] Pioneer Bus Co., Inc., 140 NLRB 54 (1962), 51 LRRM 1546.
[16] General Cable Corp., 139 NLRB 1123 (1962), 51 LRRM 1444; General Dynamics Corp., 175 NLRB No. 154 (1969), 71 LRRM 1113.
[17] 134 NLRB 662 (1961), 49 LRRM 1160.

ployment the payment of sums of money other than "periodic dues and initiation fees uniformly required."

The mere existence of a clearly unlawful union-security provision in a contract will render it no bar regardless of whether it has ever been or was intended to be enforced by the parties, unless the contract also contains a provision which clearly defers the effectiveness of the unlawful clause or such clause has been eliminated by a properly executed rescission or amendment thereto.

Contracts containing ambiguous though not clearly unlawful union-security provisions will bar representation proceedings in the absence of a determination of illegality as to the particular provision involved by this Board or a Federal court pursuant to an unfair labor practice proceeding . . . And no evidence will be admissible in a representation proceeding, where the . . . evidence is only relevant to the question of the practice under a contract urged as a bar to the proceeding.

Rule IX

A contract prematurely extended will not bar beyond the date when it would have expired originally.

The reason for this rule is to prevent contracting parties from depriving employees of the right to change bargaining representatives. A contract is prematurely extended if, before the open period, an amendment or a new contract is negotiated with a later terminal date.[18]

Rule X

A change of circumstances during the term of a contract may prevent that contract from barring an election.[19]

The Twenty-fourth Annual Report of the NLRB states the rules on changed circumstances as follows:

In the *General Extrusion* case, 121 NLRB 1165 (1959), the Board announced certain changes in the rules governing the effectiveness of contracts as a bar where changes in the employer's operations and personnel complement have occurred before the filing of the petition.

(a) Prehire   contracts
The following rules were adopted:

---

[18] DeLuxe Metal Furniture Co., *above*, note 11.
[19] General Extrusion Co., 121 NLRB 1165 (1958), 42 LRRM 1508.

(1) A contract is not a bar if executed before any employees were hired.

(2) A contract executed before a substantial increase in personnel is a bar to an election only if at least 30 percent of the work force employed at the time of the hearing was employed at the time the contract was executed, and 50 percent of the job classifications in existence at the time of the hearing were in existence at the time the contract was executed.

(b) Changed operations

The rule that a contract is removed as a bar by pre-petition major changes in the *nature,* as distinguished from the *size,* of the employer's operations continues in effect, with the added requirement that to remove the contract bar the change must have involved a considerable portion of employees. The present rule contemplates changes in the nature of operations—

involving (1) a merger of two or more operations resulting in creation of an entirely new operation with major personnel changes; or (2) resumption of operations at either the same or a new location, after an indefinite period of closing, with new employees.

It was made clear, however, that a contract bar is not removed by—

a mere relocation of operations accompanied by a transfer of a considerable proportion of the employees to another plant, without an accompanying change in the character of the jobs and the functions of the employees in the contract unit.

Also remaining in effect is the rule that—

after a contract is removed as a bar because of [changes in operations], an amendment thereto embracing the changed operation or a new agreement will, subject to the rules relating to premature extension . . . , serve as a bar to a petition filed after its execution.

Likewise the rule remains that a contract is removed as a bar by—

the assumption of the operations by a purchaser in good faith who had bound himself to assume the bargaining agreement of the prior owner of the establishment.

Applying the *General Extrusion* rules, the Board held in one case that, while the petition for a new plant was not barred by the parties' original contract executed when there was no representative and substantial employee complement, the petition was barred by an amendment to the contract made when the plant had more than 30 percent of the work complement and more than 50 percent of the job classifications in existence at the time of the hearing. In another case, the Board held that the employer's petition was barred by a contract at a plant which later was consolidated with another plant. Here, at least 20 percent of the two-plant complement had been employed when the contract was executed, and at least 50 percent of the plant job classifications were in existence at the time.

Rule XI

A contract will not operate to bar an election unless it contains substantial terms and conditions of employment.

This does not mean that wage increases provided for in a contract need be of any particular size. It does, however, mean that a so-called "collective-bargaining contract" limited only to recognition of a union,[20] "to wages only, or to one or several provisions not deemed substantial" will not operate as a bar.[21]

Rule XII

To operate as a bar, the contract must be viable and of a currency to permit the parties to look to the actual terms and conditions of their contract for guidance in their day-to-day problems.

Where, although theoretically renewing the contract, the parties allow the written document to become outdated, so that it no longer reflects the terms and conditions of employment, there will be no bar.[22]

Rule XIII

This summary does not cover all of the Board's rules. The contract-bar doctrine is tricky, variable, and intricate; so get yourself a good lawyer when you face a complicated contract-bar question.

Recognition as Bar

The Board has recently extended the web of protective doctrines to include situations where there has been no election or Board order or settlement agreement, and there is not yet a contract in existence that would act as a bar. The Board now holds that where an employer has *voluntarily* recognized a union the parties will be given a reasonable period of time in

---

[20] Central Coat, Apron & Linen Service, Inc., 126 NLRB 958 (1960), 45 LRRM 1410.

[21] Appalachian Shale Products, *above,* note 7; *but see* Keller Plastics Eastern, Inc., 157 NLRB 583 (1966), 61 LRRM 1396.

[22] Raymond's Inc., 161 NLRB 838 (1966), 63 LRRM 1363.

which to bargain and execute a contract.[23] During that period another union's petition for an election will be barred. Limitations on the doctrine are that to constitute a bar, recognition (1) must be based upon a previously demonstrated showing of a majority[24] and (2) must not have been granted at a time when organizing campaigns were being conducted by more than one union.[25]

Independent Unions

Often international union organizers come upon a situation where an independent union has a contract with an employer, but the workers seem to need and want better representation, the solidarity, and the protection they can get from a strong international union.

Assuming the workers' inclination to join the international union, there are a number of avenues of approach open to the organizer, and they are not mutually exclusive—that is, if one route fails, another may be taken.

NLRB Election

Obviously, if under the contract-bar doctrine, discussed earlier, the employer-independent union contract has only a short time to run, a quick way to win bargaining rights is to petition for an election and win it. This should be done during the "open" period of the contract-bar doctrine—that is, between the ninetieth and the sixtieth day prior to the contract's expiration date. If a contract is unlawful, or not a "real" collective bargaining contract, it will not bar an election at all, so the first step is to get a copy of the agreement for *careful analysis by the union's lawyer*. Where there is no contract bar and the filing of the petition is timely, the unit should be described pretty much in terms of the contract language; there can then be little excuse for a long delay in a Board-ordered election. Of course, once the date 60 days before the contract's expiration date arrives without the filing of the petition, the incumbent union and

---

[23] Keller Plastics Eastern, Inc., *above*, note 21.
[24] Josephine Furniture Co., 172 NLRB No. 22 (1968), 68 LRRM 1311.
[25] Superior Furniture Mfg. Co., 167 NLRB No. 40 (1967), 66 LRRM 1036.

the company are insulated from another union's petition. If they arrive at a new agreement before the old one expires, the new one will be a bar to an election.

Affiliation of Independent

Where an election petition is not timely, the organizing union has the option of trying for an affiliation of the independent union as an entity, a local of the international union. In the case of an affiliation—where, say, the Jones Company Happy Employees' Union becomes Local 2140 of the UAW—the organizing union, once it obtains recognition, is bound by the independent union's contract for its term. Sometimes the independent's contract doesn't run too long, or is advantageous, so that living under it is worthwhile. And it hardly needs saying that a strong international union can often render valuable service to workers by properly administering and servicing an existing contract.

Both the Labor Board and the courts clearly recognize that a change in name and affiliation does not affect the right of a local union to preserve recognition and contract rights with an employer. There are certain criteria that are important, however, before the NLRB. They are as follows:

1. The officers, committee chairmen, and functional leaders of the newly affiliated local should be the same, if possible.

2. A majority of the membership voting at a regular or special meeting must have voted to affiliate after proper notice specifically stating that such a vote would be taken. The international union is in the strongest position if it can point to a majority of the full membership of the independent union, so there should be a strong effort to obtain the approval of a definite majority of the members of the *independent union and, if possible, a majority of all employees in the contract unit.*

3. The constitution and by-laws of the independent union must be scrupulously followed in effectuating affiliation.

4. The union should notify the employer of the action it has taken and of its new affiliation, and request a meeting.

It is important to note that if there is a split among the

top officers of the independent on the issue of the new affiliation, the Board may find that there is sufficient confusion for
the employer to refuse recognition and to insist upon an election—or to continue to recognize the old union without affiliation as represented by the dissenting officer or officers. This
will be discussed later under schism. In other words, while only
a majority vote of the membership at a meeting is needed for
the affiliation procedure to be successful, it is best to have a
consensus among the top officers of the independent union.

Assuming that there is a consensus among the leaders of the
independent union for affiliation with the international union,
the following steps should be taken:

1. There should be notice to the membership of a special
meeting called for the purpose of considering affiliation (or a
notice informing the membership that the question of considering affiliation will be taken up at the next regular meeting).
If the constitution and by-laws of the independent union cover
notice for special votes such as this, that procedure should be
followed. If not, this notice could be posted on the bulletin
board (if the independent union has such privileges at the
plant), placed in the independent's newspaper, or mailed to
each member. Notice should be given well in advance of the
meeting at which the vote is taken and should read something
like the following:

At a (special) (regular) meeting of _____ Independent Union to be held at_____ at _____ p.m. on
_____, 19 _____, a secret ballot vote will
be taken on the issue of affiliation of this local union with the
International _____ Union. All members
are urged to be present.

2. At the meeting the officers should present the question of
affiliation with the international union (an international organizer may be invited to speak and to present the case for
affiliation). After free and untrammelled discussion, *in which
dissenters are allowed full opportunity to speak,* a resolution
providing for affiliation should be presented and voted upon
(preferably by secret ballot) in strict accordance with the independent union's constitution and bylaws.

The resolution should read something like the following:

Whereas, it is the desire of the membership and officers of this organization known as the Independent _____ Workers Union, that said organization affiliate with and become chartered by the International _____ Union, as a local union of said International because of the International Union's prestige and its ability to provide expert technical assistance and advice to the officers and membership of this organization; and Whereas, it is the desire of the officers and membership of the Independent _____ Workers Union that the organization, structure, officers, and committees of this organization continue to operate and to carry out its collective bargaining functions after said affiliation with said International Union as has been done in the past and as is presently being done;

Now, Therefore, It Is Hereby Resolved as follows:

A. That this organization presently known as Independent _____ Workers Union be and is hereafter known as Local _____ of the International _____ Union.

B. That all assets and property of this organization, including but not limited to its bank account, its collective bargaining agreement dated _____ with the _____ Company and related pension and insurance agreements, be hereafter held by this organization under the name and style of Local _____, of the International _____ Union.

C. That this organization apply promptly to International_____ Union for affiliation therewith and for a Charter evidencing such affiliation as Local _____ of said International Union.

D. That this organization continue its relationship with the _____ Company as the duly certified and recognized bargaining representative of the production and maintenance employees (or insert proper unit of said Company.

E. That the officers and committeemen of this organization take all steps necessary to accomplish the objectives set forth hereinabove.

3. Immediately after the meeting at which affiliation is voted, the president of the local should inform the employer of the change in affiliation and its continuing status as contracting party.

The letter should read something like the following:

Dear Mr. _____:
    At a meeting of the members of _____ Union which, as you know, is the exclusive collective bargaining representative of your employees and is under contract with your company, the membership, after special notice of the purpose of the meeting, voted to affiliate with the International _____ Union. A copy of the resolution of affiliation is attached.

From this date on the name of the union has been changed to _____. All officers and functional leaders remain the same, and we anticipate no change in our day-to-day relationship with the company. The continuity of organization in the local union has been completely preserved and we intend to honor fully all contractual commitments with the company. Please note for your records the change in name of the contracting union.

4. Shortly after the employer has received the letter described above, the newly affiliated local should seek a meeting with the employer. If the employer refuses to meet or to deal with the newly affiliated local, then the union is in a position to file a petition for an amendment to certification (AC petition) with the Board or to file unfair labor practice charges against the employer for refusal to bargain [8 (a) (5)]. Finally, if all the steps previously outlined have been complied with, the union might, *after consultation with its lawyers,* strike the employer to protest his unfair labor practices in refusing to recognize the union under contract. Prior to taking any dramatic action, the union should notify the employer of its rights and its legal theory.

Usually a petition to amend the certification is a much faster way to obtain recognition than a refusal-to-bargain charge. If the independent was originally certified, an amendment may be sought by the filing of an AC petition with the Board. It is a good idea for the president of the affiliating local to sign the petition and to include a summary of the procedure followed, the resolution passed, and the letter to the employer.[26]

Schism and Defunctness

Schism—If the officers and members are too badly split for simple affiliation, an NLRB election is necessary. In this case

---

[26] Some important cases on the union's right to continued recognition are the following: *NLRB v. Weyerhauser Co.,* 276 F.2d 865 (CA 7, 1960), 45 LRRM 3088; *Union Carbide & Carbon Corp.* v. *NLRB,* 224 F.2d 672 (CA 6, 1957), 40 LRRM 2084; *Carpinteria Lemon Assn.* v. *NLRB,* 240 F.2d 554 (CA 9, 1956), 39 LRRM 2185; *NLRB* v. *Harris-Woodson Co.,* 179 F.2d 720 (CA 4, 1950), 25 LRRM 2346; *Marshall Maintenance Corp.,* 154 NLRB 611 (1965), 59 LRRM 1784; *Montgomery Ward & Co., Inc.,* 137 NLRB 346 (1962), 50 LRRM 1137. Amendment-to-certification cases include the following: *Emery Industries, Inc.,* 148 NLRB 51 (1964), 56 LRRM 1449; *Minnesota Mining & Mfg. Co.,* 144 NLRB 419 (1963), 54 LRRM 1078; *Proctor & Gamble Mfg. Co.,* 130 NLRB 633 (1961), 47 LRRM 1392; and *Missouri Beef Packers, Inc.,* 175 NLRB No. 179 (1969), 71 LRRM 1177.

the organizing union would have to meet certain requirements that are necessary to remove the contract between the independent union and the employer as a bar to an election, assuming, of course, that the contract has a long time to run. If some of the top officers resist affiliation with the international but the international has a clear majority of the membership and the support of *some* leaders of the independent union, it is possible to promote a "schism" within the local union by attempting affiliation as stated previously, so as to remove its contract as a bar to an election. The following steps should be taken:

1. Obtain a majority of authorization cards.

2. Give notice of a vote for affiliation similar to the one described in the previous section.

3. At an open meeting, conducted according to the constitutional provisions and bylaws of the independent union, present a resolution exactly as set forth in the affiliation procedure. This should be passed (preferably by secret ballot) after full and free discussion in which all can participate, including the dissidents. In this case only it may be possible to get by with a majority of those present and voting rather than of the entire unit.

4. Then have one of those officers who is in favor of the affiliation write the following letter to the employer:

Dear Mr. _____:
    At a meeting called after notice of intent to vote on affiliation with the International _____ Union, the members of _____ Union voted to affiliate with the International so that the exclusive collective bargaining agent is now (name of union with new affiliation). No other labor organization is entitled to recognition.

5. If the employer bargains with the union, the problem is solved. If, on the other hand, the employer is faced with a request for continued recognition by the old union (unaffiliated) and refuses to recognize the newly affiliated union, the latter should petition the Board for an election and argue that there is a schism—that is, a split—so that an election is required to determine which union the employer should recognize. In other words, there is a question concerning representation.

However, it *is very difficult to establish a schism that will re-move a contract bar,* because the doctrine has been used largely to permit locals of unions, expelled from a parent federation for corruption or subversion, to escape. The leading Board case on schism is *Hershey Chocolate Corp.*[27] In its Twenty-fourth Annual Report the Board stated the rules it established in *Hershey*:

(a) Where a schism is found, an election will be directed whether or not the contracting representative is defunct.

(b) A schism warranting an election will be found to exist only where it arises from "a basic intraunion conflict." i.e., "any conflict over policy at the highest level of an international union, whether or not it is affiliated with a federation."

(c) Employee disaffiliation action at the local level—even though arising from a basic intraunion conflict—however will not be held to warrant an election unless the action was taken "at an *open meeting* called, without regard to any constitutional restrictions but with *due notice* to the members in the unit, for the purpose of taking disaffiliation action for reasons relating to the basic intraunion conflict," and unless the "action is taken within a reasonable period of time after the occurrence of the conflict and results in confusion unstabilizing the bargaining relationship."

(d) "[U]nstabilizing confusion" will be found whenever "the disaffiliation action . . . results in the employer being confronted with two organizations each claiming with some show of right to be the organization previously chosen by the employees as their representative."

(e) Disaffiliation action of the above kind will be held to remove the contract bar whenever—though not only where—it is coextensive with the contract unit. In the case of joint representation by two or more locals, unstabilizing confusion will also be found if disaffiliation action is taken by the members of one or more of such locals and involves a substantial number of all the employees in the contract unit.

Defunctness—Sometimes an independent union that is a party to an existing collective-bargaining agreement has really ceased to exist. In that case, if the union is *really* defunct, neither a contract with a nonexistent union nor the certification year will excuse the employer from his duty to bargain with a newly organized union. If the defunct union never made a contract, the organizing union can demand recognition; but even if there

---

[27] 121 NLRB 901 (1958), 42 LRRM 1460.

is a contract, it will *not* bar an election petition if the old union no longer exists. It should be kept in mind that the defunct union really has to cease to operate in *any* way. Moreover, the Board will not permit an independent that made an unsatisfactory contract to "play dead" just to get rid of what it now thinks is a bad deal.[28]

Conclusion

The problems of the contract-bar rules are, as previously noted, intricate and difficult. In most instances legal advice on these matters is necessary.

When, however, the contract-bar issues are settled, there is no reason why a careful professional organizer could not assist an independent union in affiliating with an international union and then, follow through with the NLRB. Where an affiliated union is involved attention should be paid to interunion agreements. (See Chapters I and VI.)

---

[28] Some leading cases in this area of the law are the following: *News Press Publishing Co.*, 145 NLRB 803 (1964), 55 LRRM 1045; *Pepsi Cola Bottling Co.*, 132 NLRB 1441 (1961), 48 LRRM 1514; *Gulf Oil Corp.*, 137 NLRB 544 (1962), 50 LRRM 1191; *Bennett Stone Co.*, 139 NLRB 1422 (1962), 51 LRRM 1518; *Rocky Mt. Phosphates, Inc.*, 138 NLRB 292 (1962), 51 LRRM 1019; *Breed Caskett Co.*, 175 NLRB No. 35 (1969), 70 LRRM 1518; and *Gate City Optical Co.*, 175 NLRB No. 172 (1969), 71 LRRM 1118.

Chapter IX

CONDUCT OF ELECTIONS

The history of the rules governing
contests between employer and employed in the several English-speaking
countries illustrates both the suscepti-
bility of such rules to change and the
variety of contemporary opinion as to
what rules will best serve the public
interest.

Mr. Justice Brandeis in
Truax v. *Corrigan,* 257
US 312, 357 (1921)

Introduction

One of the most difficult, and yet most important, subjects
for organizers, employees, employers, and the Board itself is
the regulation of the election campaign and the election itself.
This area of the law is difficult because it brings into play not
only Sections 7 and 9 of the Act, dealing with employee rights
and representational matters, but all of the unfair-labor-practice
proscriptions of Section 8, both employer and union, Section
8 (c) of the Act dealing with free speech, and, finally, the First
Amendment of the Constitution of the United States.

As we have seen, the Board has broad powers in deciding
how to handle cases dealing with the representation of employees. Indeed, these matters are hardly reviewable at all by the
federal courts. The Board's responsibility in elections extends
well beyond that of government officials in political elections,
for those officials normally deal only with the mechanics of balloting. The Board, on the other hand, must see to it, as best it

189

can, that the election is *fair* and that the workers are able to make a reasoned selection of a bargaining representative or decide against being represented at all.

To the organizer the dare is to hold onto his card majority in the face of an antiunion campaign by the employer. At the same time, he must be prepared to prove, if he can, that an election *loss* was caused by objectionable conduct by the employer and still refrain from any actions that might cause an election *victory* to be upset.

The Board-conducted election becomes the focal point for the formulation of the bargaining unit under the Act. The Board sees its role as an impartial judge of election returns whose function is simply to certify the results as an indication of what the employees desire. But it must, nevertheless, make sure that the vote is taken under civilized, reasonable conditions. It has said:

> . . . In election proceedings, it is the Board's function to *provide a laboratory in which an experiment may be conducted,* under conditions as nearly ideal as possible, to determine the uninhibited desires of the employees . . . [When] the standard drops too low, because of our fault or that of others, the requisite laboratory conditions are not present and the experiment must be conducted over again.[1]

And the Board has described its general process in representation cases as follows:

> In evaluating the interference resulting from specific conduct, the Board does not attempt to assess its actual effect on the employees, but rather concerns itself with whether it is reasonable to conclude that the conduct tended to prevent the free formation and expression of the employees' choice. In making this evaluation the Board treats each case on its facts, taking an *ad hoc* rather than a *per se* approach in resolution of the issues . . ."[2]

There are essentially two kinds of conduct that interfere sufficiently to cause an election to be set aside—speech (written or spoken words) and actions. Although speech is never divorced from other types of conduct, the history of employer speech is one tangled with shifts in Board position and legislative revision. Under the Wagner Act, as originally administered

---

[1] General Shoe Corp., 77 NLRB 124 (1948), 21 LRRM 1337.
[2] NLRB, 32nd Annual Report, pp. 69-70.

by the NLRB, *any* expression of antiunion opinion by a campaigning employer was considered to constitute illegal interference with the employee's protected right to organize.[3] This policy was based on the theory that every statement, argumentative in tone, would be coercive upon an employee. However, the Supreme Court, in *Virginia Electric & Power Co. v. NLRB*,[4] rejected that approach, holding that the expression of opinion alone cannot warrant condemnation; the Court directed the Board to look to the "totality of conduct," which meant that speech could be held illegal only if it were an integral part of a course of antiunion conduct which, in its totality, amounted to coercion.[5]

It is now settled, as a result of *Virginia Electric & Power* and the *American Tube Bending* case,[6] that an employer has a constitutional right of free speech that entitles him to speak out against unionization. The Board has recognized expressly that the employer has such a constitutionally protected right of free speech in election cases, but it has said that the right is unrelated to Section 8 (c), the so-called "free speech" provision of Taft-Hartley, which applies only to unfair labor practices.[7] An employer may, according to the Supreme Court, express his views and opinions, but he should not engage in "brinkmanship," and "at the least he can avoid coercive speech simply by avoiding conscious overstatements he has reason to believe will mislead his employees." [8]

Necessarily, in discussing permissible and legally objectionable conduct during election campaigns, one has to reconsider the effects of unfair labor practices and the kinds and varieties of such practices. If there have been unfair labor practices, such as interference, coercion, restraint, discrimination, and illegal assistance or domination of unions, there is a good chance that the Board will find that this conduct not only violated Section 8 of the Act but also interfered with the election. Consequently, most of the material dealing with employer unfair labor practices in Chapter III is also relevant here. However, in view of the re-

---

[3] Rockford Mitten & Hosiery Co., 16 NLRB 501 (1939), 5 LRRM 244.
[4] 314 US 463 (1941), 9 LRRM 405.
[5] *See* Ovalwood Dish Corp., 62 NLRB 1129 (1945), 16 LRRM 249.
[6] NLRB v. American Tube Bending Co., Inc., 134 F.2d 993 (CA 2, 1943), 12 LRRM 615, cert. denied, 320 US 768 (1943), 13 LRRM 850.
[7] Oak Mfg. Co., 141 NLRB 1323 (1963), 52 LRRM 1502.
[8] NLRB v. Gissel Packing Co., 395 US 575 (1969), 71 LRRM 2481.

quired "laboratory conditions" for elections, objectionable conduct is judged by a *different standard* than conduct alleged to be an unfair labor practice. So, what may not be an unfair labor practice may, nevertheless, be a solid ground for setting aside an election. (See Chapters II, III, IV, and V generally.)

Considerations of Time

The conduct of elections is tested by the filing of objections. These objections must be filed within five working days after the parties receive the Board's tally of election results—holidays, Saturdays, and Sundays not being counted in the five-day rule. Objections to election conduct are quite different from voter challenges, which are made orally at the time the worker tries to vote. The objections must be written (no particular form is required) and must contain a brief statement of the reasons for the objections. These objections may be made by telegram. In any case, however, they must be served on the other parties and received at the Board's regional office before the close of business on the fifth working day after the completion of the election. An original and three copies of objections should be filed.

Organizers must be familiar with the NLRB rule which sets the crucial period during which preelection conduct may be tested by objection after an election. There is now only one rule for both contested (Board-ordered) elections and elections by agreement (consent or stipulation). It is as follows: *The date of the filing of the petition is the cutoff date in considering post-election objections in elections.* Nothing done before that time can upset an election and from that time on, conduct in a Board-ordered election campaign which tends to prevent a free election is considered by the Board in a post-election objection. Conduct occurring *before* the date the petition was filed will *not* be considered.[9]

Twenty-Four Hour Rule

In a famous case, *Peerless Plywood Co.*[10] the Board laid down

---

[9] The leading cases on the cutoff date for election misconduct are *Ideal Electric & Mfg. Co.*, 134 NLRB 1275 (1961), 49 LRRM 1316, and *Goodyear Tire & Rubber Co.*, 138 NLRB 453 (1962), 51 LRRM 1070.

[10] 107 NLRB 427 (1953), 33 LRRM 1151.

its 24-hour rule, which is the law to this day. In that case the Board said:

> Accordingly, we now establish an election rule which will be applied in all election cases. This rule shall be that employers and unions alike will be prohibited from making election speeches on company time to massed assemblies of employees within 24 hours before the scheduled time for conducting an election. Violation of this rule will cause the election to be set aside whenever valid objections are filed. We institute this rule pursuant to our statutory authority and obligation to conduct elections in circumstances and under conditions which will insure employees a free and untrammeled choice. Implicit in this rule is our view that the combined circumstances of (1) the use of company time for preelection speeches and (2) the delivery of such speeches on the eve of the election tend to destroy freedom of choice and establish an atmosphere in which a free election cannot be held. Also implicit in the rule is our judgment that noncoercive speeches made prior to the proscribed period will not interfere with a free election, inasmuch as our rule will allow time for their effect to be neutralized by the impact of other media of employee persuasion.

> This rule is closely akin to, and no more than an extension of, our long-standing rule prohibiting electioneering by either party at or near the polling place. We have previously prescribed space limitations, now we prescribe time limitations as well. This rule arises from the same concept and has the same purpose of keeping our elections free. It is this same purpose which has led us recently to prohibit the use of sound trucks for the purpose of projecting voice propaganda into the polling place although the trucks are physically located outside the proscribed polling area. Likewise, it is this same purpose which caused us in another recent decision to set aside an election because an atmosphere of terror was created by individual employees, although their conduct could not be attributed either to the union or the employer.

> We believe that the application of this same concept of fair and free elections to speeches on company time on the very eve of an election will have a salutary effect, will not give undue advantage to any party, and will afford employees an opportunity to exercise their franchise in an atmosphere more truly conducive to freedom of choice.

> This rule will not interfere with the rights of unions or employers to circulate campaign literature on or off the premises at any time prior to an election, nor will it prohibit the use of any other legitimate campaign propaganda or media. It does not, of course, sanction coercive speeches or other conduct prior to the 24-hour period, nor does it prohibit an employer from making (without granting the union an opportunity to reply) campaign speeches on company time prior to the 24-hour period, provided, of course, such speeches are

not otherwise violative of Section 8(a)(1). Moreover, the rule does not prohibit employers or unions from making campaign speeches on or off company premises during the 24-hour period if employee attendance is voluntary and on the employees' own time.

In a nutshell, the rule bars *speeches* to "captive audiences" during the 24-hour period just before the election. It does *not* apply to completely voluntary meetings on or off the employer's property, nor does it apply to *written* matter like handbills, letters, or leaflets. The rule applies *only* to speeches during working hours or speeches employees are required to attend.[11] An election-eve party at which no speeches are made does not violate the rule.[12]

In *Honeywell Inc.*,[13] a Board majority of Chairman McCulloch and Members Brown and Zagoria set aside an election lost by the IUE after a supervisor conducted a question-and-answer session among the cover-room employees shortly before they were to vote. An hour and a half before certain employees were to vote, the supervisor asked them if any of them had questions about the Employer's "Facts Sheets," a compilation of antiunion propaganda previously distributed to supervisors for use in persuading employees to vote against the union. Although the employees stated they had no questions, the supervisor instructed them to cease work, and proceeded for an hour and a half, until it was time for them to vote, to read and comment upon the antiunion material and to answer resultant questions which he invited.

This captive audience meeting was conducted on company time, with the knowledge and acquiescence of higher management, and the employees were paid. Deciding to direct a second election, the majority stated:

> As the Board explained in the *Montgomery Ward* case, where a question-and-answer session was similarly involved, the *Peerless Plywood* ban is not limited to "a formal speech in the usual sense," but is designed to bar "absolutely" during the 24-hour preelection period the use of company time for campaign speeches in any form, including specifically campaign electioneering of the type engaged in by Peterson in this case.
>
> . . . [W]e think it clear that the "captive audience" of cover room

---

[11] Conroe Creosoting Co., 149 NLRB 1174 (1964), 57 LRRM 1469.
[12] Peachtree City Warehouse, Inc., 158 NLRB 97 (1966), 62 LRRM 1169.
[13] 162 NLRB 323 (1966), 64 LRRM 1002.

employees, who were required as a group to cease work and pay heed to Peterson's antiunion electioneering, constituted a massed assembly within the intent of the *Peerless Plywood* rule.

A recent case demonstrates that an *incorrect statement* of the 24-hour rule is a good reason for setting aside an election. In *General Electric Co.*,[14] the manager had said that "by law, neither the company nor the union is allowed to hold meetings, distribute campaign material, or contact employees 24 hours before the election. In other words tomorrow is a silent day."

Concluding that the statement constituted grounds for setting aside the election, the Board stated:

> . . .[I]ts mischief lies not so much in being a misrepresentation of some material fact having relevant bearing on terms and conditions of employment . . . but in being an unwarranted interference with an employee's right to receive all lawful communications reasonably concerned with the election.

> The statement, coming as it did from one of management's higher officials, could reasonably have been taken at face value by the employees and led to their rejection of literature attempted to be distributed by Petitioner or other employees during the important hours immediately preceding the election. The statement, in our opinion, therefore constituted an improper interference in the election and justifies our setting the election aside.

In a very real sense, the *GE* case points up the necessity for complete familiarity with the law. Misstatements of the law by high union or company officials can be violations of law as well as good grounds for upsetting an election.

Activity at or Near Polls

In the case of *Milchem, Inc.*[15] the Board announced a strict new rule governing conversation at the polling area. Under this rule conversations between either company or union officials and employees in the polling area will be grounds for setting aside an election *regardless of what is discussed*. In the *Milchem* case a union officer stood for several minutes near the line of employees waiting to vote, engaging them in conversation. Allegedly his conversation concerned "the weather and like

---

[14] 161 NLRB 618 (1966), 63 LRRM 1289.
[15] 170 NLRB No. 46 (1968), 67 LRRM 1395.

topics." Nonetheless, the Board set aside the election which the
union won, saying:

> Careful consideration of the problem now convinces us that the
> potential for distraction, last minute electioneering or pressure, and
> unfair advantage from prolonged conversations between representa-
> tives of any party to the election and voters waiting to cast ballots
> is of sufficient concern to warrant a strict rule against such conduct,
> without inquiry into the nature of the conversations.
>
> The final minutes before an employee casts his vote should be his
> own, as free from interference as possible. Furthermore, the standard
> here applied insures that no party gains a last minute advantage
> over the other, and at the same time deprives neither party of any
> important access to the ear of the voter. The difficulties of recap-
> turing with any precision the nature of the remarks made in the
> charged atmosphere of a polling place are self-evident, and to require
> an examination into the substance and effect of the conversations
> seems unduly burdensome and, in this situation, unnecessary. Fin-
> ally, a blanket prohibition against such conversations is easily under-
> stood and simply applied.

Sometimes even the mere *presence* of company officials, without any attempt at conversation will interfere sufficiently with
the conduct of an election to warrant setting it aside. In
Belk's Dept. Store of Savannah, Ga.[16] the presence of officials of
management near the polling place—though no electioneering
took place—was sufficient to set aside the election. The Board
said, in part:

> We are also convinced that, even though the supervisors were at
> some distance from the actual polling place, and apparently said
> nothing calculated to restrain or coerce the employees, their pres-
> ence in the area where the employees were gathered while waiting
> to vote tended to interfere with the employees' freedom of choice of
> a bargaining agent. *In particular, we regard as improper Galloway's
> conduct in walking back and forth in the space which the employees
> were required to traverse to go to the polling place.*
>
> In view of the above findings, we believe that the purposes of the
> Act will best be effectuated by setting the election aside. (Emphasis
> added)

In *Claussen Baking Co.*[17] a leadman had engaged in electioneering near the polls. However, the Board also noted that
the plant manager and sales supervisor had been seen convers-

---

[16] 98 NLRB 280 (1952), 29 LRRM 1325.
[17] 134 NLRB 111 (1961), 49 LRRM 1092.

ing with each other near the polling place—without any evidence of electioneering. The election was set aside.

Election Propaganda

Two rights must be balanced by the Board in judging campaign propaganda—the right of the parties to wage a vigorous, partisan, and free campaign and the right of employees to a fair choice, without pressure, on the honest merits of the situation.

The leading Board case balancing these rights in the situation where an employer or a union misrepresents facts to the voters is *Hollywood Ceramics Co.*,[18] in which the Board said:

> We believe that an election should be set aside only where there has been a misrepresentation or other similar campaign trickery, which involves a substantial departure from the truth, at a time which prevents the other party or parties from making an effective reply, so that the misrepresentation, whether deliberate or not, may reasonably be expected to have a significant impact on the election. However, the mere fact that a message is inartistically or vaguely worded and subject to different interpretations will not suffice to establish such misrepresentation as would lead us to set the election aside. Such ambiguities, like extravagant promises, derogatory statements about the other party, and minor distortions of some facts, frequently occur in communication between persons. But even where a misrepresentation is shown to have been substantial, the Board may still refuse to set aside the election if it finds upon consideration of all the circumstances that the statement would not be likely to have had a real impact on the election. For example, the misrepresentation might have occurred in connection with an unimportant matter so that it could only have had a *de minimis* effect. Or, it could have been so extreme as to put the employees on notice of its lack of truth under the particular circumstances so that they could not reasonably have relied on the assertion. Or, the Board may find that the employees possessed independent knowledge with which to evaluate the statements.

Unions and employers should avoid last-minute desperation "pitches" in campaigns. However, even eleventh hour misstatements may not fatally affect elections, if the misrepresentation is unimportant or one that likely would be dismissed as nonsense by the employees.

---

[18] 140 NLRB 221 (1962), 51 LRRM 1600.

The Board found in one case that misleading propaganda in a letter sent by the Teamsters two days before an election to all production employees, as well as maintenance employees, adversely affected *two* elections held the same day—one in the maintenance unit where only the Teamsters union was on the ballot and one in the producton unit where only the Meat Cutters union was on the ballot.[19]

A couple of days before the voting, the Teamsters mailed a letter to employees in both units. It pointed out that the Teamsters had already gained the right to represent the company's truck drivers, that it was now concentrating on the maintenance unit, and that it would go after the production unit later if the Meat Cutters were defeated in the forthcoming election. As an example of the benefits of representation by the Teamsters, the preelection letter boasted of a substantial hourly wage increase already won for the truck drivers (untrue).

The Teamsters won and the Meat Cutters lost their respective elections. Both results were tainted, the Board found, by the Teamsters' propaganda. The hourly wage increase won for the truck drivers was found to have been about half as big as the union claimed.

An important and instructive case is *United States Gypsum*,[20] where the Board said:

> [W]hen one of the parties deliberately misstates material facts *which are within its special knowledge, under such circumstances that the other party or parties cannot learn about them in time to point out the misstatements, and the employees themselves lack the independent knowledge to make possible a proper evaluation of the misstatements, the Board* will find that the bounds of legitimate campaign propaganda have been exceeded and *will set aside an election.* (Emphasis added)

In *United States Gypsum* the employer's misrepresentation centered about two telegrams which were widely distributed, discussed, and posted at the plant two days before the election. The telegrams dealt with the employer's bargaining relationship with the same union at another of its plants. The Board found that the telegrams contained "deliberate misrepresentations."[21]

---

[19] Ore-Ida Foods, Inc., 160 NLRB 1396 (1966), 63 LRRM 1158.

[20] 130 NLRB 901 (1961), 47 LRRM 1436.

[21] *See also* Bausch & Lomb, Inc., 2—RC—14304 (1966), 65 LRRM 1137.

The second form of suspect election propaganda is that which may contain coercion or threats, or promises of benefit. A landmark case in this area of election propaganda is *Dal-Tex Optical Company, Inc.*,[22] which overruled many previous cases permitting coercive statements under the guise of free speech, opinion, prediction, or statement of legal position. Because that case is so instructive to organizers and because it represents the most common form of objectionable employer propaganda, we reprint here generous portions of the Board's opinion.

[Quoting the employer's speech to employees:]

"Two years ago the I.U.E. Union tried to organize this plant. They went to every length to cause trouble. They misrepresented all of the facts. They conducted a vicious campaign. They did not then, nor do they now, represent any optical laboratory in Texas. Our employees were not fooled and voted against the Union by a large majority. The Union lost the election. This election was conducted by a secret ballot and was a fair election, but the Union could not stand being beaten and attempted to set aside the election. They introduced evidence before the Board, which I considered then, and do now consider, to be false and perjured. A year and a half after the election the National Labor Relations Board, based upon such evidence, decided that the election should be set aside and a new one held. After another six months the Board then decided to hold another election next week. The Company does not agree with the Board, and has maintained and is going to maintain that the election held two years ago was a valid election. And the Courts are going to have to decide whether this first election was valid. In the meantime, the Company is permitting the holding of this new election on Company property on September 22nd, because it feels that your rights can be better protected. If the Union should win this election, which I don't think it can, the Courts are still going to have to determine whether the Board was right or wrong. If the Board was wrong, which I firmly believe, the election to be held on September 22nd will not mean a thing if the Union wins it. My guess is that it will be another couple of years before this matter is settled. In the meantime, we will go on just as we are without any Union. I am explaining all of this to you so you will understand that wild promises by this Union of what is going to happen here if the Union wins don't mean a thing. I believe in law and order. When the Courts decide the matter I will abide by the decisions of the Courts."

[After detailing some of the benefits employees were receiving:]

"So, why should you want a Union to represent you? Is it because you believe they can get you more than you now have, or have you

22 137 NLRB 1782 (1962), 50 LRRM 1489.

been told the Union will run this plant? I have made it a practice of giving back in increased wages all efficiency gains during the year. During the year 1959 there were 270 individual raises given. During the year 1960 there were 298 raises given, and during this year already there have been 349 raises given. These are merit raises. These are wages that you get in addition to your profit sharing and pension plans. I not only provide for your old age and your family in case of your death, but as the efficiency improves you get the benefit of it in increased wages. Do you want to gamble all of these things? If I am required by the Court to bargain with this Union, whenever that may be, I will bargain in good faith, but I will have to bargain on a cold-blooded business basis. You may come out with a lot less than you have now. Why gamble because agitators make wild promises to you? If I am required to bargain and I cannot agree there is no power on earth that can make me sign a contract with this Union, so what will probably happen is the Union will call a strike. I will go right along running this business and replace the strikers. There has been a lot of talk about your being skilled workers. You only do one operation and in a short period I can train anybody to do any of these operations, as we trained most of you. I am not afraid of a strike. It won't hurt the Company. I will replace the strikers. They will lose all of their benefits. Strikers will draw no wages, no unemployment compensation and be out of a job. The Union won't pay you wages. The Union has nothing to lose. You do all of the losing. No employee is so important that he or she cannot be replaced. I am not afraid of threats. Before the last election this Union tried everything. Before this election is over, you will see how dirty the Union will get. It has no responsibility. It is not reasonable to believe that you would give up your individual rights to outside agitators and not be able to come to me as you have in the past with your problems. I cannot believe you want to change to the cold blooded bargaining basis that must follow."

[In another speech he stated, among other things:]

"Will the Union get you more wages? No, who pays the wages? I do. I built this plant. I invest the capital. I see to it that it runs 52 weeks a year. I see that the orders come in. I have consistently turned back to you in increased wages all efficiency gains made by the Company. I give hundreds of increases in wages that are merited. In 1960 I gave 349 raises. This year I have already given 442 raises. This is the right way to handle wages. The result is that you have the highest wages in the industry. This I can assure you, it is my position now, and it will be my position at all times, that you will get merit raises just as I have been giving them over the years. If you don't merit them, you will not get them. This is nothing new. It is the system I have operated on from the beginning. I do not have to, nor will I, change it. If you believe promises the Union makes you, you will find out the Union doesn't pay wages. I do. The Union doesn't give raises. I do. Now, please remember you have to compare your wages with those of other optical laboratories in Dallas, Texas. We are at the top. It does not make any difference what Collins Electric pays or any other industry. It is what is paid in our industry. No Union and no company in our industry in Texas can match our wages and benefits."

[The Board's reasoning:]

Even a cursory reading of these portions of the speeches of the Employer's president demonstrates that they were couched in language calculated to convey to the employees the danger and futility of their designating the Union. After listing some of the existing benefits, he queried whether they wanted "to gamble all of these things," stated that if required to bargain he would do so on "a cold-blooded business basis" so that the employees "may come out with a lot less than you have now," and emphasized his own control over wages. This was a clearcut, readily understandable threat that the Employer would bargain "from scratch" as though no economic benefits had been given, and the employees would suffer economic loss and reprisal if they selected the Union. Also, the reference to the probability of a strike accompanied by the threat to replace strikers with the emphasis upon their expendability and resultant loss of all their benefits was calculated to create a fear that there would necessarily be a loss of employment and financial security if the Union won. These latter statements had even greater meaning and weight occurring, as they did, after the Employer engaged in a series of unfair labor practices, including, most recently, the discharge of three employees for acting contrary to the Employer's wishes.

In addition to and intermingled with the above threats were statements by which the Employer clearly conveyed the idea that designation of the Union was futile and that the Employer would not sign a contract even if required to engage in bargaining. The Employer informed the employees that in the event the Union won it would not mean a thing because the "Courts are still going to have to determine" the issue and "my guess is that it will be another couple of years before this matter is settled"; that if required to bargain and unable to agree, no power on earth could make the Employer sign a contract ". . . so what will *probably* happen is the Union will call a strike" (emphasis supplied); and that the Employer did not have to and would not change its wage policy. While these comments may appear to be mere statements of the Employer's legal rights and his intention to adhere to them, in the present context they assume quite a different character. The statement that the Employer could not be compelled to sign a contract in the absence of agreement seems innocuous on the surface. But when the same sentence was completed by pointing out the probability of a strike, when the entire sentence followed immediately after the threat to abrogate existing benefits and, in effect, bargain "from scratch," and when it was succeeded by the graphic description of the results of their replacement during the predicted strike, the entire import and impact of the comment was changed to a clear message that the Employer would not sign a contract even if required to negotiate. This message was reinforced by the other statements noted above, particularly the Employer's position that it *would not* change its wage policy, undeniably it was thus announcing a predetermination not to bargain on the subject of wages.

Prior cases involving objections to elections, have held, although not uniformly, statements similar to those involved herein to the effect that the employer would not bargain, were merely an expression of the Employer's "legal position." On the other hand, it has long been well settled that the same type of statement is not within the "free speech" protection of Section 8(c) of the Act but, rather, constitutes interference, restraint, and coercion of employees within the meaning of Section 8(a)(1) of the Act. We find no logic or sound reason for this disparity of treatment depending on the nature of the proceeding in which the issue is raised before the Board. Conduct violative of Section 8(a)(1) is, *a fortiori*, conduct which interferes with the exercise of a free and untrammeled choice in an election. This is so because the test of conduct which may interfere with the laboratory conditions for an election is considerably more restrictive than the test of conduct which amounts to interference, restraint, or coercion which violates Section 8(a)(1). Accordingly, to the extent they are inconsistent herewith, we hereby overrule *National Furniture Company, Inc., supra,* and similar cases holding such statements to be privileged under Section 8(c).

To adhere to those decisions would be to sanction implied threats couched in the guise of statements of legal position. Such an approach is too mechanical, fails to consider all the surrounding circumstances, and is inconsistent with the duty of this Board to enforce and advance the statutory policy of encouraging the practice and procedure of collective bargaining by protecting the full freedom of employees to select representatives of their own choosing. Rather, we shall look to the economic realities of the employer-employee relationship and shall set aside an election where we find that the employer's conduct has resulted in substantial interference with the election, regardless of the form in which the statement was made.

However, it should not be thought that all employer predictions of dire economic consequences resulting from unionization will be grounds for setting aside an election that the union loses. Statements of a rather blander sort than those in *Dal-Tex* will be allowed. *Watson Drilling Co., Inc.*[23] is illustrative. There the Company's president spoke to assembled groups of employees two days before the election. He stated that if he entered into a

[23] 164 NLRB 357 (1967), 65 LRRM 1101.

union contract which obligated him to pay wages higher than those paid by some other drilling contractors, it would be difficult for him to bid successfully on jobs, and that in the event of higher costs resulting from a Union victory, some oil wells would not be drilled. The obvious implication was that there would be less work available for the employees. In rejecting union objections to the election the Board said that:

> In our view, the Employer in the foregoing remarks did not threaten the employees' job security. The Employer's statements, rather, set forth its economic and competitive position in the industry, and presented this information in a non-coercive manner. Hence they were within permissible limits of campaign propaganda.

The Supreme Court has said that the Board's duty is to "focus on the question 'What did the speaker intend and the listener understand.'" Although the line between permissible and impermissible employer statements may be fine, and the decision in each case might turn on the particular facts of the case, there are certain kinds of employer statements which should be watched for, as they will often constitute interference sufficient to warrant setting aside an election: [24]

1. Voting for the union will cause a loss of business and customers.[25]

2. Violent strikes or economic detriment to employees is probable if the union wins.[26]

3. If the union wins, the employer will not bargain until a court forces him to do so.[27]

4. Strikes which will probably follow a union victory will be disastrous—employees can't get unemployment compensation, they will be unable to get jobs, they will lose benefits and deplete savings, and the company will subcontract its work.[28]

---

[24] NLRB v. Gissel Packing Co., *above*, note 8. For a recent application of the *Gissel* standards of permissible company "predictions" where the NLRB found interference, *see General Electric Wiring Devices, Inc.*, 182 NLRB No. 130 (1970), 74 LRRM 1224.

[25] R. D. Cole Mfg. Co., 133 NLRB 1455 (1961), 49 LRRM 1033; TRW Semiconductors, Inc., 159 NLRB 415 (1966), 62 LRRM 1469; Carl T. Mason, Inc., 142 NLRB 480 (1963), 53 LRRM 1063.

[26] Pepperell Mfg. Co., 159 NLRB 291 (1966), 62 LRRM 1279; General Industries Electronics Co., 146 NLRB 1139 (1964), 56 LRRM 1015; *cf., e.g.*, Oak Mfg. Co., *above*, note 7.

[27] Lord Baltimore Press, 142 NLRB 328 (1963), 53 LRRM 1019.

[28] General Industries Electronics Co., *above*, note 26; *see also, e.g.*, Marsh Supermarkets, Inc., 140 NLRB 899 (1963), 52 LRRM 1134, enforced as modified, 327 F.2d 109 (CA 7, 1963), 55 LRRM 2017; Steel Equipment Co., 140 NLRB 1158 (1963), 52 LRRM 1192; Trane Co., 137 NLRB 1506 (1962), 50 LRRM 1434.

In concentrating on examples of objectionable employer propaganda we should not overlook the fact that the same rules apply to union election propaganda. Statements by union agents which are misleading or coercive may result in the overturning of a union election victory. An example is provided by the case of *NLRB* v. *A. G. Pollard Co.*[29] In that case the court of appeals reversed the Board and held that telephone calls by a union agent soon before an election, in which the agent told employees that there had been a representation election some years ago which the union had lost and that over a period of years the employer had discharged the employees, constituted grounds for setting aside the union's election victory. The court assumed, of course, that the statements were false.

Motion Pictures

Some employers have used "scare" movies as campaign propaganda. The two films that have been held improper as campaign material are "A Question of Law and Order" and "And Women Must Weep." These films grossly distort and misrepresent unions, strikes, and labor-management relations.[30] In cases involving these films the Board has noted that movies are more powerful in arousing emotions and affecting attitude than written or spoken words. Several courts have held that showing "And Women Must Weep" is not an unfair labor practice.[31] But, of course, the tests for unfair labor practices and election interference are distinct.

Cartoons or Pictures

A threat may be conveyed by a single dramatic picture. A single picture—that of a closed-down plant with its windows and doors boarded up and a "closed" sign nailed to the boarded door—was enough to cause the upsetting of a union-lost election and the ordering of a new election. The Board held in a recent case that this picture conveyed a definite threat of plant closure in the event of unionization.[32]

---

[29] 393 F.2d 239 (CA 1, 1968), 67 LRRM 2997.
[30] *See, e.g.,* Carl T. Mason, Inc. *above,* note 25; and Ideal Baking Co. of Tennessee, Inc., 143 NLRB 546 (1963), 53 LRRM 1270.
[31] Southwire Co. v. NLRB, 383 F.2d 235 (CA 5, 1967), 65 LRRM 3042; *accord* NLRB v. Hawthorn Co., 404 F.2d 1205 (CA 8, 1969), 70 LRRM 2193.
[32] Maremont Corp., 10—RC—6415 (1966), 65 LRRM 1135.

Appeals to Racial Prejudice

In this time of concern with civil rights and the so-called "backlash" problem, race propaganda and appeals to racial prejudice are not uncommon in organizing campaigns. The lead case is *Sewell Mfg. Co.*[33] in which the Board twice set aside elections in two southern communities.

In *Sewell,* the employer published, for four months before the election, a vicious, antiunion, anti-black, prosegregation newspaper and distributed other offensive materials, including a picture of a union official dancing with a black woman. The Board set aside the two elections because of this kind of conduct. It concluded that most of the racist material was irrelevant to any legitimate campaign issue and was designed only to stir race hatred and promote blind fear and hostility against the union.

The Board stated in the same case that, in the future, a party to an election who used racial messages would bear the burden of establishing that messages were *truthful and germane, and if doubt existed* as to whether all of the material were true, the doubt would be resolved *against* the party using the racial matter.

But each case involving any reference to race must be closely examined on its own peculiar facts. In *Allen-Morrison Sign Co.,*[34] the Board refused to set aside an election where the employer had injected the race issue into the campaign because, in its view, the employer's propaganda "was temperate in tone," truthful, and pertinent to the campaign. And in another case [35] the Board refused to set aside an election lost by the union because the employer had mailed to its black employees reprints of an article published in *Look* magazine entitled "A National Disgrace: What Unions Do To Blacks."

Another type of case involving racial issues occurs where the union makes discrimination an issue in its campaign and urges unionism as a means of combating such discrimination. The Board has held that such appeals are proper and allowable. The

[33] 138 NLRB 66 (1962), 50 LRRM 1532, and 140 NLRB 220 (1962), 51 LRRM 1611; *see also* Bush Hog, Inc., 161 NLRB 1575 (1966), 63 LRRM 1501, affirmed, 405 F.2d 755 (CA 5, 1968), 70 LRRM 2070.
[34] 138 NLRB 73 (1962), 50 LRRM 1535; *cf.* Bush Hog, Inc., *above,* note 33.
[35] Pittsburgh Plate Glass Co., 11—RC—2613 (1969), 70 LRRM 1359.

following quotations from the *Baltimore Luggage* case [36] outline the Board's approach to cases of this type:

> Here the employees were told that Negroes had, in the past, received lower wages and had been subject to poorer working conditions than white workers, primarily because they were Negroes; they were urged to join a union, not as an act against the white race, but to engage in lawful concerted action which could help bring Negro employees that equality with white employees which the Negroes had been denied because of their race. No suggestion was made that white workers should not be permitted the same rights as the Negroes, and a vote for the union was represented as a vote for better working conditions, not as a vote against the white race.

> . . . [C]ampaign material of this type is directed at undoing disadvantages historically imposed, [generally unlawfully] upon Negroes because of their race, through an appeal to collective action of the disadvantaged. The choice of racial basis for concerted action has been made, not by the victims who organize to seek redress, but by those who use race as a basis to impose the disadvantage. The fact that those selected for disadvantage are chosen by race can hardly justify, on some "two wrongs don't make a right" theory, preventing collective action on the basis of their race to overcome the disadvantage. For to prohibit reasonable, non-inflammatory appeals to the solidarity and economic interest of such a racial group, where its initial selection by others was on a racial basis, would allow an originally wrongful action to become immune to correction because of its original wrongfulness.

Employer Action

Change in Conditions

In regulating employer election conduct the Board has considered sudden actions which operate to the benefit or detriment of the employees in the plant. It is the changes from *prior employer conduct* which seem to be the key to condemnation, if the changes have as their purpose, or natural result, the rejection by the employees of a union.[37]

In 1964 the Supreme Court considered the case [38] of an employer who conferred economic benefits upon his employees shortly before a representation election where, in the Court's words, "the employer's purpose is to affect the outcome of the

---

[36] The Baltimore Luggage Co., 162 NLRB 1230 (1967), 64 LRRM 1145, affirmed 387 F.2d 744 (CA 4, 1967), 67 LRRM 2209.

[37] *See, e.g.,* Hudson Hosiery Co., 72 NLRB 1434 (1947), 19 LRRM 1288.

[38] NLRB v. Exchange Parts Co., 375 US 405 (1964), 55 LRRM 2098.

election." Briefly, the facts indicated that prior to November, 1959 the employees were unrepresented. On November 9, the union formally notified the company that it was in the process of an organizing campaign. On November 4 and 5, the Company, already aware of the campaign, had announced that it would grant an extra "floating holiday." On February 25, six days after the Board issued its election order, the company held a dinner for its employees at which it announced that the new floating holiday would be the employee's birthday. It further announced at this dinner that a new vacation schedule and new method of computing overtime would be adopted which would increase the rates of pay and length of vacations. This, it should be added, was its first general announcement of the revision in working conditions. The Court held that the pattern of conduct warranted setting the election aside as a violation of Section 8 (a) (1) of the Act. It stated:

> The danger inherent in well-timed increases in benefits is the suggestion of a *fist inside the velvet glove*. Employees are not likely to miss the inference that the source of benefits now conferred is also the source from which future benefits must flow and which may dry up if it is not obliged. (Emphasis added)

The Board has often used this type of reasoning to set aside elections or find unfair labor practices where benefits conferred have coincided with the holding of a Board-directed election. Among other benefits declared illegal have been promises to create a new job classification system;[39] grant of holiday;[40] hospitalization benefits;[41] working conditions (shoe allowance) ;[42] and wage and other economic benefits.[43]

Often, the key factor is the presence or absence of *antiunion animus*. If the change had already been planned for some time and the coincidence of the union election and the employer-granted benefits is, in reality, fortuitous, the election probably will not be set aside. In *American Thermos Products Co.,*[44] the company conducted its annual employee outing some three days before the representation election. To buy food and drinks

---

[39] Bernel Foam Products Co., 146 NLRB 1277 (1964), 56 LRRM 1039.
[40] Universal Packaging Corp., 149 NLRB 262 (1964), 57 LRRM 1312, affirmed 361 F.2d 384 (CA 1, 1966), 62 LRRM 2288.
[41] Cadillac Overall Supply Co., 148 NLRB 1133 (1964), 57 LRRM 1136.
[42] Performance Measurements Co., 148 NLRB 1657 (1964), 57 LRRM 1218.
[43] Baltimore Catering Co., 148 NLRB 970 (1964), 57 LRRM 1106.
[44] 119 NLRB 557 (1957), 41 LRRM 1134.

the employees used tickets furnished by the employer which had been raised 50 cents in value over the previous year. The Board held, however, that the increase was lawful when seen in the light of a continuous practice of holding such annual outings for some 18 consecutive years and where the raise in the value of the tickets had been decided upon over three months before the election at the request of an employee committee. Another type of case is seen in *Barber Colman Co.*,[45] where the employer instituted wage increases as part of a continuous and well established policy.

Obviously, employers are likely to argue that benefits issued prior to an election are in keeping with longstanding policy or that timing of new benefits is fortuitous in many more situations than the facts would warrant. For example, in one case [46] the presence of certain chemicals on the floor of a plant had been a longstanding source of difficulty because the chemicals caused the footwear of the employees to deteriorate. Although his predecessor had furnished footwear, the employer did no more than place a plastic mat on the floor and pass out plastic boots to the employees; neither step eliminated the problem. Finally, some four days before the election, the employer announced that each man would receive a six dollar allowance toward the purchase of his own footwear. The promised allowance was withheld from distribution until after the election. The Board stated:

> Although granting employees benefits during the period immediately preceding an election is not *per se* ground for setting aside an election, in the absence of a showing that the timing of the announcement was governed by factors other than the pendency of the election, the Board will regard such timing as calculated to influence the employees in their choice of a bargaining representative. The *burden of showing other factors is upon the Employer*. (Emphasis added)

In another case an election was set aside because after the Union's petition the employer formed a safety committee to which he appointed employees, and proceeded to implement some of its recommendations.[47]

In short, the employer must carry the burden of explaining away the nagging question of why an action was taken at the

---

[45] 116 NLRB 24 (1956), 38 LRRM 1184.
[46] Performance Measurements Co., *above*, note 42.
[47] Illinois Marble Co., Inc., 167 NLRB No. 147 (1967), 66 LRRM 1235.

crucial election time, even though it may have been a reasonable action in the abstract. Thus, in *Baltimore Catering Co.*,[48] there appeared to be no good reason why wage bonuses decided upon in June were not announced until November, just after an election petition had been filed with the Board.

Much the same reasoning has been used by the Board to find unfair preelection conduct in a sudden deterioration of working conditions during a union organizing drive, where the *purpose* of the change in conditions was to affect that drive. This deterioration may involve merely the transfer of an employee from one unit to another in order to impede an organizing drive,[49] or a threat to lay off,[50] or the firing of employees who are union sympathizers.[51]

On the other hand, an adverse change in working conditions, even to the point of permanently closing the plant, may be valid,[52] although if the move or closing was prompted by an antiunion animus found also in other plants which are part of a single integrated operation, the closing would be an unfair labor practice.[53] If the plant were not closed in reality, so that the transaction involved the formation of a second corporation which was an exact replica of the first, it would be a sham and similarly invalid.[54]

If an employer who owns two or more plants distinguishes in treatment of employees at the several locations in order to affect an election to be held at one plant, this will constitute interference. Thus a union-lost election was set aside because an employer had granted a wage increase at one of his plants but not another in order to impress employees at the latter plant that their union activities had cost them a similar increase.[55]

Because of the prevalence of the problem of employer "generosity" at or near the election, we discuss it in more detail.

---

[48] Baltimore Catering Co., *above*, note 43.
[49] J.W. Mays, Inc., 147 NLRB 942 (1964), 56 LRRM 1106, enforced as modified, 356 F.2d 693 (CA 2, 1966), 61 LRRM 2538.
[50] Coca-Cola Bottling of Louisville, 118 NLRB 1422 (1957), 40 LRRM 1390.
[51] *See, e.g.,* Edward G. Budd Mfg. Co. v. NLRB, 138 F.2d 86 (CA 3, 1943), 13 LRRM 512, 564.
[52] *See* NLRB v. Rapid Bindery, Inc., 293 F.2d 170 (CA 2, 1961), 45 LRRM 1524.
[53] Textile Workers Union v. Darlington Mfg. Co., 380 US 263 (1965), 58 LRRM 2657.
[54] *See* NLRB v. E.C. Brown, 184 F.2d 829 (CA 2, 1950), 27 LRRM 2022.
[55] Congdon Die Castings Co., 176 NLRB No. 60 (1969), 71 LRRM 1285.

In *Maine Fisheries Corp.*,[56] the implied promise of more work for the employees was the basis of the Board's setting aside the election. One factor was "the significant timing of the statement with respect to the imminent hour for balloting . . ." The Board added:

> The Employer argues that because Usen's statement did not explicitly or literally tie the announcement with the impending election, no finding may be made that his promise of improved conditions bore any relationship to the employees' union activities. But, as the Board has heretofore held, it is immaterial whether coercive statements be direct or indirect, explicit or implied. It suffices, so far as the issue raised by the objections is concerned, that the employees, in the circumstances of the moment, had reasonable cause to believe that Usen's statement was a promise provoked by their union activity. Accordingly, in agreement with the Regional Director, we find merit in the objections, and we shall, therefore, set aside the results of the election and direct that a new election be held at such time as the Regional Director may deem proper.

In *Food Fair Stores of Florida*,[57] the Board discussed an employer's explanation of the timing of an announcement of benefit as follows:

> In the instant case, we can perceive no reason why, if the sole purpose of the announcement was to inform the employees that the promised wage increase had been granted, the announcement could not have been made in the form of a general announcement, on December 16, the day the increases became effective, or made at a date after the election. The mere fact that the Employer had previously promised its employees that they would get the same wage increases as was negotiated for employees in the east coast stores, and the fact that the information as to how the increase affected individual employees was not available until December 18, when weighed against the fact that the announcement was made to individual employees called away from their work stations, and was so scheduled as to coincide with the election hours at the Tampa and Clearwater stores, and the day before the election at St. Petersburg store, when it would have the "maximum possible impact upon the minds of the employees," does not constitute a credible explanation for the timing or manner of the announcement.

In *Coca-Cola Bottling Company of Memphis*,[58] the Board affirmed the trial examiner's findings that $10 payments "made during the critical period" to certain employees were sufficient

[56] 99 NLRB 604 (1952), 30 LRRM 1101.
[57] 120 NLRB 1669 (1958), 42 LRRM 1242.
[58] 132 NLRB 481 (1961), 48 LRRM 1370.

to justify a finding that the employer had interfered with the election. The payments in that case were to be used for beer for other employees.

An employer who holds back paychecks beyond the normal pay hour until after employees vote is pressuring them.[59]

In *Direct Laboratories, Inc.*[60] the company's promise of a wage increase "regardless of the outcome of the election" was sufficient to justify setting aside the election. The Board said:

> We find that the announcement did not conform with any established company practice, and that it was timed solely in connection with the pending election. As the Board has repeatedly held, such a promise of wage increase improperly influences the results of an election and prevents an untrammelled expression of choice by the employees.

An entirely different kettle of fish is found in *Montgomery Ward & Co.*,[61] where the union had been representing the employees for some time. The existing union contract evidently required the employer to grant a five-cent hourly wage increase on June 1, 1962. At a meeting in April, 1962, an employee who was also a union steward asked the company manager if the employees would receive the five-cent increase under the contract if the union were not the representative on June 1. *The company manager acknowledged that the company would have no obligation to grant the five-cent increase if the union were not the representative on that date,* but he also indicated that he would be critical of the store manager if this were used as an excuse not to give the increase. This statement was held not to be a promise of benefit that would justify setting aside the election.

But such a situation is quite different from one where an employer conditions benefits on employees remaining unrepresented by a union or on employees remaining represented by a particular union. Such conduct obviously interferes with employees' free choice.[62]

Other Employer Action

The Board has held that an employer may not interview

---

[59] *See* R.H. Osbrink Mfg. Co., 104 NLRB 42 (1953), 32 LRRM 1043.
[60] 94 NLRB 380 (1951), 28 LRRM 1053.
[61] 7—RD—430 (1962), 50 LRRM 1553.
[62] *See* Humble Oil and Refining Co., 160 NLRB 1088 (1966), 62 LRRM 1593.

employees in small groups in private, nonwork areas in order to influence them in a coming election.[63] Nor may he visit employees at their homes.[64]

The distribution of *marked,* official NLRB sample ballots before the election will be a good ground for setting aside an election,[65] because the voters might be led to believe that the NLRB favors a particular result in the election. But if the marked sample ballots are sufficiently different from the official Board ballots and are distributed or shown to employees in a context that does not indicate that the Board favors voting in the indicated manner, they may be allowed.[66]

Similarly, other distortion or misrepresentation of Board policy will constitute interference. Elections have been set aside because a union distributed handbills which contained a partial reprint of the Board's Notice of Election along with a general statement of the purposes and functions of unions[67] and because an employer posted the Board's Notice of Election with the "Rights of Employees" section turned under so as not to be visible.[68]

Straw votes or private polling of employees by an employer just before an election interferes with the election,[69] and listing those who actually vote also is not permissible.[70]

The NLRB recently set aside an election where an employer made antiunion T-shirts and buttons available to employees in such a way that the workers were forced to show the employer how they felt about the union.[71] Each supervisor wore a T-shirt and employees were told they could order one for a nickel. Antiunion buttons, which were free, were also pushed hard by the supervisors. As a result of the employer's campaign it was easy to pick out the union supporters—those who refused to

---

[63] Aragon Mills, 135 NLRB 859 (1962), 49 LRRM 1669; Great A & P Tea Co., 140 NLRB 133 (1962), 51 LRRM 1570.

[64] General Shoe Corp., 77 NLRB 124 (1948), 21 LRRM 1337.

[65] Allied Electric Products, 109 NLRB 1270 (1954), 34 LRRM 1538.

[66] Burnside Steel Foundry Co., 178 NLRB No. 32 (1969), 72 LRRM 1045; Rett Electronics, Inc., 169 NLRB No. 168 (1968), 67 LRRM 1461.

[67] Rebmar, Inc., 173 NLRB No. 215 (1968), 70 LRRM 1018. But the appearance of altered Board literature will not *automatically* result in the setting aside of an election (Bush Hog, Inc., 420 F.2d 1266 (CA 5, 1969), 73 LRRM 2066).

[68] Overland Hauling, Inc., 168 NLRB No. 115 (1967), 67 LRRM 1003.

[69] Offner Electronics Inc., 127 NLRB 991 (1960), 46 LRRM 1136.

[70] Belk's Dept. Store of Savannah, Ga., Inc., *above,* note 16.

[71] Macklanburg-Duncan Co., 179 NLRB No. 143 (1969), 72 LRRM 1523.

wear the T-shirts and buttons. The vice was that the boss had put the workers in a position where, by electing to wear or not wear the employer's shirts and buttons, they had to disclose their choice as to union.

The intentional "loading" of an employee eligibility list with supervisors to get a larger vote against the union will cause an election to be set aside.[72]

An employer device the Board has sanctioned is placing an amount equal to union dues in an envelope separate from the balance of the paycheck and informing workers that this money is theirs *now* but would be the monthly cost to each one for union dues if the union won and the employee joined it.[73] But if the employer misrepresents the amount of the dues or a legal rule, an election can be overturned.[74]

Employers may try to get out the vote and may offer transportation to voters—but they cannot concentrate on antiunion workers only.

No-Solicitation Rules

All of the material discussed under distribution and solicitation in Chapter II is most relevant to preelection conduct. We will not repeat it here. Attention should also focus on the *Montgomery Ward* case.[75] The Montgomery Ward no-solicitation rule barred union solicitation and distribution of union literature on company time, but permitted such activity by employees on company property *only if both* the soliciting and solicited employees were on their own time and the solicitation was conducted in an orderly manner and did not interfere with the business of the store. The company's written rule barred all employee meetings and speeches, and was supplemented by an oral rule, announced and read at a meeting, stating that employees were not to discuss the union from 8:30 in the morning until 5:30 in the afternoon, including lunch and coffeebreak time, and that if they did they "would be fired."

---

[72] Vail Mfg. Co., 61 NLRB 181 (1945), 16 LRRM 85, enforced 158 F.2d 664 (CA 7, 1947), 19 LRRM 2177, cert. denied 331 US 835 (1947), 20 LRRM 2185.

[73] Mosler Safe Co., 129 NLRB 747 (1960), 47 LRRM 1058.

[74] Trane Co., *above*, note 28.

[75] Montgomery Ward and Co., Inc., 145 NLRB 846 (1964), 55 LRRM 1063, enforced as modified, 339 F.2d 889 (CA 6, 1965), 58 LRRM 2115.

The company for *its* part, however, made antiunion speeches to groups of employees on paid time, on the company premises. When the union asked for permission to speak to the employees during company working hours in answer to the employer speeches, the company refused.

The Board, in holding the company's rule unlawful, said that the company

> seriously impaired lawful solicitation activities at the natural site where employees are accessible for organizational efforts. Quite clearly, Respondent's broad and unlawful no-solicitation rule, coupled with its own use of company time and property to impress its anti-union propaganda on employees, created a glaring imbalance in organizational communication that justified the union's request to address employees under the same circumstances as had Respondent.

In another no-solicitation rule case a court enforced a Board finding that an employer violated Section 8 (a) (1) by having a rule prohibiting employees, when on nonworking time and in nonworking areas of the plant, from distributing any leaflets, handbills, circulars, or other literature on behalf of the union.[76]

Union Acts of Interference With Elections

Everything that has been said about campaign propaganda, the 24-hour rule, and electioneering at the polls applies with equal force to unions and employers. Certain kinds of conduct that have been held to interfere with elections, however, are peculiarly the acts of unions. It goes without saying that any conduct that violates Section 8 (b) (1) (A), such as violence or the threat of violence aimed at nonsupporters of a union, is automatically a sufficient basis upon which to set aside an election.[77]

In *Vickers, Inc.,*[78] an election was set aside because the shop committeemen of an incumbent union threatened employees with expulsion from the union and the probable loss of jobs if they supported the rival union.

---

[76] United Aircraft Corp., 139 NLRB 39 (1962), 51 LRRM 1259, enforced, 324 F.2d 128 (CA 2, 1962), 54 LRRM 2492.

[77] *See, e.g.,* The Gabriel Co., 137 NLRB 1252 (1962), 50 LRRM 1369.

[78] 152 NLRB 793 (1965), 59 LRRM 1196; *see also* Hurwitz Electrical Co., 146 NLRB 1265 (1964), 56 LRRM 1032.

A common tactic used by unions during organizing drives is the offer to waive initiation fees for unrepresented employees. However, the Board has held this to be an unfair device if the offer is made with certain kinds of qualifications. In *Gilmore Industries, Inc.,*[79] the Board stated that a union may announce that it will waive initiation fees if it wins the election, provided the waiver is to apply to *all* employees and does not depend on how the individual employees vote. Some courts have taken a more restrictive view of this device, however. One refused to enforce the Board's policy,[80] holding that the waiver was objectionable because it was dependent on the union's winning the election. The Board, however, continues to follow the rule that a waiver that is contingent on an election victory is permissible if granted to all employees regardless of how they vote.[81] A waiver offer dependent on how an employee votes, on the other hand, is viewed as being a coercive attempt to buy votes. Similarly, it would not be permissible for a union to garner authorization cards by saying that those who signed would pay less if the union won than those who did not.

The organizer must also be careful about other kinds of economic inducements. Union victories have been set aside where the union offered free life insurance to those becoming members[82] and where a union gave five-dollar gift certificates to potential voters.[83] However, the Board refused to set aside an election because the union had distributed turkeys to employees before the election.[84]

In many cases the Board has set aside elections because of deliberate attempts by unions to misinform and mislead voters. In *Walgreen Co.,*[85] the union distributed leaflets which exaggerated the wages and benefits being received by employees who were already represented by the union. Since the leaflet was distributed on the eve of the election, the employer did not have sufficient time in which to refute the statements made by the union. The employees also had no other means to obtain

---

[79] 140 NLRB 100 (1962), 51 LRRM 1562.
[80] NLRB v. Gilmore Industries, Inc., 341 F.2d 240 (CA 6, 1965), 58 LRRM 2419.
[81] Weyerhaeuser Co., 146 NLRB 1 (1964), 56 LRRM 116; *see* Dit-M Co., Inc., 163 NLRB 147 (1967), 64 LRRM 1476.
[82] Wagner Electric Corp., 167 NLRB No. 75 (1967), 66 LRRM 1072.
[83] General Cable Corp., 170 NLRB No. 172 (1968), 67 LRRM 1635.
[84] Jacqueline Cochran, Inc., 177 NLRB No. 39 (1969), 71 LRRM 1395.
[85] 140 NLRB 1141 (1963), 53 LRRM 1193.

information as to the veracity of the union statements, and for these reasons the election was set aside.

The *Walgreen* case should be contrasted with *Sam Belz Upholstered Products Co.*,[86] in which a union distributed leaflets which falsely claimed that an earlier election had been set aside because of certain acts of misconduct committed by the employer. The Board refused to set aside the election because the employer had an opporutnity to reply to the union statements, and the assertions in the leaflets were not within the sole knowledge of the union.[87]

In another case an election was set aside because a union agent substantially misrepresented the union's legal bargaining obligation. The agent told employees prior to the vote that if the union won it would not have to bargain very hard for employees in classifications from which no authorization cards were obtained.[88]

Another tactic which the Board has held to be objectionable is the use of sound trucks or similar devices during the 24-hour period immediately preceding the election. In *U. S. Gypsum Co.*,[89] union sound trucks beamed campaign speeches and other propaganda directly into plant work areas for a period of seven and a half hours on the day before the election. The Board held this conduct to be objectionable under the 24-hour rule, which prohibits campaign speeches to massed assemblies of workers.[90] However, this standard was relaxed somewhat by the Board in a recent decision.[91] In that case the Board did not condemn the use of a car equipped with loudspeakers parked outside the plant on the day before the election. The car was used for only about one hour, and the union messages were designed mainly as part of a "get out the vote" drive. Also, the messages were intended to reach employees as they entered or left the plant, and were not intended to be beamed directly into the plant, as was the case in *U. S. Gypsum*.

The conduct discussed above is usually part of a conscious effort on the part of a union; however, if very serious miscon-

---

[86] 138 NLRB 433 (1962), 51 LRRM 1073.
[87] *See* Hollywood Ceramics Co., *above*, note 18.
[88] Joseph L. Rozier Machinery Co., 174 NLRB No. 176 (1969), 70 LRRM 1393.
[89] 115 NLRB 734 (1956), 37 LRRM 1374.
[90] Peerless Plywood Co., *above*, note 10.
[91] Crown Paper Board Co., 158 NLRB 440 (1966), 62 LRRM 1041.

duct occurs, an election can be set aside even though the objectionable conduct cannot be traced directly to the union. For example, in *Poinsett Lumber & Mfg. Co.*,[92] prounion employees were responsible for a number of threats of violence and other forms of intimidation directed against some of their fellow employees. The Board held:

> We are convinced that the threats of personal retaliation and of physical violence made to employees and the concomitant coercive effect thereof, constituted such serious conduct as to interfere with a free and untrammeled choice of representatives contemplated by the Act. Moreover, we find it unnecessary to determine whether or not such serious and coercive conduct can be attributed to the Union because the important fact is that an atmosphere of fear and reprisal existed and that a free election was thereby rendered impossible.

In another case an election was set aside because of repeated and extensive sabotage of the employer's trucks which were driven by employees who had not signed authorization cards. Although the Board did not find that the union was responsible for the sabotage it held that the actions had frustrated a "rational uncoerced expression of choice."[93]

Interference by Outsiders

As we have pointed out earlier, the Board views its role as one of maintaining laboratory conditions for the experiment of the representation election. It stands to reason then that if the atmosphere in which the election is held is unfair and destroys the chance for a free election, the election should be set aside and held again, regardless of whether the poor atmosphere was caused by one of the parties. The important thing is that a fair election could not be held, not who made it impossible.

Accordingly, if a Board agent, even innocently, gives the appearance of partiality, the Board will set aside the election.[94] Even an innocent mistake by the Board that interferes with the employees free choice will be ground for overturning an election. Such was the situation in a recent case where the regional director failed to provide bilingual Notices of Election and ballots to accommodate Portuguese-speaking employees.[95]

---

[92] 116 NLRB 1732 (1956), 39 LRRM 1083.
[93] IBT, Local 980, 170 NLRB No. 51 (1969), 72 LRRM 1126.
[94] NLRB v. Fresh'nd-Aire Co., 226 F.2d 737 (CA 7, 1955), 36 LRRM 2732.
[95] Fibre Leather Mfg. Co., 167 NLRB No. 51 (1967), 66 LRRM 1056.

The Twenty-ninth Annual Report of the NLRB (1964) well describes the Board's attitude toward community interference with elections. It states:

> In two cases, the Board was called upon to evaluate the impact of statements made by members of the community, during the union's preelection campaign, upon the exercise of the employees' free choice in an election. Differing results were reached in the two cases. In *Utica-Herbrand Tool Division of Kelsey-Hayes Co.,* [145 NLRB 1717 (1964)] the Board set an election aside where official and influential citizens of the community, through letters, visits to employees' homes, leaflet distribution, radio newscasts and spot announcements, and newspaper editorials and advertisements, reiterated the themes that selection of the union would cause the employer to move, the city to become a distressed area, and would deprive employees of job opportunities because other companies would not locate in the area. The Board viewed this massive campaign conducted by third parties in the community, in the context of the employer's statements developing the same theme, as creating an atmosphere of fear of reprisal and loss of job opportunity if the employees selected the union as their bargaining representative. The Board noted that such pressures as home calls by local police officers and the mayor of the city, and the distribution of antiunion propaganda at all banks in the community, although not emanating from the employer, exerted a coercive effect upon the employees' free choice.

> In the second case, *Claymore Mfg. Co.,* [145 NLRB 1400 (1964)] the Board refused to set an election aside, notwithstanding the preelection statements of the employer and the activities of prominent and influential members of the community who attempted to dissuade employees from voting for the union by spreading rumors that the plant would close if the union won the election. The Board pointed out that, at the union's request, the employer had issued a letter to the employees disavowing the rumors of the plant closing, and that there was no showing that the union was dissatisfied with the disavowal. In concluding that neither the campaign of the community leaders nor the employer's statements interfered with the election, the Board also noted the give-and-take of the campaign, the fact that the campaign propaganda occurred in the context of the employer operating at a loss, and the employer's straight-forward assurances to the employees that it had dealt fairly with them, hoped to do better by them, and intended to keep the plant operating regardless of the outcome of the election.

Actions of outsiders need not, however, be on a grand scale to constitute improper interference with an election. For instance, where a newspaper, completely on its own, printed a full-page message to employees on the day before the election warning them to vote against the union or suffer economic harm, the election was voided.[96] The NLRB also set aside an election because of the arrest of the organizer on the morning of the election in front of many of the voters.[97]

Conclusion

It is impossible to cover every kind of situation that will upset an election. Within the general area of election conduct this chapter has made an attempt at supplying guidelines only. Each case turns on its own facts. And that brings us back to where we started in this book. The organizer is the person closest to the facts. He must pay careful attention to detail, keeping scrupulous records and avoiding mistakes. That throws the responsibility squarely on his shoulders.

We hope this book can help him better discharge this awesome responsibility.

---

[96] Monarch Rubber Co., 121 NLRB 81 (1958), 42 LRRM 1294; *see also* Dean Industries, Inc., 162 NLRB 1078 (1967), 64 LRRM 1193.
[97] Great A & P Tea Co., 120 NLRB 765 (1958), 42 LRRM 1042.

Appendix A

GLOSSARY OF SELECTED TERMS
USED BY NLRB*

Backpay—Amounts of money paid or to be paid employees by Board order as reimbursement for wages lost because they were discriminatorily discharged or unlawfully denied employment or because of other violations of the Act. Interest on such moneys, payment for bonuses, vacation, other fringe benefits, etc., lost because of the discriminatory acts are also included.

Backpay Hearing—After an employer or a union, or both, have been found guilty of unfair practices, a supplementary hearing is held to receive evidence and testimony as to the amounts of backpay due workers under the prior Board order or court decree.

Backpay Specification—The formal document, or paper, is served on the parties when the regional office and the charged party do not agree as to the amounts of backpay due workers pursuant to a Board order or court decree requiring payment of such backpay. It sets forth in detail the amounts held by the regional director to be owing each worker and the method of computation employed. The specification is accompanied by a notice of hearing setting a date for a backpay hearing.

Case—A "case" is the general term used in referring to a charge or petition filed with the Board. Each case is numbered and carries a letter designation indicating the type of case.

Certification—A certification of the results of an election is is-

---

* This glossary is taken almost word for word from the Board's Thirtieth Annual Report (1965). Changes have been made only for purposes of simplification and clarity.

sued by the regional director or the Board. If a union has been chosen as the exclusive bargaining representative by a majority of the employees, a certification of representatives is issued. If no union has received a majority vote, a certification of results of the election is issued.

Challenges—The parties to an NLRB election are entitled to challenge any voter. At the election site, the challenged ballots are segregated and not counted when the other ballots are tallied. Most frequently, the tally of unchallenged ballots determines the election, and the challenged ballots are insufficient in number to affect the results of the election. The challenges in such a case are never resolved, and the certification is based upon the tally of (unchallenged) ballots.

When challenged ballots are determinative of the results, a determination as to whether they are to be counted rests with the regional director in the first instance, subject to possible appeal to the Board. Often, however, the "determinative" challenges are resolved informally by the parties by mutual agreement. No record is kept of nondeterminative challenges or determinative challenges which are resolved by agreement prior to issuance of the first tally of ballots.

Charge—A document filed by an employee, an employer, a union, or an individual alleging that an unfair labor practice has been committed.

Charging Party—The union, employer, individual, or group filing an unfair labor practice charge.

Complaint—The document which initiates "formal" proceedings in an unfair labor practice case. It is issued by the regional director when he concludes on the basis of a completed investigation that some or all of the allegations contained in the charge have merit and an adjustment or settlement has not been achieved by the parties. The complaint sets forth all allegations and information necessary to bring a case to hearing before a trial examiner pursuant to due process of law. The complaint contains a notice of hearing, specifying the time and place of hearing. It is served on the charging party as well as the respondent.

Compliance—The carrying out of remedial action as agreed upon by the parties in writing (see "Formal Agreement," "Informal Agreement"); as recommended by the trial examiner in his decision; as ordered by the Board in its Decision and Order; or as decreed by the court. Usually each NLRB regional office has one or more agents assigned solely to compliance matters.

Dismissed Cases—Cases may be dismissed at any stage. They are dismissed informally when, following investigation, the regional director concludes that there has been no violation of the law, that there is insufficient evidence to support further action, or for a variety of other reasons. Before a charge is dismissed, however, the charging party is given the opportunity to withdraw the charge voluntarily. Cases may also be dismissed by the trial examiner, by the Board, or by the courts through their refusal to enforce orders of the Board.

Election, Board Directed—An election conducted by the regional director pursuant to a decision and direction of election by the Board. Post-election rulings are made by the regional director or by the Board.

Election, Consent—An election conducted by the regional director pursuant to an agreement signed by all parties concerned. The agreement provides for the waiving of a hearing, the establishment of the appropriate unit by mutual consent, and for the final determination of all post-election issues by the regional director.

Election, Expedited—An election conducted by the regional director pursuant to a petition filed within 30 days of the commencement of picketing in a situation in which a meritorious 8(b) (7) (C) charge has been filed. The election is conducted under priority conditions and without a hearing unless the regional director believes the proceeding raises questions which cannot be decided without a hearing. Post-election rulings on objections and/or challenges are made by the regional director and are final and binding unless the Board grants an appeal on application by one of the parties.

Election, Regional Director Directed—An election conducted by the regional director pursuant to a decision and direction of election issued by the regional director after a hearing. Post-election rulings are made by the regional director or by the Board.

Election, Rerun—An election held after an initial election has been set aside either by the regional director or by the Board.

Election, Runoff—An election conducted by the regional director after an initial election, having three or more choices on the ballot and in which none of the choices received a majority of the valid votes cast. The regional director conducts the runoff election between the choices on the original ballot which received the highest and the next highest number of votes.

Election, Stipulated—An election held by the regional director pursuant to an agreement signed by all the parties concerned. The agreement provides for the waiving of hearing and the establishment of the appropriate unit by mutual consent. Post-election rulings are made by the Board.

Eligible Voters—Employees within an appropriate bargaining unit who were employed as of a fixed date prior to an election, or are otherwise qualified to vote under the Board's eligibility rules.

Formal Agreement (in unfair labor practice cases)—A written agreement between the Board and the other parties to a case in which hearing is waived and the specific terms of a Board order agreed upon. The agreement may also provide for the entry of a consent court decree enforcing the Board order.

Informal Agreement (in unfair labor practice cases)—A written agreement entered into by the party charged with committing an unfair labor practice, the regional director, and (in most cases) the charging party, requiring the charged party to take certain specific remedial action as a basis for the closing of the case.

Injunction Petitions—Petitions filed by the Board with U.S. district courts for injunctive relief under Section 10(j) (discretionary) or Section 10(1) (mandatory) of the Act pending hearing and adjudication of unfair labor practice charges before the Board. Also, petitions filed with a U.S. court of appeals under Section 10(e) of the Act.

Jurisdictional Disputes—Controversies between unions or groupings of employees as to which will perform specific work. Cases involving jurisdictional disputes are received by the

Board through the filing of charges alleging a violation of Section 8(b) (4) (D). They are initially processed under Section 10(k) of the Act, which is concerned with the determination of the jurisdictional dispute itself rather than with a finding as to whether an unfair labor practice has been committed. Thereafter, the failure of a party to comply with the Board's determination of the dispute is the basis for the issuance of an unfair labor practice complaint and the processing of the case through the usual unfair labor practice procedures.

Objections—Any party to an election may file objections alleging that either the conduct of the election or the conduct of a party to the election failed to meet the Board's standards. An election will be set aside if eligible employee-voters have not been given an adequate opportunity to cast their ballots, in secrecy and without hindrance from fear or other interference with the expression of their free choice.

Representation Case—This term applies to all kinds of election cases bearing the alphabetical designations RC, RM, or RD. (See "R Cases" under "Types of Cases," below, for specific definitions of these terms.) All three types of cases are included in the term "representation," which deals generally with the problem of which union, if any, shall represent employees in negotiations with their employer. The cases are initiated by the filing of a petition by a union, an employer, or a group of employees.

Representation Election—An election by secret ballot conducted by the Board among the employees in an appropriate collective-bargaining unit to determine whether the employees wish to be represented by a particular labor organization for purposes of collective bargaining.

Request to Proceed—NLRB's Form No. 4551, by which one party charging another with unfair labor practices asks the Board to go ahead with an election and agrees not to object to the election on the basis of any conduct of the charged party occurring before the "Request" was filed. This form is really a waiver of the right to object because of *anything* done before the date on it. It prevents a charge from blocking an election at the instance of the charging party.

Respondent—One charged with the commission of an unfair labor practice.

Types of Cases—C cases (unfair labor practice cases): A case number which contains the first letter designation C, in combination with another letter, *i.e.,* CA, CB, etc., indicates that it involves a charge that an unfair labor practice has been committed in violation of one or more subsections of Section 8.

CA: A charge that an employer has committed unfair labor practices in violation of Section 8(a) (1), (2), (3), (4), or (5), or any combination thereof.

CB: A charge that a labor organization has committed unfair labor practices in violation of Section 8 (b) (1), (2), (3), (5), or (6), or any combination thereof.

CC: A charge that a labor organization has committed unfair labor practices under Section 8(b) (4) (i) and/or (ii), (A), (B), or (C), or any combination thereof, usually involving a secondary boycott.

CD: A charge that a labor organization has committed an unfair labor practice in violation of Section 8(b) (4) (i) or (ii) (D). Preliminary actions under Section 10(k) for the determination of jurisdictional disputes are processed as CD cases. (See "Jurisdictional Disputes," above.)

CE: A charge that either a labor organization or an employer, or both jointly, have committed an unfair labor practice in violation of Section 8(e) (hot cargo).

CP: A charge that a labor organization has committed an unfair labor practice in violation of Section 8(b) (7) (A), (B), or (C), or any combination thereof (recognition picketing).

R Cases (representation cases): A case number which contains the first letter designation R, in combination with another letter, *i.e.,* RC, RD, RM, indicates that it is a petition for investigation and determination of a question concerning representation of employees, filed under Section 9(c) of the Act.

RC: A petition by a labor organization or an employee alleging that a question concerning representation has arisen and seeking an election for the determination of a collective-bargaining representative.

RD: A petition filed by employees alleging that the union previously certified or currently recognized by the employer as their collective bargaining representative no longer represents a majority of the employees in the appropriate unit and seeking an election to determine this. An RD petition is a decertification petition. It must be filed by employees, not an employer.

RM: A petition filed by an employer alleging that a question concerning representation has arisen and seeking an election for the determination of a collective-bargaining representative.

Other Cases:

AC (Amendment of Certification cases): A petition filed by a labor organization or an employer for amendment of an existing certification to reflect changed circumstances, such as changes in the name or affiliation of the labor organization involved or in the name or location of the employer involved.

AO (Advisory Opinion cases): As distinguished from the other types of cases described above, which are filed in and processed by regional offices of the Board, AO or "advisory opinion" cases are filed directly with the Board in Washington and seek a determination as to whether the Board would or would not assert jurisdiction in any given situation, on the basis of its current standards, over the party or parties to a proceeding pending before a State or territorial agency or a court.

UC (Unit Clarification cases) : A petition filed by a labor organization or an employer seeking a determination as to whether certain classifications of employees should or should not be included within a presently existing bargaining unit.

UD (Union Deauthorization cases): A petition filed by employees pursuant to Section 9(e)(1) requesting that the Board conduct a referendum to determine whether a union's authority to enter into a union-shop contract should be rescinded.

Union-Shop Agreement—An agreement between an employer and a labor organization which requires membership in the union as a condition of employment on or after the 30th day, or a later date, following (1) the beginning of such employment or (2) the effective date of the agreement, whichever is the later.

Unit, Appropriate Bargaining—A grouping of employees in a plant, firm, or industry recognized by the employer, agreed upon by the parties to a case, or designated by the Board or its regional director, as appropriate for the purposes of collective bargaining.

Valid Vote—A secret ballot on which the choice of the voter is clearly shown.

Withdrawn Cases—Cases are closed as "withdrawn" when the charging party or petitioner, for whatever reasons, requests withdrawal of the charge or the petition and such request is approved.

Appendix B

TEXT OF LABOR MANAGEMENT
RELATIONS ACT

*Public Law No. 101, 80th Congress of the United States, Chapter
120, First Session, H.R. 3020, Passed June 23, 1947, over the
President's Veto; Amended by Public Law No. 189,
82d Congress, October 22, 1951; by Judicial Review Act,
August 28, 1958; by the Labor-Management
Reporting and Disclosure Act of 1959; and
by Public Law 91-86, October 14, 1969.*

AN ACT

*To amend the National Labor Relations Act, to provide addi-
tional facilities for the mediation of labor disputes affecting
commerce, to equalize legal responsibilities of labor organizations and employers, and for other purposes.*
*Be it enacted by the Senate and House of Representatives of the
United States of America in Congress assembled,*
Short Title and Declaration of Policy

Section 1. (a) This Act may be cited as the "Labor Management Relations Act, 1947."

(b) Industrial strife which interferes with the normal flow
of commerce and with the full production of articles and commodities for commerce, can be avoided or substantially minimized if employers, employees, and labor organizations each recognize under law one another's legitimate rights in their relations with each other, and above all recognize under law that
neither party has any right in its relations with any other to
engage in acts or practices which jeopardize the public health,
safety, or interest.

It is the purpose and policy of this Act, in order to promote the full flow of commerce, to prescribe the legitimate rights of both employees and employers in their relations affecting commerce, to provide orderly and peaceful procedures for preventing the interference by either with the legitimate rights of the other, to protect the rights of individual employees in their relations with labor organizations whose activities affect commerce, to define and proscribe practices on the part of labor and management which affect commerce and are inimical to the general welfare, and to protect the rights of the public in connection with labor disputes affecting commerce.

Title I—Amendment of National Labor Relations Act

Sec. 101. The National Labor Relations Act is hereby amended to read as follows:

"Findings and Policies

"Section 1. The denial by some employers of the right of employees to organize and the refusal by some employers to accept the procedure of collective bargaining lead to strikes and other forms of industrial strife or unrest, which have the intent or the necessary effect of burdening or obstructing commerce by (a) impairing the efficiency, safety, or operation of the instrumentalities of commerce; (b) occurring in the current of commerce; (c) materially affecting, restraining, or controlling the flow of raw materials or manufactured or processed goods from or into the channels of commerce, or the prices of such materials or goods in commerce; or (d) causing diminution of employment and wages in such volume as substantially to impair or disrupt the market for goods flowing from or into the channels of commerce.

"The inequality of bargaining power between employees who do not possess full freedom of association or actual liberty of contract, and employers who are organized in the corporate or other forms of ownership association substantially burdens and affects the flow of commerce, and tends to aggravate recurrent business depressions, by depressing wage rates and the purchasing power of wage earners in industry and by preventing the stabilization of competitive wage rates and working conditions within and between industries.

"Experience has proved that protection by law of the right of employees to organize and bargain collectively safeguards commerce from injury, impairment, or interruption, and promotes the flow of commerce by removing certain recognized sources of industrial strife and unrest, by encouraging practices fundamental to the friendly adjustment of industrial disputes arising out of differences as to wages, hours, or other working conditions, and by restoring equality of bargaining power between employers and employees.

"Experience has further demonstrated that certain practices by some labor organizations, their officers, and members have the intent or the necessary effect of burdening or obstructing commerce by preventing the free flow of goods in such commerce through strikes and other forms of industrial unrest or through concerted activities which impair the interest of the public in the free flow of such commerce. The elimination of such practices is a necessary condition to the assurance of the rights herein guaranteed.

"It is hereby declared to be the policy of the United States to eliminate the causes of certain substantial obstructions to the free flow of commerce and to mitigate and eliminate these obstructions when they have occurred by encouraging the practice and procedure of collective bargaining and by protecting the exercise by workers of full freedom of association, self-organization, and designation of representatives of their own choosing, for the purpose of negotiating the terms and conditions of their employment or other mutual aid or protection.

"Definitions

"Sec. 2. When used in this Act—

" (1) The term 'person' includes one or more individuals, labor organizations, partnerships, associations, corporations, legal representatives, trustees, trustees in bankruptcy, or receivers.

" (2) The term 'employer' includes any person acting as an agent of an employer, directly or indirectly, but shall not include the United States or any wholly owned Government corporation, or any Federal Reserve Bank, or any State or political subdivision thereof, or any corporation or association operating a hospital, if no part of the net earnings inures to the benefit of any private shareholder or individual, or any person subject to the Railway Labor Act, as amended from time to time, or any labor organization (other than when acting as an employer), or anyone acting in the capacity of officer or agent of such labor organization.

" (3) The term 'employee' shall include any employee, and shall not be limited to the employees of a particular employer, unless the Act explicitly states otherwise, and shall include any individual whose work has ceased as a consequence of, or in connection with, any current labor dispute or because of any unfair labor practice, and who has not obtained any other regular and substantially equivalent employment, but shall not include any individual employed as an agricultural laborer, or in the domestic service of any family or person at his home, or any individual employed by his parent or spouse, or any individual having the status of an independent contractor, or any individual employed as a supervisor, or any individual employed by an employer subject to the Railway Labor Act, as amended from time to time, or by any other person who is not an employer as herein defined.

" (4) The term 'representatives' includes any individual or labor organization.

" (5) The term 'labor organization' means any organization of any kind, or any agency or employee representation committee or plan, in which employees participate and which exists for the purpose, in whole or in part, of dealing with employers concerning grievances, labor disputes, wages, rates of pay, hours of employment, or conditions of work.

" (6) The term 'commerce' means trade, traffic, commerce, transportation, or communication among the several States, or between the District of Columbia or any Territory of the United States and any State or other Territory, or between any foreign country and any State, Territory, or the District of Columbia, or within the District of Columbia or any Territory, or between points in the same State but through any other State or any Territory or the District of Columbia or any foreign country.

" (7) The term 'affecting commerce' means in commerce, or burdening or obstructing commerce or the free flow of commerce, or having led or tending to lead to a labor dispute burdening or obstructing commerce or the free flow of commerce.

" (8) The term 'unfair labor practice' means any unfair labor practice listed in section 8.

" (9) The term 'labor dispute' includes any controversy concerning terms, tenure or conditions of employment, or concerning the association or representation of persons in negotiating, fixing, maintaining, changing, or seeking to arrange terms or conditions of employment, regardless of whether the disputants stand in the proximate relation of employer and employee.

" (10) The term 'National Labor Relations Board' means the National Labor Relations Board provided for in section 3 of this Act.

" (11) The term 'supervisor' means any individual having authority, in the interest of the employer, to hire, transfer, suspend, lay off, recall, promote, discharge, assign, reward, or discipline other employees, or responsibly to direct them, or to adjust their grievances, or effectively to recommend such action, if in connection with the foregoing the exercise of such authority is not of a merely routine or clerical nature, but requires the use of independent judgment.

" (12) The term 'professional employee' means—

" (a) any employee engaged in work (i) predominantly intellectual and varied in character as opposed to routine mental, manual, mechanical, or physical work; (ii) involving the consistent exercise of discretion and judgment in its performance; (iii) of such a character that the output produced or the result accomplished cannot be standardized in relation to a given period of time; (iv) requiring knowledge of an advanced type in a field of science or learning customarily acquired by a prolonged course of specialized intellectual instruction and study in an institution of higher learning or a hospital, as distinguished from a general academic education or from an apprenticeship or from training in the performance of routine mental, manual, or physical processes; or

" (b) any employee, who (i) has completed the courses of specialized intellectual instruction and study described in clause (iv) of paragraph (a), and (ii) is performing related work under the supervision of a professional person to qualify himself to become a professional employee as defined in paragraph (a).

" (13) In determining whether any person is acting as an 'agent' of another person so as to make such other person responsible for his acts, the question of whether the specific acts performed were actually authorized or subsequently ratified shall not be controlling.

"National Labor Relations Board

"Sec. 3. (a) The National Labor Relations Board (hereinafter called the 'Board') created by this Act prior to its amendment by the Labor Management Relations Act, 1947, is hereby continued as an agency of the United States, except that the Board shall consist of five instead of three members, appointed by the President by and with the advice and consent of the Senate. Of the two additional members so provided for, one shall be appointed for a term of five years and the other for a term of two years. Their successors, and the successors of the other members, shall be appointed for terms of five years each, excepting that any individual chosen to fill a vacancy shall be appointed only for the unexpired term of the member whom he shall succeed. The President shall designate one member to serve as Chairman of the Board. Any member of the Board may be removed by the President, upon notice and hearing, for neglect of duty or malfeasance in office, but for no other cause.

" (b) The Board is authorized to delegate to any group of three or more members any or all of the powers which it may itself exercise. The Board is also authorized to delegate to its regional directors its powers under section 9 to determine the unit appropriate for the purpose of collective bargaining, to investigate and provide for hearings, and determine whether a question of representation exists, and to direct an election or take a secret ballot under subsection (c) or (e) of section 9 and certify the results thereof, except that upon the filing of a request therefor with the Board by any interested person, the Board may review any action of a regional director delegated to him under this paragraph, but such a review shall not, unless specifically ordered by the Board, operate as a stay of any action taken by the regional director. A vacancy in the Board shall not impair the right of the remaining members to exercise all of the powers of the Board, and three members of the Board shall, at all times, constitute a quorum of the Board, except that two members shall constitute a quorum of any group designated pursuant to the first sentence hereof. The Board shall have an official seal which shall be judicially noticed.

" (c) The Board shall at the close of each fiscal year make a report in writing to Congress and to the President stating in detail the cases it has heard, the decisions it has rendered, the names, salaries, and duties of all employees and officers in the employ or under the supervision of the Board, and an account of all moneys it has disbursed.

" (d) There shall be a General Counsel of the Board who shall be appointed by the President, by and with the advice and consent of the Senate, for a term of four years. The General Counsel of the Board shall exercise general supervision over all attorneys employed by the Board (other than trial examiners and legal assistants to Board members) and over the officers and employees in the regional offices. He shall have final authority, on behalf of the Board, in respect of the investigation of charges and issuance of complaints under section 10, and in respect of the prosecution of such complaints before the Board, and shall have such other duties as the Board may prescribe or as may be provided by law. In case of a vacancy in the office of the General Counsel the President is authorized to designate the officer or employee who shall act as General Counsel during such vacancy, but no person or persons so designated shall so act (1) for more than forty days when the Congress is in session unless a nomination to fill such vacancy shall have been submitted to the Senate, or (2) after the adjournment sine die of the session of the Senate in which such nomination was submitted.

"Sec. 4. (a) Each member of the Board and the General Counsel of the Board shall receive a salary of $12,000 a year, shall be eligible for reappointment, and shall not engage in any other business, vocation, or employment. The Board shall appoint an executive secretary, and such attorneys, examiners and regional directors, and such other employees as it may from time to time find necessary for the proper performance of its duties. The Board may not employ any attorneys for the purpose of reviewing transcripts of hearings or preparing drafts of opinions except that any attorney employed for assignment as a legal assistant to any Board member may for such Board member review such transcripts and prepare such drafts. No trial examiner's report shall be reviewed, either before or after its publication, by any person other than a member of the Board or his legal assistant, and no trial examiner shall advise or consult with the Board with respect to exceptions taken to his findings, rulings or recommendations. The Board may establish or utilize such regional, local, or other agencies, and utilize such voluntary and uncompensated services, as may from time to time be needed. Attorneys appointed under this section may, at the direction of the Board, appear for and represent the Board in any case in court. Nothing in this Act shall be construed to authorize the Board to appoint individuals for the purpose of conciliation or mediation, or for economic analysis.

" (b) All of the expenses of the Board, including all necessary traveling and subsistence expenses outside the District of Columbia incurred by the members or employees of the Board under its orders, shall be allowed and paid on the presentation of itemized vouchers, therefor approved by the Board or by any individual it designates for that purpose.

"Sec. 5. The principal office of the Board shall be in the District of Columbia, but it may meet and exercise any or all of its powers at any other place. The Board may, by one or more of its members or by such agents or agencies as it may designate, prosecute any inquiry necessary to its functions in any part of the United States. A member who participates in such an inquiry shall not be disqualified from subsequently participating in a decision of the Board in the same case.

"Sec. 6. The Board shall have authority from time to time to make, amend, and rescind, in the manner prescribed by the Administrative Procedure Act, such rules and regulations as may be necessary to carry out the provisions of this Act.

"Rights of Employees

"Sec. 7. Employees shall have the right to self-organization, to form, join or assist labor organizations, to bargain collectively through representatives of their own choosing, and to engage in other concerted activities for the purpose of collective bargaining or other mutual aid or protection, and shall also have the right to refrain from any or all of such activities except to the extent that such right may be affected by an agreement requiring membership in a labor organization as a condition of employment as authorized in section 8 (a) (3) .

"Unfair Labor Practices

"Sec. 8. (a) It shall be an unfair labor practice for an employer—

" (1) to interfere with, restrain, or coerce employees in the exercise of the rights guaranteed in section 7;

" (2) to dominate or interfere with the formation or administration of any labor organization or contribute financial or other support to it: *Provided,* That subject to rules and regulations made and published by the Board pursuant to section 6, an employer shall not be prohibited from permitting employees to confer with him during working hours without loss of time or pay;

" (3) by discrimination in regard to hire or tenure of employment or any term or condition of employment to encourage or discourage membership in any labor organization: *Provided,* That nothing in this Act, or any other statute of the United States, shall preclude an employer from making an agreement with a labor organization (not established, maintained, or assisted by any action defined in section 8 (a) of this Act as an unfair labor practice) to require as a condition of employment membership therein on or after the thirtieth day following the beginning of such employment or the effective date of such agreement, whichever is the later, (i) if such labor organization is the representative of the employees as provided in section 9 (a), in the appropriate collective-bargaining unit covered by such agreement when made; and (ii) unless following an election held as provided in section 9 (e) within one year preceding the effective date of such agreement the Board shall have certified that at least a majority of the employees eligible to vote in such election have voted to rescind the authority of such labor organization to make such an agreement: *Provided further,* That no employer shall justify any discrimination against an employee for nonmembership in a labor organization (A) if he has reasonable grounds for believing that such membership was not available to the employee on the same terms and conditions generally applicable to other members or (B) if he has reasonable grounds for believing that membership was denied or terminated for reasons other than the failure of the employee to tender the periodic dues and the initiation fees uniformly required as a condition of acquiring or retaining membership;

" (4) to discharge or otherwise discriminate against an employee because he has filed charges or given testimony under this Act;

" (5) to refuse to bargain collectively with the representatives of his employees, subject to the provisions of section 9 (a) .

" (b) It shall be an unfair labor practice for a labor organization or its agents—

" (1) to restrain or coerce (A) employees in the exercise of the rights guaranteed in section 7: *Provided,* That this paragraph shall not impair the right of a labor organization to prescribe its own rules with respect to the acquisition or retention of membership therein; or (B) an employer in the selection of his representatives for the purposes of collective bargaining or the adjustment of grievances;

" (2) to cause or attempt to cause an employer to discriminate against an employee in violation of subsection (a) (3) or to discriminate against an employee with respect to whom membership in such organization has been denied or terminated on some ground other than his failure to tender the periodic dues and the initiation fees uniformly required as a condition of acquiring or retaining membership;

" (3) to refuse to bargain collectively with an employer, provided it is the representative of his employees subject to the provisions of section 9 (a) ;

" (4) (i) to engage in, or to induce or encourage any individual employed by any person engaged in commerce or in an industry affecting commerce to engage in, a strike or a refusal in the course of his employment to use, manufacture, process, transport or otherwise handle or work on any goods, articles, materials or commodities or to perform any services; or (ii) to threaten, coerce, or restrain any person engaged in commerce or in an industry affecting commerce where in either case an object thereof is:

" (A) forcing or requiring any employer or self-employed person to join any labor or employer organization or to enter into any agreement which is prohibited by section 8 (e) ;

" (B) forcing or requiring any person to cease using, selling, handling, transporting, or otherwise dealing in the products of any other producer, processor, or manufacturer, or to cease doing business with any other person, or forcing or requiring any other employer to recognize or bargain with a labor organization as the representative of his employees unless such labor organization has been certified as the representative of such employees under the provisions of section 9: *Provided,* That nothing contained in this clause (B) shall be construed to make unlawful, where not otherwise unlawful, any primary strike or primary picketing;

"(C) forcing or requiring any employer to recognize or bargain with a particular labor organization as the representative of his employees if another labor organization has been certified as the representative of such employees under the provisions of section 9;

"(D) forcing or requiring any employer to assign particular work to employees in a particular labor organization or in a particular trade, craft, or class rather than to employees in another labor organization or in another trade, craft, or class, unless such employer is failing to conform to an order or certification of the Board determining the bargaining representative for employees performing such work:

Provided, That nothing contained in this subsection (b) shall be construed to make unlawful a refusal by any person to enter upon the premises of any employer (other than his own employer), if the employees of such employer are engaged in a strike ratified or approved by a representative of such employees whom such employer is required to recognize under this Act: *Provided further,* That for the purposes of this paragraph (4) only, nothing contained in such paragraph shall be construed to prohibit publicity, other than picketing, for the purpose of truthfully advising the public, including consumers and members of a labor organization, that a product or products are produced by an employer with whom the labor organization has a primary dispute and are distributed by another employer, as long as such publicity does not have an effect of inducing any individual employed by any person other than the primary employer in the course of his employment to refuse to pick up, deliver, or transport any goods, or not to perform any services, at the establishment of the employer engaged in such distribution.

" (5) to require of employees covered by an agreement authorized under subsection (a) (3) the payment, as a condition precedent to becoming a member of such organization, of a fee in an amount which the Board finds excessive or discriminatory under all the circumstances. In making such a finding, the Board shall consider, among other relevant factors, the practices and customs of labor organizations in the particular industry, and the wages currently paid to the employees affected;

" (6) to cause or attempt to cause an employer to pay or deliver or agree to pay or deliver any money or other thing of value, in the nature of an exaction, for services which are not performed or not to be performed; and

" (7) to picket or cause to be picketed, or threaten to picket or cause to be picketed, any employer where an object thereof is forcing or requiring an employer to recognize or bargain with a labor organization as the representative of his employees, or forcing or requiring the employees of an employer to accept or select such labor organization as their collective bargaining representative, unless such labor organization is currently certified as the representative of such employees:

" (A) where the employer has lawfully recognized in accordance with this Act any other labor organization and a question concerning representation may not appropriately be raised under section 9 (c) of this Act,

" (B) where within the preceding twelve months a valid election under section 9 (c) of this Act has been conducted, or

" (C) where such picketing has been conducted without a petition under section 9 (c) being filed within a reasonable period of time not to exceed thirty days from the commencement of such picketing: *Provided,* That when such a petition has been filed the Board shall forthwith, without regard to the provisions of section 9 (c) (1) or the absence of a showing of a substantial interest on the part of the labor organization, direct an election in such unit as the Board finds to be appropriate and shall certify the results thereof: *Provided further,* That nothing in this subparagraph (C) shall be construed to prohibit any picketing or other publicity for the purpose of truthfully advising the public (including consumers) that an employer does not employ members of, or have a contract with, a labor organization, unless an effect of such picketing is to induce any individual employed by any other person in the course of his employment, not to pick up, deliver or transport any goods or not to perform any services.

"Nothing in this paragraph (7) shall be construed to permit any act which would otherwise be an unfair labor practice under this section (8) (b).

" (c) The expressing of any views, argument, or opinion, or the dissemination thereof, whether in written, printed, graphic, or visual form, shall not constitute or be evidence of an unfair labor practice under any of the provisions of this Act, if such expression contains no threat of reprisal or force or promise of benefit.

" (d) For the purposes of this section, to bargain collectively is the performance of the mutual obligation of the employer and the representative of the employees to meet at reasonable times and confer in good faith with respect to wages, hours, and other terms and conditions of employment, or the negotiation of an agreement, or any question arising thereunder, and the execution of a written contract incorporating any agreement reached if requested by either party, but such obligation does not compel either party to agree to a proposal or require the making of a concession: *Provided,* That where there is in effect a collective-bargaining contract covering employees in an industry affecting commerce, the duty to bargain collectively shall also mean that no party to such contract shall terminate or modify such contract, unless the party desiring such termination or modification—

" (1) serves a written notice upon the other party to the contract of the proposed termination or modification sixty days prior to the expiration date thereof, or in the event such contract contains no expiration date, sixty days prior to the time it is proposed to make such termination or modification;

" (2) offers to meet and confer with the other party for the purpose of negotiating a new contract or a contract containing the proposed modifications;

" (3) notifies the Federal Mediation and Conciliation Service within thirty days after such notice of the existence of a dispute, and simultaneously therewith notifies any State or Territorial agency established to mediate and conciliate disputes within the State or Territory where the dispute occurred, provided no agreement has been reached by that time; and

" (4) continues in full force and effect, without resorting to strike or lock-out, all the terms and conditions of the existing contract for a period of sixty days after such notice is given or until the expiration date of such contract, whichever occurs later:

The duties imposed upon employers, employees and labor organizations by paragraphs (2), (3), and (4) shall become inapplicable upon an intervening certification of the Board, under which the labor organization or individual, which is a party to the contract, has been superseded as or ceased to be the representative of the employees subject to the provisions of section 9 (a), and the duties so imposed shall not be construed as requiring either party to discuss or agree to any modification of the terms and conditions contained in a contract for a fixed period, if such modification is to become effective before such terms and conditions can be reopened under the provisions of the contract. Any employee who engages in a strike within the sixty-day period specified in this subsection shall lose his status as an employee of the employer engaged in the particular labor dispute, for the purposes of sections 8, 9, and 10 of this Act, as amended, but such loss of status for such employee shall terminate if and when he is reemployed by such employer.

" (e) It shall be an unfair labor practice for any labor organization and any employer to enter into any contract or agreement, express or implied, whereby such employer ceases or refrains or agrees to cease or refrain from handling, using, selling, transporting or otherwise dealing in any of the products of any other employer, or to cease doing business with any other person, and any contract or agreement entered into heretofore or hereafter containing such an agreement shall be to such extent unenforcible and void: *Provided,* That nothing in this subsection (e) shall apply to an agreement between a labor organization and an employer in the construction industry relating to the contracting or subcontracting of work to be done at the site of the construction, alteration, painting, or repair of a buldiing, structure, or other work: *Provided further,* That for the purposes of this subsection (e) and section 8 (b) (4) (B) the terms 'any employer,' 'any person engaged in commerce or an industry affecting commerce,' and 'any person' when used in relation to the terms 'any other producer, processor, or manufacturer,' 'any other employer,' or 'any other person' shall not include persons in the relation of a jobber, manufacturer, contractor, or subcontractor working on the goods or premises of the jobber or manufacturer or performing parts of an integrated process of production in the apparel and clothing industry: *Provided further,* That nothing in this Act shall prohibit the enforcement of any agreement which is within the foregoing exception.

" (f) It shall not be an unfair labor practice under subsections (a) and (b) of this section for an employer engaged primarily in the building and construction industry to make an agreement covering employees engaged (or who, upon their employment, will be engaged) in the building and construction industry with a labor organization of which building and construction employees are members (not established, maintained, or assisted by any action defined in section 8 (a) of this Act as an unfair labor practice) because (1) the majority status of such labor organization has not been established under the provisions of section 9 of this Act prior to the making of such agreement, or (2) such agreement requires as a condition of employment, membership in such labor organization after the seventh day following the beginning of such employment or the effective date of the agreement, whichever is later, or (3) such agreement requires the employer to notify such labor organization of opportunities for employment with such employer, or gives such labor organization an opportunity to refer qualified applicants for such employment, or (4) such agreement specifies minimum training or experience qualifications for employment or provides for priority in opportunities for employment based upon length of service with such employer, in the industry or in the particular geographic area: *Provided,* That nothing in this subsection shall set aside the final proviso to section 8 (a) (3) of this Act: *Provided further,* That any agreement which would be invalid but for clause (1) of this subsection, shall not be a bar to a petition filed pursuant to section 9 (c) (or 9 (e) .

"Representatives and Elections

"Sec. 9 (a) Representatives designated or selected for the purposes of collective bargaining by the majority of the employees in a unit appropriate for such purposes, shall be the exclusive representatives of all the employees in such unit for the purposes of collective bargaining in respect to rates of pay, wages, hours of employment, or other conditions of employment: *Provided*, That any individual employee or a group of employees shall have the right at any time to present grievances to their employer and to have such grievances adjusted, without the intervention of the bargaining representative, as long as the adjustment is not inconsistent with the terms of a collective-bargaining contract or agreement then in effect: *Provided further,* That the bargaining representative has been given opportunity to be present at such adjustment.

" (b) The Board shall decide in each case whether, in order to assure to employees the fullest freedom in exercising the rights guaranteed by this Act, the unit appropriate for the purposes of collective bargaining shall be the employer unit, craft unit, plant unit, or subdivision thereof: *Provided,* That the Board shall not (1) decide that any unit is appropriate for such purposes if such unit includes both professional employees and employees who are not professional employees unless a majority of such professional employees vote for inclusion in such unit; or (2) decide that any craft unit is inappropriate for such purposes on the ground that a different unit has been established by a prior Board determination, unless a majority of the employees in the proposed craft unit vote against separate representation or (3) decide that any unit is appropriate for such purposes if it includes, together with other employees, any individual employed as a guard to enforce against employees and other persons rules to protect property of the employer or to protect the safety of persons on the employer's premises; but no labor organization shall be certified as the representative of employees in a bargaining unit of guards if such organization admits to membership, or is affiliated directly or indirectly with an organization which admits to membership, employees other than guards.

" (c) (1) Whenever a petition shall have been filed, in accordance with such regulations as may be prescribed by the Board—

"(A) by an employee or group of employees or any individual or labor organization acting in their behalf alleging that a substantial number of employees (i) wish to be represented for collective bargaining and that their employer declines to recognize their representative as the representative defined in section 9 (a) , or (ii) assert that the individual or labor organization, which has been certified or is being currently recognized by their employer as the bargaining representative, is no longer a representative as defined in section 9 (a) ; or

"(B) by an employer, alleging that one or more individuals or labor orgnizations have presented to him a claim to be recognized as the representative defined in section 9 (a) ;

the Board shall investigate such petition and if it has reasonable cause to believe that a question of representation affecting commerce exists shall provide for an appropriate hearing upon due notice. Such hearing may be conducted by an officer or employee of the regional office, who shall not make any recommendations with respect thereto. If the Board finds upon the record of such hearing that such a question of representation exists, it shall direct an election by secret ballot and shall certify the results thereof.

"(2) In determining whether or not a question of representation affecting commerce exists, the same regulations and rules of decision shall apply irrespective of the identity of the persons filing the petition or the kind of relief sought and in no case shall the Board deny a labor organization a place on the ballot by reason of an order with respect to such labor organization or its predecessor not issued in conformity with section 10 (c) .

"(3) No election shall be directed in any bargaining unit or any subdivision within which, in the preceding twelve-month period, a valid election shall have been held. Employees engaged in an economic strike who are not entitled to reinstatement shall be eligible to vote under such regulations as the Board shall find are consistent with the purposes and provisions of this Act in any election conducted within twelve months after the commencement of the strike. In any election where none of the choices on the ballot receives a majority, a run-off shall be conducted, the ballot providing for a selection between the two choices receiving the largest and second largest number of valid votes cast in the election.

"(4) Nothing in this section shall be construed to prohibit the waiving of hearings by stipulation for the purpose of a consent election in conformity with regulations and rules of decision of the Board.

"(5) In determining whether a unit is appropriate for the purposes specified in subsection (b) the extent to which the employees have organized shall not be controlling.

"(d) Whenever an order of the Board made pursuant to section 10 (c) is based in whole or in part upon facts certified following an investigation pursuant to subsection (c) of this section and there is a petition for the enforcement or review of such order, such certification and the record of such investigation shall be included in the transcript of the entire record required to be filed under section 10 (e) or 10 (f), and thereupon the decree of the court enforcing, modifying, or setting aside in whole or in part the order of the Board shall be made and entered upon the pleadings, testimony, and proceedings set forth in such transcript.

"(e) (1) Upon the filing with the Board, by 30 per centum or more of the employees in a bargaining unit covered by an agreement between their employer and a labor organization made pursuant to section 8 (a) (3), of a petition alleging the desire that such authority be rescinded, the Board shall take a secret ballot of the employees in such unit and certify the results thereof to such labor organization and to the employer.

"(2) No election shall be conducted pursuant to this subsection in any bargaining unit or any subdivision within which, in the preceding twelve-month period, a valid election shall have been held.

"Prevention of Unfair Labor Practices

"Sec. 10. (a) The Board is empowered, as hereinafter provided, to prevent any person from engaging in any unfair labor practice (listed in section 8) affecting commerce. This power shall not be affected by any other means of adjustment or prevention that has been or may be established by agreement, law, or otherwise: *Provided,* That the Board is empowered by agreement with any agency of any State or Territory to cede to such agency jurisdiction over any cases in any industry (other than mining, manufacturing, communications, and transportation except where predominantly local in character) even though such cases may involve labor disputes affecting commerce, unless the provision of the State or Territorial statute applicable to the determination of such cases by such agency is inconsistent with the corresponding provision of this Act or has received a construction inconsistent therewith.

" (b) Whenever it is charged that any person has engaged in or is engaging in any such unfair labor practice, the Board, or any agent or agency designated by the Board for such purposes, shall have power to issue and cause to be served upon such person a complaint stating the charges in that respect, and containing a notice of hearing before the Board or a member thereof, or before a designated agent or agency, at a place therein fixed, not less than five days after the serving of said complaint: *Provided,* That no complaint shall issue based upon any unfair labor practice occurring more than six months prior to the filing of the charge with the Board and the service of a copy thereof upon the person against whom such charge is made, unless the person aggrieved thereby was prevented from filing such charge by reason of service in the armed forces, in which event the six-month period shall be computed from the day of his discharge. Any such complaint may be amended by the member, agent, or agency conducting the hearing or the Board in its discretion at any time prior to the issuance of an order based thereon. The person so complained of shall have the right to file an answer to the original or amended complaint and to appear in person or otherwise and give testimony at the place and time fixed in the complaint. In the discretion of the member, agent, or agency conducting the hearing or the Board, any other person may be allowed to intervene in the said proceeding and to present testimony. Any such proceeding shall, so far as practicable, be conducted in accordance with the rules of evidence applicable in the district courts of the United States under the rules of civil procedure for the district courts of the United States, adopted by the Supreme Court of the United States pursuant to the Act of June 19, 1934 (U.S.C., title 28, secs. 723-B, 723-C) .

" (c) The testimony taken by such member, agent, or agency or the Board shall be reduced to writing and filed with the Board. Thereafter, in its discretion, the Board upon notice may take further testimony or hear argument. If upon the preponderance of the testimony taken the Board shall be of the opinion that any person named in the complaint has engaged in or is engaging in any such unfair labor practice, then the Board shall state its findings of fact and shall issue and cause to be served on such person an order requiring such person to cease and desist from such unfair labor practice, and to take such affirmative action including reinstatement of employees with or without back pay, as will effectuate the policies of this Act: *Provided,* That where an order directs reinstatement of an employee, back pay may be required of the employer or labor organization, as the case may be, responsible for the discrimination suffered by him: *And provided further,* That in determining whether a complaint shall issue alleging a violation of section 8 (a) (1) or section 8 (a) (2), and in deciding such cases, the same regulations and rules of decision shall apply irrespective of whether or not the labor organization affected is affiliated with a labor organization national or international in scope. Such order may further require such person to make reports from time to time showing the extent to which it has complied with the order. If upon the preponderance of the testimony taken the Board shall not be of the opinion that the person named in the complaint has engaged in or is engaging in any such unfair labor practice, then the Board shall state its findings of fact and shall issue an order dismissing the said complaint. No order of the Board shall require the reinstatement of any individual as an employee who has been suspended or discharged, or the payment to him of any back pay, if such individual was suspended or discharged for cause. In case the evidence is presented before a member of the Board, or before an examiner or examiners thereof, such member, or such examiner or examiners, as the case may be, shall issue and cause to be served on the parties to the proceedings a proposed report, together with a recommended order, which shall be filed with the Board, and if no exceptions are filed within twenty days after service thereof upon such parties, or within such further period as the Board may authorize, such recommended order shall become the order of the Board and become effective as therein prescribed.

" (d) Until the record in a case shall have been filed in a court, as hereinafter provided, the Board may at any time upon reasonable notice and in such manner as it shall deem proper, modify or set aside, in whole or in part, any finding or order made or issued by it.

" (e) The Board shall have power to petition any court of appeals of the United States, or if all the courts of appeals to which application may be made are in vacation, any district court of the United States, within any circuit or district, respectively, wherein the unfair labor practice in question occurred or wherein such person resides or transacts business, for the enforcement of such order and for appropriate temporary relief or restraining order, and shall file in the court the record in the proceedings, as provided in section 2112 of title 28, United States Code. Upon the filing of such petition, the court shall cause notice thereof to be served upon such person, and thereupon shall have jurisdiction of the proceeding and of the question determined therein, and shall have power to grant such temporary relief or restraining order as it deems just and proper, and to make and enter a decree enforcing, modifying, and enforcing as so modified, or setting aside in whole or in part the order of the Board. No objection that has not been urged before the Board, its member, agent, or agency, shall be considered by the court, unless the failure or neglect to urge such objection shall be excused because of extraordinary circumstances. The findings of the Board with respect to questions of fact if supported by substantial evidence on the record considered as a whole shall be conclusive. If either party shall apply to the court for leave to adduce additional evidence and shall show to the satisfaction of the court that such additional evidence is material and that there were reasonable grounds for the failure to adduce such evidence in the hearing before the Board, its member, agent, or agency, the court may order such additional evidence to be taken before the Board, its member, agent, or agency, and to be made a part of the record. The Board may modify its findings as to the facts, or make new findings, by reason of additional evidence so taken and filed, and it shall file such modified or new findings, which findings with respect to questions of fact if supported by substantial evidence on the record considered as a whole shall be conclusive, and shall file its recommendations, if any, for the modification or setting aside of its original order. Upon the filing of the record with it the jurisdiction of the court shall be exclusive and its judgment and decree shall be final, except that the same shall be subject to review by the appropriate United States court of appeals if application was made to the district court as herein-above provided, and by the Supreme Court of the United States upon writ of certiorari or certification as provided in section 1254 of title 28.

" (f) Any person aggrieved by a final order of the Board granting or denying in whole or in part the relief sought may obtain a review of such order in any United States court of appeals in the circuit wherein the unfair labor practice in question was alleged to have been engaged in or wherein such person resides or transacts business, or in the United States Court of Appeals for the District of Columbia, by filing in such court a written petition praying that the order of the Board be modified or set aside. A copy of such petition shall be forthwith transmitted by the clerk of the court to the Board, and thereupon the aggrieved party shall file in the court the record in the proceeding, certified by the Board, as provided in section 2112 of title 28, United States Code. Upon the filing of such petition, the court shall proceed in the same manner as in the case of an application by the Board under subsection (e) of this section, and shall have the same jurisdiction to grant to the Board such temporary relief or restraining order as it deems just and proper, and in like manner to make and enter a decree enforcing, modifying, and enforcing as so modified, or setting aside in whole or in part the order of the Board; the findings of the Board with respect to questions of fact if supported by substantial evidence on the record considered as a whole shall in like manner be conclusive.

" (g) The commencement of proceedings under subsection (e) or (f) of this section shall not, unless specifically ordered by the court, operate as a stay of the Board's order.

" (h) When granting appropriate temporary relief or a restraining order, or making and entering a decree enforcing, modifying, and enforcing as so modified, or setting aside in whole or in part an order of the Board, as provided in this section, the jurisdiction of courts sitting in equity shall not be limited by the Act entitled 'An Act to amend the Judicial Code and to define and limit the jurisdiction of courts sitting in equity and for other purposes,' approved March 23, 1932 (U.S.C. Supp. VII, title 29, secs. 101-115).

"(i) Petitions filed under this Act shall be heard expeditiously, and if possible within ten days after they have been docketed.

"(j) The Board shall have power, upon issuance of a complaint as provided in subsection (b) charging that any person has engaged in or is engaging in an unfair labor practice, to petition any United States district court within any district wherein the unfair labor practice in question is alleged to have occurred or wherein such person resides or transacts business, for appropriate temporary relief or restraining order. Upon the filing of any such petition the court shall cause notice thereof to be served upon such person, and thereupon shall have jurisdiction to grant to the Board such temporary relief or restraining order as it deems just and proper.

"(k) Whenever is is charged that any person has engaged in an unfair labor practice within the meaning of paragraph (4) (D) of section 8 (b), the Board is empowered and directed to hear and determine the dispute out of which such unfair labor practice shall have arisen, unless, within ten days after notice that such charge has been filed, the parties to such dispute submit to the Board satisfactory evidence that they have adjusted, or agreed upon methods for the voluntary adjustment of, the dispute. Upon compliance by the parties to the dispute with the decision of the Board or upon such voluntary adjustment of the dispute, such charge shall be dismissed.

"(l) Whenever it is charged that any person has engaged in an unfair labor practice within the meaning of paragraph (4) (A), (B), or (C) of section 8 (b) or section 8 (e) or section 8 (b) (7), the preliminary investigation of such charge shall be made forthwith and given priority over all other cases except cases of like character in the office where it is filed or to which it is referred. If, after such investigation, the officer or regional attorney to whom the matter may be referred has reasonable cause to believe such charge is true and that a complaint should issue, he shall, on behalf of the Board, petition any United States district court within any district where the unfair labor practice in question has occurred, is alleged to have occurred, or wherein such person resides or transacts business, for appropriate injunctive relief pending the final adjudication of the Board with respect to such matter. Upon the filing of any such petition the district court shall have jurisdiction to grant such injunctive relief or temporary restraining order as it deems just and proper, notwithstanding any other provision of law: *Provided further,* That no temporary restraining order shall be issued without notice unless a petition alleges that substantial and irreparable injury to the charging party will be unavoidable and such temporary restraining order shall be effective for no longer than five days and will become void at the expiration of such period: *Provided further,* that such officer or regional attorney shall not apply for any restraining order under section 8 (b) (7) if a charge against the employer under 8 (a) (2) has been filed and after the preliminary investigation, he has reasonable cause to believe that such charge is true and that a complaint should issue. Upon filing of any such petition, the courts shall cause notice thereof to be served upon any person involved in the charge and such person, including the charging party, shall be given an opportunity to appear by counsel, and present any relevant testimony: *Provided further,* That for the purposes of this subsection district courts shall be deemed to have jurisdiction of a labor organization (1) in the district in which such organization maintains its principal office, or (2) in any district in which its duly authorized officers or agents are engaged in promoting or protecting the interests of employee members. The service of legal process upon such officer or agent shall constitute service upon the labor organization and make such organization a party to the suit. In situations where such relief is appropriate the procedure specified herein shall apply to charges with respect to section 8 (b) (4) (D).

"(m) Whenever it is charged that any person has engaged in an unfair labor practice within the meaning of subsection (a) (3) or (b) (2) of section 8, such charge shall be given priority over all other cases except cases of like character in the office where it is filed or to which it is referred and cases given priority under subsection (l).

"Investigatory Powers

"Sec. 11. For the purpose of all hearings and investigations, which, in the opinion of the Board, are necessary and proper for the exercise of the powers vested in it by section 9 and section 10—

" (1) The Board, or its duly authorized agents or agencies, shall at all reasonable times have access to, for the purpose of examination, and the right to copy any evidence of any person being investigated or proceeded against that relates to any matter under investigation or in question. The Board, or any member thereof, shall upon application of any party to such proceedings, forthwith issue to such party subpenas requiring the attendance and testimony of witnesses or the production of any evidence in such proceeding or investigation requested in such application. Within five days after the service of a sub- pena on any person requiring the production of any evidence in his possession or under his control, such person may petition the Board to revoke, and the Board shall revoke, such subpena if in its opinion the evidence whose production is required does not relate to any matter under investigation, or any matter in question in such proceedings, or if in its opinion such subpena does not describe with sufficient particularity the evidence whose production is required. Any member of the Board, or any agent or agency designated by the Board for such purposes, may administer oaths and affirmations, examine witnesses, and re- ceive evidence. Such attendance of witnesses and the produc- tion of such evidence may be required from any place in the United States or any Territory or possession thereof, at any des- ignated place of hearing.

" (2) In case of contumacy or refusal to obey a subpena issued to any person, any district court of the United States or the United States courts of any Territory or possession, within the jurisdiction of which the inquiry is carried on or within the juris- diction of which said person guilty of contumacy or refusal to obey is found or resides or transacts business, upon application by the Board shall have jurisdiction to issue to such person an order requiring such person to appear before the Board, its member, agent, or agency, there to produce evidence if so ordered, or there to give testimony touching the matter under investigation or in question; and any failure to obey such order of the court may be punished by said court as a contempt thereof.

" (3) No person shall be excused from attending and testifying or from producing books, records, correspondence, documents, or other evidence in obedience to the subpena of the Board, on the ground that the testimony or evidence required of him may tend to incriminate him or subject him to a penalty or forfeiture; but no individual shall be prosecuted or subjected to any penalty or forfeiture for or on account of any transaction, matter, or thing concerning which he is compelled, after having claimed his privilege against self-incrimination, to testify or produce evidence, except that such individual so testifying shall not be exempt from prosecution and punishment for perjury committed in so testifying.

" (4) Complaints, orders, and other process and papers of the Board, its member, agent, or agency, may be served either personally or by registered mail or by telegraph or by leaving a copy thereof at the principal office or place of business of the person required to be served. The verified return by the individual so serving the same setting forth the manner of such service shall be proof of the same, and the return post office receipt or telegraph receipt therefor when registered and mailed or telegraphed as aforesaid shall be proof of service of the same. Witnesses summoned before the Board, its member, agent, or agency, shall be paid the same fees and mileage that are paid witnesses in the courts of the United States, and witnesses whose depositions are taken and the persons taking the same shall severally be entitled to the same fees as are paid for like services in the courts of the United States.

" (5) All process of any court to which application may be made under this Act may be served in the judicial district wherein the defendant or other person required to be served resides or may be found.

" (6) The several departments and agencies of the Government, when directed by the President, shall furnish the Board, upon its request, all records, papers, and information in their possession relating to any matter before the Board.

"Sec. 12. Any person who shall willfully resist, prevent, impede, or interfere with any member of the Board or any of its agents or agencies in the performance of duties pursuant to this Act shall be punished by a fine of not more than $5,000 or by imprisonment for not more than one year, or both.

"Limitations

"Sec. 13. Nothing in this Act, except as specifically provided for herein, shall be construed so as either to interfere with or impede or diminish in any way the right to strike, or to affect the limitations or qualifications on that right.

"Sec. 14. (a) Nothing herein shall prohibit any individual employed as a supervisor from becoming or remaining a member of a labor organization, but no employer subject to this Act shall be compelled to deem individuals defined herein as supervisors as employees for the purpose of any law, either national or local, relating to collective bargaining.

"(b) Nothing in this Act shall be construed as authorizing the execution or application of agreements requiring membership in a labor organization as a condition of employment in any State or Territory in which such execution or application is prohibited by State or Territorial law.

"Federal-State Jurisdiction

"(c) (1) The Board, in its discretion, may, by rule of decision or by published rules adopted pursuant to the Administrative Procedure Act, decline to assert jurisdiction over any labor dispute involving any class or category of employers, where, in the opinion of the Board, the effect of such labor dispute on commerce is not sufficiently substantial to warrant the exercise of its jurisdiction: *Provided,* That the Board shall not decline to assert jurisdiction over any labor dispute over which it would assert jurisdiction under the standards prevailing upon August 1, 1959.

"(2) Nothing in this Act shall be deemed to prevent or bar any agency or the courts of any State or Territory (including the Commonwealth of Puerto Rico, Guam, and the Virgin Islands), from assuming and asserting jurisdiction over labor disputes over which the Board declines, pursuant to paragraph (1) of this subsection, to assert jurisdiction.

"Sec. 15. Wherever the application of the provisions of section 272 of chapter 10 of the Act entitled 'An Act to establish a uniform system of bankruptcy throughout the United States', approved July 1, 1898, and Acts amendatory thereof and supplementary thereto (U.S.C., title 11, sec. 672), conflicts with the application of the provisions of this Act, this Act shall prevail: *Provided,* That in any situation where the provisions of this Act cannot be validly enforced, the provisions of such other Acts shall remain in full force and effect.

"Sec. 16. If any provision of this Act, or the application of such provision to any person or circumstances, shall be held invalid, the remainder of this Act, or the application of such a provision to persons or circumstances other than those as to which it is held invalid, shall not be affected thereby.

"Sec. 17. This Act may be cited as the 'National Labor Relations Act.'

"Sec. 18. No petition entertained, no investigation made, no election held, and no certification issued by the National Labor Relations Board, under any of the provisions of section 9 of the National Labor Relations Act, as amended, shall be invalid by reason of the failure of the Congress of Industrial Organizations to have complied with the requirements of section 9 (f), (g), or (h) of the aforesaid Act prior to December 22, 1949, or by reason of the failure of the American Federation of Labor to have complied with the provisions of section 9 (f), (g), or (h) of the aforesaid Act prior to November 7, 1947: *Provided,* That no liability shall be imposed under any provision of this Act upon any person for failure to honor any election or certificate referred to above, prior to the effective date of this amendment; *Provided, however,* That this proviso shall not have the effect of setting aside or in any way affecting judgments or decrees heretofore entered under section 10 (e) or (f) and which have become final."

Effective Date of Certain Changes

Sec. 102. No provision of this title shall be deemed to make an unfair labor practice any act which was performed prior to the date of the enactment of this Act which did not constitute an unfair labor practice prior thereto, and the provisions of section 8 (a) (3) and section 8 (b) (2) of the National Labor Relations Act as amended by this title shall not make an unfair labor practice the performance of any obligation under a collective-bargaining agreement entered into prior to the date of the enactment of this Act, or (in the case of an agreement for a period of not more than one year) entered into on or after such date of enactment, but prior to the effective date of this title, if the performance of such obligation would not have constituted an unfair labor practice under section 8 (3) of the National Labor Relations Act prior to the effective date of this title, unless such agreement was renewed or extended subsequent thereto.

Sec. 103. No provisions of this title shall affect any certification of representatives or any determination as to the appropriate collective-bargaining unit, which was made under section 9 of the National Labor Relations Act prior to the effective date of this title until one year after the date of such certification or if, in respect of any such certification, a collective-bargaining contract was entered into prior to the effective date of this title, until the end of the contract period or until one year after such date, whichever first occurs.

Sec. 104. The amendments made by this title shall take effect sixty days after the date of the enactment of this Act except that the authority of the President to appoint certain officers conferred upon him by section 3 of the National Labor Relations Act as amended by this title may be exercised forthwith.

Title II—Conciliation of Labor Disputes in Industries Affecting Commerce; National Emergencies

Sec. 201. It is the policy of the United States that—

(a) sound and stable industrial peace and the advancement of the general welfare, health, and safety of the Nation and of the best interests of employers and employees can most satisfactorily be secured by the settlement of issues between employers and employees through the processes of conference and collective bargaining between employers and the representatives of their employees;

(b) the settlement of issues between employers and employees through collecctive bargaining may be advanced by making available full and adequate governmental facilities for conciliation, mediation, and voluntary arbitration to aid and encourage employers and the representatives of their employees to reach and maintain agreements concerning rates of pay, hours, and working conditions, and to make all reasonable efforts to settle their differences by mutual agreement reached through conferences and collective bargaining or by such methods as may be provided for in any applicable agreement for the settlement of disputes; and

(c) certain controversies which arise between parties to collective-bargaining agreements may be avoided or minimized by making available full and adequate governmental facilities for furnishing assistance to employers and the representatives of their employees in formulating for inclusion within such agreements provision for adequate notice of any proposed changes in the terms of such agreements, for the final adjustment of grievances or questions regarding the application or interpretation of such agreements, and other provisions designed to prevent the subsequent arising of such controversies.

Sec. 202. (a) There is hereby created an independent agency to be known as the Federal Mediation and Conciliation Service (herein referred to as the "Service," except that for sixty days after the date of the enactment of this Act such term shall refer to the Conciliation Service of the Department of Labor). The Service shall be under the direction of a Federal Mediation and Conciliation Director (hereinafter referred to as the "Director"), who shall be appointed by the President by and with the advice and consent of the Senate. The Director shall receive compensation at the rate of $12,000 per annum. The Director shall not engage in any other business, vocation, or employment.

(b) The Director is authorized, subject to the civil-service laws, to appoint such clerical and other personnel as may be necessary for the execution of the functions of the Service, and shall fix their compensation in accordance with the Classification Act of 1923, as amended, and may, without regard to the provisions of the civil-service laws and the Classification Act of 1923, as amended, appoint and fix the compensation of such conciliators and mediators as may be necessary to carry out the functions of the Service. The Director is authorized to make such expenditures for supplies, facilities, and services as he deems necessary. Such expenditures shall be allowed and paid upon presentation of itemized vouchers therefor approved by the Director or by any employee designated by him for that purpose.

(c) The principal office of the Service shall be in the District of Columbia, but the Director may establish regional offices convenient to localities in which labor controversies are likely to arise. The Director may by order, subject to revocation at any time, delegate any authority and discretion conferred upon him by this Act to any regional director, or other officer or employee of the Service. The Director may establish suitable procedures for cooperation with State and local mediation agencies. The Director shall make an annual report in writing to Congress at the end of the fiscal year.

(d) All mediation and conciliation functions of the Secretary of Labor or the United States Conciliation Service under section 8 of the Act entitled "An Act to create a Department of Labor," approved March 4, 1913 (U.S.C., title 29, sec. 51), and all functions of the United States Conciliation Service under any other law are hereby transferred to the Federal Mediation and Conciliation Service, together with the personnel and records of the United States Conciliation Service. Such transfer shall take effect the sixtieth day after the date of enactment of this Act. Such transfer shall not affect any proceedings pending before the United States Conciliation Service or any certification, order, rule, or regulation theretofore made by it or by the Secretary of Labor. The Director and the Service shall not be subject in any way to the jurisdiction or authority of the Secretary of Labor or any official or division of the Department of Labor.

Functions of the Service

Sec. 203. (a) It shall be the duty of the Service, in order to prevent or minimize interruptions of the free flow of commerce growing out of labor disputes, to assist parties to labor disputes in industries affecting commerce to settle such disputes through conciliation and mediation.

(b) The Service may proffer its services in any labor dispute in any industry affecting commerce, either upon its own motion or upon the request of one or more of the parties to the dispute, whenever in its judgment such dispute threatens to cause a substantial interruption of commerce. The Director and the Service are directed to avoid attempting to mediate disputes which would have only a minor effect on interstate commerce if State or other conciliation services are available to the parties. Whenever the Service does proffer its services in any disputes, it shall be the duty of the Service promptly to put itself in communication with the parties and to use its best efforts, by mediation and conciliation, to bring them to agreement.

(c) If the Director is not able to bring the parties to agreement by conciliation within a reasonable time, he shall seek to induce the parties voluntarily to seek other means of settling the dispute without resort to strike, lock-out, or other coercion, including submission to the employees in the bargaining unit of the employer's last offer of settlement for approval or rejection in a secret ballot. The failure or refusal of either party to agree to any procedure suggested by the Director shall not be deemed a violation of any duty or obligation imposed by this Act.

(d) Final adjustment by a method agreed upon by the parties is hereby declared to be the desirable method for settlement of grievance disputes arising over the application or interpretation of an existing collective-bargaining agreement. The Service is directed to make its conciliation and mediation services available in the settlement of such grievance disputes only as a last resort and in exceptional cases.

Sec. 204. (a) In order to prevent or minimize interruptions of the free flow of commerce growing out of labor disputes, employers and employees and their representatives, in any industry affecting commerce, shall—

(1) exert every reasonable effort to make and maintain agreements concerning rates of pay, hours, and working conditions, including provision for adequate notice of any proposed change in the terms of such agreements;

(2) whenever a dispute arises over the terms or application of a collective-bargaining agreement and a conference is requested by a party or prospective party thereto, arrange promptly for such a conference to be held and endeavor in such conference to settle such dispute expeditiously; and

(3) in case such dispute is not settled by conference, participate fully and promptly in such meetings as may be un-

dertaken by the Service under this Act for the purpose of aiding in a settlement of the dispute.

Sec. 205. (a) There is hereby created a National Labor-Management Panel which shall be composed of twelve members appointed by the President, six of whom shall be selected from among persons outstanding in the field of management and six of whom shall be selected from among persons outstanding in the field of labor. Each member shall hold office for a term of three years, except that any member appointed to fill a vacancy occurring prior to the expiration of the term for which his predecessor was appointed shall be appointed for the remainder of such term, and the terms of office of the members first taking office shall expire, as designated by the President at the time of appointment, four at the end of the first year, four at the end of the second year, and four at the end of the third year after the date of appointment. Members of the panel, when serving on business of the panel, shall be paid compensation at the rate of $25 per day, and shall also be entitled to receive an allowance for actual and necessary travel and subsistence expenses while so serving away from their places of residence.

(b) It shall be the duty of the panel, at the request of the Director, to advise in the avoidance of industrial controversies and the manner in which mediation and voluntary adjustment shall be administered, particularly with reference to controversies affecting the general welfare of the country.

National Emergencies

Sec. 206. Whenever in the opinion of the President of the United States, a threatened or actual strike or lockout affecting an entire industry or a substantial part thereof engaged in trade, commerce, transportation, transmission, or communication among the several States or with foreign nations, or engaged in the production of goods for commerce, will, if permitted to occur or to continue, imperil the national health or safety, he may appoint a board of inquiry to inquire into the issues involved in the dispute and to make a written report to him within such time as he shall prescribe. Such report shall include a statement of the facts with respect to the dispute, including each party's statement of its position but shall not contain any recommendations. The President shall file a copy of such report with the Service and shall make its contents available to the public.

Sec. 207. (a) A board of inquiry shall be composed of a chairman and such other members as the President shall determine, and shall have power to sit and act in any place within the United States and to conduct such hearings either in public or in private, as it may deem necessary or proper, to ascertain the facts with respect to the causes and circumstances of the dispute.

(b) Members of a board of inquiry shall receive compensation at the rate of $50 for each day actually spent by them in the work of the board, together with necessary travel and subsistence expenses.

(c) For the purpose of any hearing or inquiry conducted by any board appointed under this title, the provisions of sections 9 and 10 (relating to the attendance of witnesses and the production of books, papers, and documents) of the Federal Trade Commission Act of September 16, 1914, as amended (U.S.C. 19, title 15, secs. 49 and 50, as amended), are hereby made applicable to the powers and duties of such board.

Sec. 208. (a) Upon receiving a report from a board of inquiry the President may direct the Attorney General to petition any district court of the United States having jurisdiction of the parties to enjoin such strike or lock-out or the continuing thereof, and if the court finds that such threatened or actual strike or lockout—

(i) affects an entire industry or a substantial part thereof engaged in trade, commerce, transportation, transmission, or communication among the several States or with foreign nations, or engaged in the production of goods for commerce; and

(ii) if permitted to occur or to continue, will imperil the national health or safety, it shall have jurisdiction to enjoin any such strike or lock-out, or the continuing thereof, and to make such other orders as may be appropriate.

(b) In any case, the provisions of the Act of March 23, 1932, entitled "An Act to amend the Judicial Code and to define and limit the jurisdiction of courts sitting in equity, and for other purposes," shall not be applicable.

(c) The order or orders of the court shall be subject to review by the appropriate court of appeals and by the Supreme Court upon writ of certiorari or certification as provided in sections 239 and 240 of the Judicial Code, as amended (U.S.C., title 29, secs. 346 and 347).

Sec. 209. (a) Whenever a district court has issued an order under section 208 enjoining acts or practices which imperil or threaten to imperil the national health or safety, it shall be the duty of the parties to the labor dispute giving rise to such order to make every effort to adjust and settle their differences, with the assistance of the Service created by this Act. Neither party shall be under any duty to accept, in whole or in part, any proposal of settlement made by the Service.

(b) Upon the issuance of such order, the President shall reconvene the board of inquiry which has previously reported with respect to the dispute. At the end of a sixty-day period (unless the dispute has been settled by that time), the board of inquiry shall report to the President the current position of the parties and the efforts which have been made for settlement, and shall include a statement by each party of its position and a statement of the employer's last offer of settlement. The President shall make such report available to the public. The National Labor Relations Board, within the succeeding fifteen days, shall take a secret ballot of the employees of each employer involved in the dispute on the question of whether they wish to accept the final offer of settlement made by their employer as stated by him and shall certify the results thereof to the Attorney General within five days thereafter.

Sec. 210. Upon the certification of the results of such ballot or upon a settlement being reached, whichever happens sooner, the Attorney General shall move the court to discharge the injunction, which motion shall then be granted and the injunction discharged. When such motion is granted, the President shall submit to the Congress a full and comprehensive report of the proceedings, including the findings of the board of inquiry and the ballot taken by the National Labor Relations Board, together with such recommendations as he may see fit to make for consideration and appropriate action.

Compilation of Collective Bargaining Agreements, etc.

Sec. 211. (a) For the guidance and information of interested representatives of employers, employees, and the general public, the Bureau of Labor Statistics of the Department of Labor shall maintain a file of copies of all available collective bargaining agreements and other available agreements and actions thereunder settling or adjusting labor disputes. Such file shall be open to inspection under appropriate conditions prescribed by the Secretary of Labor, except that no specific information submitted in confidence shall be disclosed.

(b) The Bureau of Labor Statistics in the Department of Labor is authorized to furnish upon request of the Service, or employers, employees, or their representatives, all available data and factual information which may aid in the settlement of any labor dispute, except that no specific information submitted in confidence shall be disclosed.

Exemption of Railway Labor Act

Sec. 212. The provisions of this title shall not be applicable with respect to any matter which is subject to the provisions of the Railway Labor Act, as amended from time to time.

Title III

Suits by and Against Labor Organizations

Sec. 301. (a) Suits for violation of contracts between an employer and a labor organization representing employees in an industry affecting commerce as defined in this Act, or between any such labor organizations, may be brought in any district court of the United States having jurisdiction of the parties, without respect to the amount in controversy or without regard to the citizenship of the parties.

(b) Any labor organization which represents employees in an industry affecting commerce as defined in this Act and any employer whose activities affect commerce as defined in this Act shall be bound by the acts of its agents. Any such labor organization may sue or be sued as an entity and in behalf of the employees whom it represents in the courts of the United States. Any money judgment against a labor organization in a district court of the United States shall be enforceable only against the organization as an entity and against its assets, and shall not be enforceable against any individual member or his assets.

(c) For the purposes of actions and proceedings by or against labor organizations in the district courts of the United States, district courts shall be deemed to have jurisdiction of a labor organization (1) in the district in which such organization maintains its principal office, or (2) in any district in which its duly authorized officers or agents are engaged in representing or acting for employee members.

(d) The service of summons, subpena, or other legal process of any court of the United States upon an officer or agent of a labor organization, in his capacity as such, shall constitute service upon the labor organization.

(e) For the purposes of this section in determining whether any person is acting as an "agent" of another person so as to make such other person responsible for his acts, the question of whether the specific acts performed were actually authorized or subsequently ratified shall not be controlling.

Restrictions on Payments to Employee Representatives

Sec. 302. (a) It shall be unlawful for any employer or association of employers or any person who acts as a labor relations expert, adviser, or consultant to an employer or who acts in the interest of an employer to pay, lend, or deliver, or agree to pay, lend, or deliver, any money or other thing of value—

(1) to any representative of any of his employees who are employed in an industry affecting commerce; or

(2) to any labor organization or any officer or employee thereof, which represents, seeks to represent, or would admit to membership, any of the employees of such employer who are employed in an industry affecting commerce; or

(3) to any employee or group or committee of employees of such employer employed in an industry affecting commerce in excess of their normal compensation for the purpose of causing such employee or group or committee directly or indirectly to influence any other employees in the exercise of the right to organize and bargain collectively through representatives of their own choosing; or

(4) to any officer or employee of a labor organization engaged in an industry affecting commerce with intent to influence him in respect to any of his actions, decisions, or duties as a representative of employees or as such officer or employee of such labor organization.

(b) (1) It shall be unlawful for any person to request, demand, receive, or accept, or agree to receive or accept, any payment, loan, or delivery of any money or other thing of value prohibited by subsection (a).

(2) It shall be unlawful for any labor organization, or for any person acting as an officer, agent, representative, or employee of such labor organization to demand or accept from the operator of any motor vehicle (as defined in part II of the Interstate Commerce Act) employed in the transportation of property in commerce, or the employer of any such operator, any money or other thing of value payable to such organization or to an officer, agent, representative or employee thereof as a fee or charge for the unloading, or in connection with the unloading, of the cargo of such vehicle: *Provided,* That nothing in this paragraph shall be construed to make unlawful any payment by an employer to any of his employees as compensation for their services as employees.

(c) The provisions of this section shall not be applicable (1) in respect to any money or other thing of value payable by an employer to any of his employees whose established duties include acting openly for such employer in matters of labor relations or personnel administration or to any representative of his employees, or to any officer or employee of a labor organization, who is also an employee or former employee of such employer, as compensation for, or by reason of, his service as an employee of such employer; (2) with respect to the payment or delivery of any money or other thing of value in satisfaction of a judgment of any court or a decision or award of an arbitrator or impartial chairman or in compromise, adjustment, settlement, or release of any claim, complaint, grievance, or dispute in the absence of fraud or duress; (3) with respect to the sale or purchase of an article or commodity at the prevailing market price in the regular course of business; (4) with respect to money deducted from the wages of employees in payment of membership dues in a labor organization: *Provided,*

That the employer has received from each employee, on whose
account such deductions are made, a written assignment which
shall not be irrevocable for a period of more than one year, or
beyond the termination date of the applicable collective agreement, whichever occurs sooner; (5) with respect to money or
other thing of value paid to a trust fund established by such
representative, for the sole and exclusive benefit of the employees of such employer, and their families and dependents (or
of such employees, families, and dependents jointly with the
employees of other employers making similar payments, and
their families and dependents) : *Provided,* That (A) such payments are held in trust for the purpose of paying, either from
principal or income or both, for the benefit of employees, their
families and dependents, for medical or hospital care, pensions on retirement or death of employees, compensation for injuries or illness resulting from occupational activity or insurance to provide any of the foregoing, or unemployment benefits or life insurance, disability and sickness insurance, or accident insurance; (B) the detailed basis on which such payments
are to be made is specified in a written agreement with the employer, and employees and employers are equally represented
in the administration of such fund, together with such neutral
persons as the representatives of the employers and the representatives of employees may agree upon and in the event the
employer and employee groups deadlock on the administration
of such fund and there are no neutral persons empowered to
break such deadlock, such agreement provides that the two
groups shall agree on an impartial umpire to decide such dispute, or in event of their failure to agree within a reasonable
length of time, an impartial umpire to decide such dispute shall,
on petition of either group, be appointed by the district court
of the United States for the district where the trust fund has its
principal office, and shall also contain provisions for an annual
audit of the trust fund, a statement of the results of which shall
be available for inspection by interested persons at the principal office of the trust fund and at such other places as may be
designated in such written agreement; and (C) such payments
as are intended to be used for the purpose of providing pensions or annuities for employees are made to a separate trust
which provides that the funds held therein cannot be used for
any purpose other than paying such pensions or annuities; or

(6) with respect to money or other thing of value paid by any employer to a trust fund established by such representative for the purpose of pooled vacation, holiday, severance or similar benefits, or defraying costs of apprenticeship or other training programs: *Provided,* That the requirements of clause (B) of the proviso to clause (5) of this subsection shall apply to such trust funds; or (7) with respect to money or other thing of value paid by any employer to a pooled or individual trust fund established by such representative for the purpose of (A) scholarships for the benefit of employees, their families, and dependents for study at educational institutions or (B) child care centers for preschool and school age dependents of employees: *Provided,* That no labor organization or employer shall be required to bargain on the establishment of any such trust fund, and refusal to do so shall not constitute an unfair labor practice: *Provided further,* That the requirements of clause (B) of the proviso to clause (5) of this subsection shall apply to such trust funds.

(d) Any person who willfully violates any of the provisions of this section shall, upon conviction thereof, be guilty of a misdemeanor and be subject to a fine of not more than $10,000 or to imprisonment for not more than one year, or both.

(e) The district courts of the United States and the United States courts of the Territories and possessions shall have jurisdiction, for cause shown, and subject to the provisions of section 17 (relating to notice to opposite party) of the Act entitled "An Act to supplement existing laws against unlawful restraints and monopolies, and for other purposes," approved October 15, 1914, as amended (U.S.C., title 28, sec. 381), to restrain violations of this section, without regard to the provisions of sections 6 and 20 of such Act of October 15, 1914, as amended (U.S.C., title 15, sec. 17, and title 29, sec. 52), and the provisions of the Act entitled "An Act to amend the Judicial Code and to define and limit the jurisdiction of courts sitting in equity, and for other purposes," approved March 23, 1932 (U.S.C., title 29, secs. 101-115).

(f) This section shall not apply to any contract in force on the date of enactment of this Act, until the expiration of such contract, or until July 1, 1948, whichever first occurs.

(g) Compliance with the restrictions contained in subsection

(c) (5) (B) upon contributions to trust funds, otherwise lawful, shall not be applicable to contributions to such trust funds established by collective agreement prior to January 1, 1946, nor shall subsection (c) (5) (A) be construed as prohibiting contributions to such trust funds if prior to January 1, 1947, such funds contained provisions for pooled vacation benefits.

Boycotts and Other Unlawful Combinations

Sec. 303 (a) It shall be unlawful, for the purpose of this section only, in an industry or activity affecting commerce, for any labor organization to engage in any activity or conduct defined as an unfair labor practice in section 8 (b) (4) of the National Labor Relations Act, as amended.

(b) Whoever shall be injured in his business or property by reason of any violation of subsection (a) may sue therefor in any district court of the United States subject to the limitations and provisions of section 301 hereof without respect to the amount in controversy, or in any other court having jurisdiction of the parties, and shall recover the damages by him sustained and the cost of the suit.

Restriction on Political Contributions

Sec. 304. Section 313 of the Federal Corrupt Practices Act, 1925 (U.S.C., 1940 edition, title 2, sec. 251; Supp. V, title 50, App., sec. 1509), as amended, is amended to read as follows:

"Sec. 313. It is unlawful for any national bank, or any corporation organized by authority of any law of Congress, to make a contribution or expenditure in connection with any election to any political office, or in connection with any primary election or political convention or caucus held to select candidates for any political office, or for any corporation whatever, or any labor organization to make a contribution or expenditure in connection with any election at which Presidential and Vice Presidential electors or a Senator or Representative in, or a Delegate or Resident Commissioner to Congress are to be voted for, or in connection with any primary election or political convention or caucus held to select candidates for any of the foregoing offices, or for any candidates, political committee, or other person to accept or receive any contribution prohibited by this section. Every corporation or labor organization which makes any contribution or expenditure in violation of this section shall be fined not more than $5,000; and every officer or director of any corporation, or officer of any labor organization, who consents to any contribution or expenditure by the corporation or labor organization, as the case may be, in violation of this section shall be fined not more than $1,000 or imprisoned for not more than one year, or both. For the purposes of this section 'labor organization' means any organization of any kind, or any agency or employee representation committee or plan, in which employees participate and which exists for the purpose, in whole or in part, of dealing with employers concerning grievances, labor disputes, wages, rates of pay, hours of employment, or conditions of work.''

Strikes by Government Employees

Sec. 305. [Repealed by Ch. 690, 69 Stat. 624, effective August 9, 1955. Sec. 305 made it unlawful for government employees to strike and made strikers subject to immediate discharge, forfeiture of civil-service status, and three-year blacklisting for federal employment.]

Title IV

Creation of Joint Committee to Study and Report on Basic Problems Affecting Friendly Labor Relations and Productivity

Sec. 401. There is hereby established a joint congressional committee to be known as the Joint Committee on Labor-Management Relations (hereafter referred to as the committee), and to be composed of seven Members of the Senate Committee on Labor and Public Welfare, to be appointed by the President pro tempore of the Senate, and seven Members of the House of Representatives Committee on Education and Labor, to be appointed by the Speaker of the House of Representatives. A vacancy in membership of the committee, shall not affect the powers of the remaining members to execute the functions of the committee, and shall be filled in the same manner as the original selection. The committee shall select a chairman and a vice chairman from among its members.

Sec. 402. The committee, acting as a whole or by subcommittee shall conduct a thorough study and investigation of the entire field of labor-management relations, including but not limited to—

(1) the means by which permanent friendly cooperation between employers and employees and stability of labor relations may be secured throughout the United States;

(2) the means by which the individual employee may achieve a greater productivity and higher wages, including plans for guaranteed annual wages, incentive profit-sharing and bonus systems;

(3) the internal organization and administration of labor unions, with special attention to the impact on individuals of collective agreements requiring membership in unions as a condition of employment;

(4) the labor relations policies and practices of employers and associations of employers;

(5) the desirability of welfare funds for the benefit of employees and their relation to the social-security system;

(6) the methods and procedures for best carrying out the collective-bargaining processes, with special attention to the effects of industrywide or regional bargaining upon the national economy;

(7) the administration and operation of existing Federal laws relating to labor relations; and

(8) such other problems and subjects in the field of labor-management relations as the committee deems appropriate.

Sec. 403. The committee shall report to the Senate and the House of Representatives not later than March 15, 1948, the results of its study and investigation, together with such recommendations as to necessary legislation and such other recommendations as it may deem advisable, and shall make its final report not later than January 2, 1949,

Sec. 404. The committee shall have the power, without regard to the civil-service laws and the Classification Act of 1923, as amended, to employ and fix the compensation of such officers, experts, and employees as it deems necessary for the performance of its duties, including consultants who shall receive compensation at a rate not to exceed $35 for each day actually spent by them in the work of the committee, together with their necessary travel and subsistence expenses. The committee is further authorized with the consent of the head of the department or agency concerned, to utilize the services, information, facilities, and personnel of all agencies in the executive branch of the Government and may request the governments of the several States, representatives of business, industry, finance, and labor, and such other persons, agencies, organizations, and instrumentalities as it deems appropriate to attend its hearings and to give and present information, advice, and recommendations.

Sec. 405. The committee, or any subcommittee thereof, is authorized to hold such hearings; to sit and act at such times and places during the sessions, recesses, and adjourned periods of the Eightieth Congress; to require by subpena or otherwise the attendance of such witnesses and the production of such books, papers, and documents; to administer oaths; to take such testimony; to have such printing and binding done; and to make such expenditures within the amount appropriated therefor; as it deems advisable. The cost of stenographic services in reporting such hearings shall not be in excess of 25 cents per one hundred words. Subpenas shall be issued under the signature of the chairman or vice chairman of the committee and shall be served by any person designated by them.

Sec. 406. The members of the committee shall be reimbursed for travel, subsistence, and other necessary expenses incurred by them in the performance of the duties vested in the committee, other than expenses in connection with meetings of the committee held in the District of Columbia during such times as the Congress is in session.

Sec. 407. There is hereby authorized to be appropriated the sum of $150,000, or so much thereof as may be necessary, to carry out the provisions of this title, to be disbursed by the Secretary of the Senate on vouchers signed by the chairman.

Title V

Definitions

Sec. 501. When used in this Act—

(1) The term "industry affecting commerce" means any industry or activity in commerce or in which a labor dispute

would burden or obstruct commerce or tend to burden or obstruct commerce or the free flow of commerce.

(2) The term "strike" includes any strike or other concerted stoppage of work by employees (including a stoppage by reason of the expiration of a collective-bargaining agreement) and any concerted slowdown or other concerted interruption of operations by employees.

(3) The terms "commerce," "labor disputes," "employer," "employee," "labor organization," "representative," "person," and supervisor" shall have the same meaning as when used in the National Labor Relations Act as amended by this Act.

Saving Provision

Sec. 502. Nothing in this Act shall be construed to require an individual employee to render labor or service without his consent, nor shall anything in this Act be construed to make the quitting of his labor by an individual employee an illegal act; nor shall any court issue any process to compel the performance by an individual employee of such labor or service, without his consent; nor shall the quitting of labor by an employee or employees in good faith because of abnormally dangerous conditions for work at the place of employment of such employee or employees be deemed a strike under this Act.

Separability

Sec. 503. If any provision of this Act, or the application of such provision to any person or circumstance, shall be held invalid, the remainder of this Act, or the application of such provision to persons or circumstances other than those as to which it is held invalid, shall not be affected thereby.

Appendix C

DIRECTORY OF BOARD'S REGIONAL OFFICES

REGIONAL OFFICES SERVING VARIOUS STATES

Region No.	State	Region No.	State	Region No.	State
10, 15	Alabama	15	Louisiana	16	Oklahoma
19	Alaska	1	Maine	19, 36	Oregon
28	Arizona	5	Maryland	4, 6	Pennsylvania
26	Arkansas	1	Massachusetts	24	Puerto Rico
20, 21, 31	California	7, 30	Michigan	1	Rhode Island
27	Colorado	18	Minnesota	11	South Carolina
1, 2	Connecticut	15, 26	Mississippi	18	South Dakota
4, 5	Delaware	14, 17	Missouri	5, 10, 26	Tennessee
5	Dist. of Col.	19	Montana	16, 23, 28	Texas
12, 15	Florida	17	Nebraska	27	Utah
10	Georgia	20, 31	Nevada	1	Vermont
37, 20	Hawaii	1	New Hampshire	24	Virgin Islands
19	Idaho	4, 22	New Jersey	5	Virginia
13, 14, 38	Illinois	28	New Mexico	19, 36	Washington
9, 13, 25	Indiana	2, 3, 29	New York	5, 6, 9	West Virginia
18, 38	Iowa	11	North Carolina	18, 30	Wisconsin
17	Kansas	18	North Dakota	27	Wyoming
9, 25	Kentucky	8, 9	Ohio		

Region 1

Address: Boston, Mass. 02203 — 7th Floor, Bulfinch Bldg., 15 New Chardon St., Tel.: 223-3330

Connecticut Counties:

Hartford	New Haven	Tolland
Litchfield	New London	Windham
Middlesex		

Maine
Massachusetts
New Hampshire
Rhode Island
Vermont

Region 2

Address: New York, N.Y. 10007 — 36th Floor, Federal Bldg., 26 Federal Plaza, Tel.: 264-0300

Connecticut County:
Fairfield

New York Counties:

Bronx	Orange	Rockland
New York	Putnam	Westchester

Region 3

Address: Buffalo, N.Y. 14202—120 Delaware Ave., Tel.: 842-3100

New York Counties:

Albany	Genesee	Rensselaer
Allegany	Greene	St. Lawrence
Broome	Hamilton	Saratoga
Cattaraugus	Herkimer	Schenectady
Cayuga	Jefferson	Schoharie
Chautauqua	Lewis	Schuyler
Chemung	Livingston	Seneca
Chenango	Madison	Steuben
Clinton	Monroe	Sullivan
Columbia	Montgomery	Tioga
Cortland	Niagara	Tompkins
Delaware	Oneida	Ulster
Dutchess	Onondaga	Warren
Erie	Ontario	Washington
Essex	Orleans	Wayne
Franklin	Oswego	Wyoming
Fulton	Otsego	Yates

Resident Office

Address: Albany, N.Y. 12207 — 60 Chapel St., Tel.: 472-2215

Area served: Counties in eastern half of state, excluding counties served by New York City office.

Region 4

Address: Philadelphia, Pa. 19107—
1700 Bankers' Sec. Bldg., Walnut and
Juniper Sts. Tel.: 597-7601

Delaware County:
New Castle

New Jersey Counties:

Atlantic	Cumberland
Burlington	Gloucester
Camden	Ocean
Cape May	Salem

Pennsylvania Counties:

Adams	Monroe
Berks	Montgomery
Bradford	Montour
Bucks	Northampton
Carbon	Northumberland
Chester	Perry
Columbia	Philadelphia
Cumberland	Pike
Dauphin	Schuylkill
Delaware	Snyder
Juniata	Sullivan
Lackawanna	Susquehanna
Lancaster	Tioga
Lebanon	Union
Lehigh	Wayne
Luzerne	Wyoming
Lycoming	York

Region 5

Address: Baltimore, Md. 21201—Federal Building, Room 1019, Charles
Center, Tel.: 962-2822

Delaware Counties:

Kent	Sussex

District of Columbia

Maryland

Tennessee
City of Bristol (Sullivan County)

Virginia

West Virginia Counties:

Berkeley	Jefferson
Grant	Mineral
Hampshire	Morgan
Hardy	Pendelton

Region 6

Address: Pittsburgh, Pa. 15222—1536
Federal Bldg., 1000 Liberty Ave.,
Tel.: 644-2977

Pennsylvania Counties:

Allegheny	Franklin
Armstrong	Fulton
Beaver	Greene
Bedford	Huntingdon
Blair	Indiana
Butler	Jefferson
Cambria	Lawrence
Cameron	McKean
Centre	Mercer
Clarion	Mifflin
Clearfield	Potter
Clinton	Somerset
Crawford	Venango
Elk	Warren
Erie	Washington
Fayette	Westmoreland
Forest	

West Virginia Counties:

Barbour	Ohio
Brooke	Pocahontas
Doddridge	Preston
Hancock	Randolph
Harrison	Taylor
Lewis	Tucker
Marion	Upshur
Marshall	Webster
Monongalia	Wetzel

Region 7

Address: Detroit, Mich. 48226—500
Book Bldg., 1249 Washington Blvd.
Tel.: 226-3200

Michigan Counties:

Alcona	Lapeer
Allegan	Leelanau
Alpena	Lenawee
Antrim	Livingston
Arenac	Macomb
Barry	Manistee
Bay	Mason
Benzie	Mecosta
Berrien	Midland
Branch	Missaukee
Calhoun	Monroe
Cass	Montcalm
Charlevoix	Montmorency
Cheboygan	Muskegon
Clare	Newaygo
Clinton	Oakland
Crawford	Oceana
Eaton	Ogemaw
Emmet	Osceola
Genesee	Oscoda
Gladwin	Otsego
Grand Traverse	Ottawa
Gratiot	Presque Isle
Hillsdale	Roscommon
Huron	Saginaw
Ingham	St. Clair
Ionia	St. Joseph
Iosco	Sanilac
Isabella	Shiawassee
Jackson	Tuscola
Kalamazoo	Van Buren
Kalkaska	Washtenaw
Kent	Wayne
Lake	Wexford

Region 8

Address: Cleveland, Ohio 44199—1695
Fed. Office Bldg., 1240 East 9th St.,
Tel.: 522-3715

Ohio Counties:

Allen	Logan
Ashland	Lorain
Ashtabula	Lucas
Auglaize	Mahoning
Belmont	Marion
Carroll	Medina
Champaign	Mercer
Columbiana	Miami
Coshocton	Morrow
Crawiord	Muskingum
Cuyahoga	Ottawa
Darke	Paulding
Defiance	Portage
Delaware	Putnam
Erie	Richland
Fulton	Sandusky
Geauga	Seneca
Guernsey	Shelby
Hancock	Stark
Hardin	Summit
Harrison	Trumbull
Henry	Tuscarawas
Holmes	Union
Huron	Van Wert
Jefferson	Wayne
Knox	Williams
Lake	Wood
Licking	Wyandot

Region 9

Address: Cincinnati, Ohio 45202—
Room 2407, Federal Office Bldg., 550
Main St., Tel.: 684-3686

Indiana Counties:

Clark	Floyd
Dearborn	

Kentucky except counties:

Daviess	Henderson

Ohio Counties:

Adams	Lawrence
Athens	Madison
Brown	Meigs
Butler	Monroe
Clark	Montgomery
Clermont	Morgan
Clinton	Noble
Fairfield	Perry
Fayette	Pickaway
Franklin	Pike
Gallia	Preble
Greene	Ross
Hamilton	Scioto
Highland	Vinton
Hocking	Warren
Jackson	Washington

West Virginia Counties:

Boone	Mingo
Braxton	Monroe
Cabell	Nicholas
Calhoun	Pleasants
Clay	Putnam
Fayette	Raleigh
Gilmer	Ritchie
Greenbrier	Roane
Jackson	Summers
Kanawha	Tyler
Lincoln	Wayne
Logan	Wirt
McDowell	Wood
Mason	Wyoming
Mercer	

Region 10

Address: Atlanta, Ga. 30308 — 730
Peachtree St., N.E., Tel.: 526-5760

Alabama Counties:

Autauga	Lamar
Bibb	Lauderdale
Blount	Lawrence
Calhoun	Lee
Chambers	Limestone
Cherokee	Madison
Chilton	Marion
Clay	Marshall
Cleburne	Morgan
Colbert	Perry
Coosa	Pickens
Cullman	Randolph
DeKalb	St. Clair
Elmore	Shelby
Etowah	Sumter
Fayette	Talladega
Franklin	Tallapoosa
Greene	Tuscaloosa
Hale	Walker
Jackson	Winston
Jefferson	

Georgia

Tennessee Counties:

Anderson	McMinn
Bledsoe	Marion
Blount	Meigs
Bradley	Monroe
Campbell	Morgan
Carter	Overton
Claiborne	Pickett
Clay	Polk
Cocke	Putnam
Cumberland	Rhea
Fentress	Roane
Grainger	Scott
Greene	Sequatchie
Grundy	Sevier
Hamblen	Sullivan
Hamilton	(except City of
Hancock	Bristol)
Hawkins	Unicoi
Jackson	Union
Jefferson	Van Buren
Johnson	Warren
Knox	Washington
Loudon	White

Resident Office

Address: Birmingham, Ala. 35203—2026 2nd Ave. North, Rm 1203, Tel.: 325-3877

Region 11

Address: Winston-Salem, N.C. 27101—1624 Wachovia Bldg., 301 North Main St., Tel.: 723-2300

North Carolina
South Carolina

Region 12

Address: Tampa, Fla. 33602—706 Federal Office Bldg., 500 Zack St., Tel.: 228-7227

Florida Counties:

Alachua	Lee
Baker	Leon
Bradford	Levy
Brevard	Madison
Broward	Manatee
Charlotte	Marion
Citrus	Martin
Clay	Monroe
Collier	Nassau
Columbia	Okeechobee
Dade	Orange
De Soto	Osceola
Dixie	Palm Beach
Duval	Pasco
Flagler	Pinellas
Gadsden	Polk
Gilchrist	Putnam
Glades	St. Johns
Hamilton	St. Lucie
Hardee	Sarasota
Hendry	Seminole
Hernando	Sumter
Highlands	Suwannee
Hillsborough	Taylor
Indian River	Union
Jefferson	Volusia
Lafayette	Wakulla
Lake	

Resident Offices

Address: Miami, Fla. 33130—Room 826 Federal Office Bldg., 51 S.W. First Ave., Tel.: 350-5391
Address: Jacksonville, Fla. 32202—Federal Building, 400 West Bay Street, Tel.: 791-2168

Region 13

Address: Chicago, Ill., 60604—Rm. 881, Everett McKinley Dirksen Bldg., 219 South Dearborn St., Tel.: 828-7572

Illinois Counties:

Cook	Lake
Du Page	Will
Kane	

Indiana County:

Lake

Sub-Region 38

Address: Peoria, Ill. 61602—10th Floor, Savings Center Tower, 411 Hamilton Blvd., Tel.: 673-9282

Illinois Counties:

Boone	Marshall
Bureau	Mason
Carroll	McDonough
Cass	McHenry
Champaign	McLean
De Kalb	Menard
De Witt	Mercer
Douglas	Morgan
Ford	Moultrie
Fulton	Ogle
Grundy	Peoria
Hancock	Piatt
Henderson	Putnam
Henry	Rock Island
Iroquois	Sangamon
Jo Daviess	Schuyler
Kankakee	Stark
Kendall	Stephenson
Knox	Tazewell
La Salle	Vermillion
Lee	Warren
Livingston	Whiteside
Logan	Winnebago
Macon	Woodford

Iowa Counties:

Clinton	Lee
Des Moines	Louisa
Dubuque	Muscatine
Jackson	Scott

Region 14

Address: St. Louis, Mo. 63102—1040 Boatmen's Bank Bldg., 314 N. Broadway, Tel.: 622-4167

Illinois Counties:

Adams	Johnson
Alexander	Lawrence
Bond	Macoupin
Brown	Madison
Calhoun	Marion
Christian	Massac
Clark	Monroe
Clay	Montgomery
Clinton	Perry
Coles	Pike
Crawford	Pope
Cumberland	Pulaski
Edgar	Randolph
Edwards	Richland
Effingham	St. Clair
Fayette	Saline
Franklin	Scott
Gallatin	Shelby
Greene	Union
Hamilton	Wabash
Hardin	Washington
Jackson	Wayne
Jasper	White
Jefferson	Williamson
Jersey	

Missouri Counties:

Audrain	Montgomery
Bollinger	New Madrid
Butler	Oregon
Callaway	Osage
Cape Girardeau	Pemiscot
Carter	Perry
City of St. Louis	Phelps
Clark	Pike
Crawford	Ralls
Dent	Reynolds
Dunklin	Ripley
Franklin	St. Charles
Gasconade	St. Francois
Iron	St. Louis
Jefferson	Ste. Genevieve
Knox	Scotland
Lewis	Scott
Lincoln	Shannon
Madison	Shelby
Maries	Stoddard
Marion	Warren
Mississippi	Washington
Monroe	Wayne

Region 15

Address: New Orleans, La. 70113—T6024 Federal Bldg., 701 Loyola Ave. Tel.: 527-6361

Louisiana

Alabama Counties:

Baldwin	Geneva
Barbour	Henry
Bullock	Houston
Butler	Lowndes
Choctaw	Macon
Clarke	Marengo
Coffee	Mobile
Conecuh	Monroe
Covington	Montogomery
Crenshaw	Pike
Dale	Russell
Dallas	Washington
Escambia	Wilcox

Florida Counties:

Bay	Jackson
Calhoun	Liberty
Escambia	Okaloosa
Franklin	Santa Rosa
Gulf	Walton
Holmes	Washington

Mississippi Counties:

Adams	Jefferson
Amite	Jefferson Davis
Claiborne	Jones
Clarke	Kemper
Copia	Lamar
Covington	Lauderdale
Forrest	Lawrence
Franklin	Leake
George	Lincoln
Greene	Madison
Hancock	Marion
Harrison	Neshoba
Hinds	Newton
Issaquena	Pearl River
Jackson	Perry
Jasper	Pike

Mississippi Counties—Contd.

Rankin	Stone
Scott	Walthall
Stone	Warren
Sharkey	Wayne
Simpson	Wilkinson
Smith	Yazoo

Region 16

Address: Fort Worth, Tex. 76102—8A24 Federal Office Bldg., 819 Taylor Street, Tel.: 334-2921

Oklahoma

Texas: Except counties under jurisdiction of Regions 23 and 28

Region 17

Address: Kansas City, Mo. 64106—610 Federal Bldg., 601 E. 12th St., Tel.: 334-2921

Nebraska

Kansas

Missouri Counties:

Adair	Jasper
Andrew	Johnson
Atchison	Laclede
Barry	Lafayette
Barton	Lawrence
Bates	Linn
Benton	Livingston
Boone	McDonald
Buchanan	Macon
Caldwell	Mercer
Camden	Miller
Carroll	Moniteau
Cass	Morgan
Cedar	Newton
Chariton	Nodaway
Christian	Ozark
Clay	Pettis
Clinton	Platte
Cole	Polk
Cooper	Pulaski
Dade	Putnam
Dallas	Randolph
Daviess	Ray
De Kalb	St. Clair
Douglas	Saline
Gentry	Schuyler
Greene	Stone
Grundy	Sullivan
Harrison	Taney
Henry	Texas
Hickory	Vernon
Holt	Webster
Howard	Worth
Howell	Wright
Jackson	

Region 18

Address: Minneapolis, Minn. 55401—316 Federal Bldg., 110 So. 4th St. Tel.: 334-2611

Iowa: Except counties under jurisdiction of Sub-Region 38

Minnesota

North Dakota

South Dakota

Wisconsin Counties:

Ashland	Jackson
Barron	Pepin
Bayfield	Pierce
Buffalo	Polk
Burnett	Price
Chippewa	Rusk
Clark	St. Croix
Douglas	Sawyer
Dunn	Taylor
Eau Claire	Trempealeau
Iron	Washburn

Region 19

Address: Seattle, Wash. 98101 — 10th Floor, Republic Bldg., 1511 Third Ave., Tel.: 583-4532

Alaska

Idaho

Montana

Washington: Except Clark County

Sub-Region 36

Address: Portland, Ore. 97205—310 Six Ten Broadway Building, 610 S.W. Broadway, Tel.: 226-3431

Oregon

Washington County:

Clark

Region 20

Address: San Francisco, Calif., 94102 —450 Golden Gate Ave., Box 36047, Tel.: 556-3197

California Counties:

Alameda	Merced
Alpine	Modoc
Amador	Mono
Butte	Monterey
Calaveras	Napa
Colusa	Nevada
Contra Costa	Placer
Del Norte	Plumas
Eldorado	Sacramento
Fresno	San Benito
Glenn	San Francisco
Humboldt	San Joaquin
Kings	San Mateo
Lake	Santa Clara
Lasson	Santa Cruz
Madera	Shasta
Marin	Sierra
Mariposa	Siskiyou
Mendocino	Solano

California Counties—Contd.

Sononia	Tuolumne
Stanislaus	Tulare
Sutter	Yolo
Tehama	Yuba
Trinity	

Nevada (except Clark, Lincoln and Nye Counties)

Sub-Region 37

Address: Honolulu, Hawaii 96814— Suite 308, 1311 Kapiolani Blvd., Tel.: 546-5797

Hawaii

Region 21

Address: Los Angeles, Calif. 90014— Eastern Columbia Bldg., 849 South Broadway, Tel.: 688-5200

California Counties:

Imperial	Riverside
Los Angeles*	San Diego
Orange	

* That portion of Los Angeles County lying to the east and south of the Harbor Freeway, the Pasadena Freeway, Arroyo Boulevard, and U.S. Highway 66 to the county line.

Region 22

Address: Newark, N.J. 07102 — 16th Floor, Federal Bldg., 970 Broad Street Tel.: 645-2100

New Jersey Counties:

Bergen	Morris
Essex	Passaic
Hudson	Somerset
Hunterdon	Sussex
Mercer	Union
Middlesex	Warren
Monmouth	

Region 23

Address: Houston, Tex., 77002 — 4th Floor, Dallas Brazos Bldg., 1125 Brazos St., Tel.: 226-4296

Texas Counties:

Aransas	Calhoun
Atascosa	Cameron
Austin	Chambers
Bandera	Colorado
Bastrop	Comal
Bee	De Witt
Bexar	Dimmit
Blanco	Duval
Brazoria	Edwards
Brazos	Fayette
Brooks	Fort Bend
Burleson	Frio
Caldwell	Galveston

Texas Counties—Contd.

Gillespie	McMullen
Goliad	Medina
Gonzales	Montgomery
Grimes	Newton
Guadalupe	Nueces
Hardin	Orange
Harris	Polk
Hays	Real
Hidalgo	Refugio
Jackson	San Jacinto
Jasper	San Patricio
Jefferson	Starr
Jim Hogg	Travis
Jim Wells	Tyler
Karnes	Uvalde
Kendall	Valverde
Kenedy	Victoria
Kerr	Walker
Kinney	Waller
Kleberg	Washington
La Salle	Webb
Lavaca	Wharton
Lee	Willacy
Liberty	Wilson
Live Oak	Zapata
Matagorda	Zavala
Maverick	

Region 24

Address: Hato Rey, P.R.—7th Floor, Pan Am Bldg., 225 Ponce de Leon Avenue. Mailing address: P.O. Box UU, Tel.: 765-0404

Puerto Rico

U.S. Virgin Islands

Region 25

A d d r e s s: Indianapolis, Ind.—46204 614 ISTA Center, 150 W. Market St., Tel.: MElrose 3-8921

Indiana: All except Lake, Clark, Dearborn, Floyd

Kentucky Counties:

Davies	Henderson

Region 26

Address: Memphis, Tenn. 38103—746 Federal Office Bldg., 167 N. Main St., Tel.: 534-3161

Arkansas

Mississippi Counties:

Alcorn	Coahoma
Attala	De Sota
Benton	Grenada
Bolivar	Holmes
Calhoun	Humphreys
Carroll	Itawamba
Chickasaw	Lafayette
Choctaw	Lee
Clay	Leflore

Mississippi Counties—Contd.

Lowndes	Tallahatchie
Marshall	Tate
Monroe	Tippah
Montgomery	Tishomingo
Noxubee	Tunica
Oktibbeha	Union
Panola	Washington
Pontotoc	Webster
Prentiss	Winston
Quitman	Yalobusha
Sunflower	

Tennessee Counties:

Bedford	Lake
Benton	Lauderdale
Cannon	Lawrence
Carroll	Lewis
Cheatham	Lincoln
Chester	McNairy
Coffee	Macon
Crockett	Madison
Davidson	Marshall
Decatur	Maury
DeKalb	Montgomery
Dickson	Moore
Dyer	Obion
Fayette	Perry
Franklin	Robertson
Gibson	Rutherford
Giles	Shelby
Hardeman	Smith
Hardin	Stewart
Haywood	Sumner
Henderson	Tipton
Henry	Trousdale
Hickman	Wayne
Houston	Weakley
Humphreys	Williamson
	Wilson

Resident Offices

Address: Little Rock, Ark. 72201— 3507 Federal Bldg., 700 W. Capitol Ave., Tel.: 372-5512

Address: Nashville, Tenn. 37203 — 562 Federal Courthouse Bldg., 801 Broadway, Tel.: 242-5922

Region 27

Address: Denver, Colo. 80202—Federal Bldg., U.S. Custom House, Rm. 260, 721 19th St., Tel.: 297-3551

Wyoming

Colorado

Utah

Region 28

Address: Albuquerque, N.M. 87101— 7011 Federal Bldg., U.S. Courthouse, 500 Gold Ave., S.W., Tel.: 843-2507

Arizona

New Mexico

Texas Counties:

Culberson   Hudspeth
El Paso

Resident Offices

Address: Phoenix, Ariz. 85013—Room
207 Camelback Bldg., 110 W. Camelback Rd. Tel.: 261-3717

Address: El Paso, Tex. 79901—The
Mills Bldg., Room 1205, 303 North
Oregon, Tel.: 533-5381

Region 29

Address: Brooklyn, N.Y. 11201—Fourth
Floor, 16 Court St. Tel.: 596-3535

New York Counties:

Kings   Richmond
Nassau   Suffolk
Queens

Region 30

Address: Milwaukee, W i s c. 53203—
2nd Floor Commerce Bldg., 744 North
Fourth St., Tel.: 272-3861

George F. Squillacote, Director; Wil-
liam C. Humphrey, Regional Attorney

Michigan Counties:

Alger   Keweenaw
Baraga   Luce
Chippewa   Mackinac
Delta   Marquette
Dickinson   Menominee
Gogebic   Ontonagon
Houghton   Schoolcraft
Iron

Wisconsin Counties:

Adams	Marinette
Brown	Marquette
Calumet	Menominee
Columbia	Milwaukee
Crawford	Monroe
Dane	Oconto
Dodge	Oneida
Door	Outagamie
Florence	Ozaukee
Fond Du Lac	Portage
Forest	Racine
Grant	Richland
Green	Rock
Green Lake	Sauk
Iowa	Shawano
Jefferson	Sheboygan
Juneau	Vernon
Kenosha	Vilas
Kewaunee	Walworth
La Crosse	Washington
Lafayette	Waukesha
Langlade	Waupaca
Lincoln	Waushara
Manitowoc	Winnebago
Marathon	Wood

Region 31

Address: Los Angeles, Calif. 90024—
Federal Bldg., Room 12100, 11000
Wilshire Blvd., Tel.: 824-7351

California Counties

Inyo   San Luis Obispo
Kern   Santa Barbara
Los Angeles*   Ventura
San Bernardino

* That portion of Los Angeles County
that lies west and north of the Harbor
Freeway, the Pasadena Freeway, Arroyo
Boulevard, and U.S. Highway 66 eastward
to the county line.

Nevada Counties:

Clark   Nye
Lincoln

Appendix D

SELECTED NLRB FORMS

FORM NLRB-501
(2-67)

Form Approved
Budget Bureau No. 64-R001.12

UNITED STATES OF AMERICA
NATIONAL LABOR RELATIONS BOARD

CHARGE AGAINST EMPLOYER

INSTRUCTIONS: *File an original and 4 copies of this charge with NLRB regional director for the region in which the alleged unfair labor practice occurred or is occurring.*

DO NOT WRITE IN THIS SPACE
Case No.
Date Filed

1. EMPLOYER AGAINST WHOM CHARGE IS BROUGHT

a. Name of Employer

b. Number of Workers Employed

c. Address of Establishment (Street and number, city, State, and ZIP code)

d. Employer Representative to Contact

e. Phone No.

f. Type of Establishment (Factory, mine, wholesaler, etc.)

g. Identify Principal Product or Service

h. The above-named employer has engaged in and is engaging in unfair labor practices within the meaning of section 8(a), subsections (1) and _____ of the National Labor Relations Act,
(List subsections)
and these unfair labor practices are unfair labor practices affecting commerce within the meaning of the Act.

2. Basis of the Charge (Be specific as to facts, names, addresses, plants involved, dates, places, etc.)

By the above and other acts, the above-named employer has interfered with, restrained, and coerced employees in the exercise of the rights guaranteed in Section 7 of the Act.

3. Full Name of Party Filing Charge (If labor organization, give full name, including local name and number)

4a. Address (Street and number, city, State, and ZIP code)

4b. Telephone No.

5. Full Name of National or International Labor Organization of Which It Is an Affiliate or Constituent Unit (To be filled in when charge is filed by a labor organization)

6. DECLARATION

I declare that I have read the above charge and that the statements therein are true to the best of my knowledge and belief.

By _____   _____
    (Signature of representative or person filing charge)   (Title, if any)

Address _____   _____   _____
                                              (Telephone number)   (Date)

WILLFULLY FALSE STATEMENTS ON THIS CHARGE CAN BE PUNISHED BY FINE AND IMPRISONMENT (U.S. CODE, TITLE 18, SECTION 1001)

GPO 904-534

FORM NLRB-508
(12-65)

Form Approved
Budget Bureau No. 64-R003.12

UNITED STATES OF AMERICA
NATIONAL LABOR RELATIONS BOARD

CHARGE AGAINST LABOR ORGANIZATION OR ITS AGENTS

INSTRUCTIONS: File an original and 3 copies of this charge and an additional copy for each organization, each local and each individual named in item 1 with the NLRB regional director for the region in which the alleged unfair labor practice occurred or is occurring.	DO NOT WRITE IN THIS SPACE
	Case No.
	Date Filed

1. LABOR ORGANIZATION OR ITS AGENTS AGAINST WHICH CHARGE IS BROUGHT

a. Name	b. Union Representative to Contact	c. Phone No.

d. Address (Street, city, State and ZIP code)

e. The above-named organization(s) or its agents has (have) engaged in and is (are) engaging in unfair labor practices within the meaning of section 8 (b), subsection(s) ——————— (List Subsections) ——————— of the National Labor Relations Act, and these unfair labor practices are unfair labor practices affecting commerce within the meaning of the Act.

2. Basis of the Charge (Be specific as to facts, names, addresses, plants involved, dates, places, etc.)

3. Name of Employer

4. Location of Plant Involved (Street, city, State and ZIP code)

5. Type of Establishment (Factory, mine, wholesaler, etc.)	6. Identify Principal Product or Service	7. No. of Workers Employed

8. Full Name of Party Filing Charge

9. Address of Party Filing Charge (Street, city, State and ZIP code)	10. Telephone No.

11. DECLARATION

I declare that I have read the above charge and that the statements therein are true to the best of my knowledge and belief.

By _____   _____
   (Signature of representative or person making charge)   (Title or office, if any)

Address _____   _____
                                            (Telephone number)   (Date)

WILLFULLY FALSE STATEMENTS ON THIS CHARGE CAN BE PUNISHED BY FINE AND IMPRISONMENT (U.S. CODE, TITLE 18, SECTION 1001)

GPO 911-597

FORM NLRB-509
(12-65)

Form Approved
Budget Bureau No. 64-R009.2

UNITED STATES OF AMERICA
NATIONAL LABOR RELATIONS BOARD

CHARGE ALLEGING UNFAIR LABOR PRACTICE UNDER SECTION 8(e) OF THE ACT

INSTRUCTIONS: *File an original and 3 copies of this charge, and an additional copy for each organization, each local and each individual named in item 1 with the NLRB regional director for the region in which the alleged unfair labor practice occurred or is occurring.*

Case No.

Date Filed

1. CHARGE FILED AGAINST: Employer and Labor Organization ☐   Employer ☐   Labor Organization ☐

a. Name of Labor Organization (Give full name, including local name and number)	b. Union Representative to Contact	c. Phone No.
d. Address (Street and number, city, State and ZIP code)		
e. Name of Employer	f. Employer Representative to Contact	g. Phone No.
h. Location of Plant Involved (Street, city, State and ZIP code)		

i. Type of Establishment (Factory, mine, wholesaler, etc.)	j. Identify Principal Product or Service	k. No. of Workers Employed

The above-named labor organization or its agents, and/or employer has (have) engaged in and is (are) engaging in unfair labor practices within the meaning of section 8(e) of the National Labor Relations Act, and these unfair labor practices are unfair labor practices affecting commerce within the meaning of the Act.

2. Basis of the Charge (Be specific as to facts, names, plants involved, dates, places, etc.)

3. Full Name of Party Filing Charge (If labor organization, give full name, including local name and number)

4a. Address (Street and number, city, State and ZIP code)	4b. Telephone No.

5. Full Name of National or International Labor Organization of Which It is an Affiliate or Constituent Unit (To be filled in when charge is filed by a labor organization)

6. DECLARATION

I declare that I have read the above charge and that the statements therein are true to the best of my knowledge and belief.

By _____   _____
   (Signature of representative or person filing charge)   (Title, if any)

Address _____   _____
                        (Telephone number)   (Date)

WILLFULLY FALSE STATEMENTS ON THIS CHARGE CAN BE PUNISHED BY FINE AND IMPRISONMENT (U.S. CODE, TITLE 18, SECTION 1001)

GPO 911-594

Form NLRB-502
(11-64)

Form Approved.
Budget Bureau No. 64-R002.14

UNITED STATES OF AMERICA
NATIONAL LABOR RELATIONS BOARD

PETITION

DO NOT WRITE IN THIS SPACE
CASE NO.
DATE FILED

INSTRUCTIONS.—Submit an original and four (4) copies of this Petition to the NLRB Regional Office in the Region in which the employer concerned is located.

If more space is required for any one item, attach additional sheets, numbering item accordingly.

The Petitioner alleges that the following circumstances exist and requests that the National Labor Relations Board proceed under its proper authority pursuant to Section 9 of the National Labor Relations Act.

1. Purpose of this Petition (*If box RC, RM, or RD is checked and a charge under Section 8(b)(7) of the Act has been filed involving the Employer named herein, the statement following the description of the type of petition shall not be deemed made.*)

(*Check one*)

☐ RC—CERTIFICATION OF REPRESENTATIVE—A substantial number of employees wish to be represented for purposes of collective bargaining by Petitioner and Petitioner desires to be certified as representative of the employees.

☐ RM—REPRESENTATION (EMPLOYER PETITION)—One or more individuals or labor organizations have presented a claim to Petitioner to be recognized as the representative of employees of Petitioner.

☐ RD—DECERTIFICATION—A substantial number of employees assert that the certified or currently recognized bargaining representative is no longer their representative.

☐ UD—WITHDRAWAL OF UNION SHOP AUTHORITY—Thirty percent (30%) or more of employees in a bargaining unit covered by an agreement between their employer and a labor organization desire that such authority be rescinded.

☐ UC—UNIT CLARIFICATION—A labor organization is currently recognized by employer, but petitioner seeks clarification of placement of certain employees: (*Check one*)   ☐ In unit not previously certified   ☐ In unit previously certified in Case No. _____

☐ AC—AMENDMENT OF CERTIFICATION—Petitioner seeks amendment of certification issued in Case No. _____

Attach statement describing the specific amendment sought.

2. NAME OF EMPLOYER	EMPLOYER REPRESENTATIVE TO CONTACT	PHONE NO.

3. ADDRESS(ES) OF ESTABLISHMENT(S) INVOLVED (*Street and number, city, State, and ZIP Code*)

4a. TYPE OF ESTABLISHMENT (*Factory, mine, wholesaler, etc.*)	4b. IDENTIFY PRINCIPAL PRODUCT OR SERVICE

5. Unit Involved (*In UC petition, describe PRESENT bargaining unit and attach description of proposed clarification.*)

Included

Excluded

6a. NUMBER OF EMPLOYEES IN UNIT.
PRESENT
PROPOSED (BY UC/AC)

6b. IS THIS PETITION SUPPORTED BY 30% OR MORE OF

(If you have checked box RC in 1 above, check and complete EITHER item 7a or 7b, whichever is applicable)

7a. ☐ Request for recognition as Bargaining Representative was made on .... (Month, day, year) and Employer

declined recognition on or about .... (If no reply received, so state)
(Month, day, year)

7b. ☐ Petitioner is currently recognized as Bargaining Representative and desires certification under the act.

8. Recognized or Certified Bargaining Agent (If there is none, so state)

NAME	AFFILIATION
ADDRESS	DATE OF RECOGNITION OR CERTIFICATION

9. DATE OF EXPIRATION OF CURRENT CONTRACT, IF ANY (Show month, day, and year)

10. IF YOU HAVE CHECKED BOX UD IN 1 ABOVE, SHOW HERE THE DATE OF EXECUTION OF AGREEMENT GRANTING UNION SHOP (Month, day, and year)

11a. IS THERE NOW A STRIKE OR PICKETING AT THE EMPLOYER'S ESTABLISHMENT(S) INVOLVED?   YES .... NO ....

11b. IF SO, APPROXIMATELY HOW MANY EMPLOYEES ARE PARTICIPATING?

11c. THE EMPLOYER HAS BEEN PICKETED BY OR ON BEHALF OF .... A LABOR
(Insert name)

ORGANIZATION, OF .... SINCE ....
(Insert address)   (Month, day, year)

12. ORGANIZATIONS OR INDIVIDUALS OTHER THAN PETITIONER (AND OTHER THAN THOSE NAMED IN ITEMS 8 AND 11c), WHICH HAVE CLAIMED RECOGNITION AS REPRESENTATIVES AND OTHER ORGANIZATIONS AND INDIVIDUALS KNOWN TO HAVE A REPRESENTATIVE INTEREST IN ANY EMPLOYEES IN THE UNIT DESCRIBED IN ITEM 5 ABOVE.   (IF NONE, SO STATE.)

NAME	AFFILIATION	ADDRESS	DATE OF CLAIM (Required only if Petition is filed by Employer)

I declare that I have read the above petition and that the statements therein are true to the best of my knowledge and belief.

....
(Petitioner and affiliation, if any)

By ....
(Signature of representative or person filing petition)   (Title, if any)

Address ....
(Street and number, city, state, and ZIP Code)   (Telephone number)

WILLFULLY FALSE STATEMENT ON THIS PETITION CAN BE PUNISHED BY FINE AND IMPRISONMENT (U.S. CODE, TITLE 18, SECTION 1001)

GP O 886-427

FORM NLRB-4551
(10-62)

UNITED STATES OF AMERICA
NATIONAL LABOR RELATIONS BOARD

REQUEST TO PROCEED

In the matter of _____ _____

(Name of Case)   (Number of Case)

The undersigned hereby requests the Regional Director to proceed with the above-captioned representation case, notwithstanding the charges of unfair labor practices filed in Case No. _____ . It is understood that the Board will not entertain objections to any election in this matter based upon conduct occurring prior to the filing of the petition.

Date _____

By _____

_____

(Title)

GPO 911-506

NLRB-651
(12-61)

UNITED STATES OF AMERICA
NATIONAL LABOR RELATIONS BOARD

AGREEMENT FOR CONSENT ELECTION

Pursuant to a Petition duly filed under Section 9 of the National Labor Relations Act as amended, and subject to the approval of the Regional Director for the National Labor Relations Board (herein called the Regional Director), the undersigned parties hereby waive a hearing and AGREE AS FOLLOWS:

1. SECRET BALLOT.—An election by secret ballot shall be held under the supervision of the said Regional Director, among the employees of the undersigned Employer in the unit defined below, at the indicated time and place, to determine whether or not such employees desire to be represented for the purpose of collective bargaining by (one of) the undersigned labor organization(s).   Said election shall be held in accordance with the National Labor Relations Act, the Board's Rules and Regulations, and the applicable procedures and policies of the Board, provided that the determination of the Regional Director shall be final and binding upon any question, including questions as to the eligibility of voters, raised by any party hereto relating in any manner to the election, and provided further that rulings or determinations by the Regional Director in respect of any amendment of any certification resulting therefrom shall also be final.

2. ELIGIBLE VOTERS.—The eligible voters shall be those employees included within the Unit described below, who were employed during the payroll period indicated below, including employees who did not work during said payroll period because they were ill or on vacation or temporarily laid off, employees in the military services of the United States who appear in person at the polls, employees engaged in an economic strike which commenced less than twelve (12) months before the election date and who retained their status as such during the eligibility period and their replacements, but excluding any employees who have since quit or been discharged for cause and employees engaged in a strike who have been discharged for cause since the commencement thereof, and who have not been rehired or reinstated prior to the date of the election, and employees engaged in an economic strike which commenced more than 12 months prior to the date of the election and who have been permanently replaced.   At a date fixed by the Regional Director, the parties, as requested, will furnish to the Regional Director, an accurate list of all the eligible voters, together with a list of the employees, if any, specifically excluded from eligibility.

3. NOTICES OF ELECTION.—The Regional Director shall prepare a Notice of Election and supply copies to the parties describing the manner and conduct of the election to be held and incorporating therein a sample ballot. The parties, upon the request of and at a time designated by the Regional Director, will post such Notice of Election at conspicuous and usual posting places easily accessible to the eligible voters.

4. OBSERVERS.—Each party hereto will be allowed to station an equal number of authorized observers, selected from among the nonsupervisory employees of the Employer, at the polling places during the election to assist in its conduct, to challenge the eligibility of voters, and to verify the tally.

5. TALLY OF BALLOTS.—As soon after the election as feasible, the votes shall be counted and tabulated by the Regional Director, or his agent or agents.   Upon the conclusion of the counting, the Regional Director shall furnish a Tally of Ballots to each of the parties.   When appropriate, the Regional Director shall issue to the parties a certification of representatives or of results of election, as may be indicated.

6. OBJECTIONS, CHALLENGES, REPORTS THEREON.—Objections to the conduct of the election or conduct affecting the results of the election, or to a determination of representatives based on the results thereof, may be filed with the Regional Director within 5 days after issuance of the Tally of Ballots.   Copies of such objections must be served upon the other parties at the time of filing with the Regional Director.   The Regional Director shall investigate the matters contained in the objections and issue a report thereon.   If objections are sustained, the Regional Director may in his report include an order voiding the results of the election and, in that event, shall be empowered to conduct a new election under the terms and provisions of this agreement at a date, time, and place to be determined by him.   If the challenges are determinative of the results of the election, the Regional Director shall investigate the challenges and issue a report thereon.   The method of investigation of objections and challenges, including the question whether a hearing should be held in connection therewith, shall be determined by the Regional Director, whose decision shall be final and binding.

7. RUN-OFF PROCEDURE.—In the event more than one labor organization is signatory to this agreement, and in the event that no choice on the ballot in the election receives a majority of the valid ballots cast, the Regional Director shall proceed in accordance with the Board's Rules and Regulations.

8. COMMERCE.—The Employer is engaged in commerce within the meaning of Section 2 (6) (7) of the National Labor Relations Act.

16—47689-7

9. WORDING ON THE BALLOT.—Where only one labor organization is signatory to this agreement, the name of the organization shall appear on the ballot and the choice shall be "Yes" or "No." In the event more than one labor organization is signatory to this agreement, the choices on the ballot will appear in the wording indicated below and in the order enumerated below, reading from left to right on the ballot, or if the occasion demands, from top to bottom. (If more than one union is to appear on the ballot, any union may have its name removed from the ballot by the approval of the Regional Director of a timely request, in writing, to that effect.)

First.

Second.

Third.

10. PAYROLL PERIOD FOR ELIGIBILITY.—

11. DATE, HOURS, AND PLACE OF ELECTION.—

12. THE APPROPRIATE COLLECTIVE BARGAINING UNIT.—

If Notice of Representation Hearing has been issued in this case, the approval of this agreement by the Regional Director shall constitute withdrawal of the Notice of Representation Hearing heretofore issued.

....
(Employer)

By ....
(Name and title)   (Date)

Recommended:

....
(Board Agent)   (Date)

Date approved ....

....
Regional Director,
National Labor Relations Board.

Case No. ....

....
(Name of Organization)

By ....
(Name and title)   (Date)

....
(Name of other Organization)

By ....
(Name and title)   (Date)

GPO 937-446

NLRB-652
(1-63)

UNITED STATES OF AMERICA
NATIONAL LABOR RELATIONS BOARD

STIPULATION FOR CERTIFICATION UPON CONSENT ELECTION

Pursuant to a Petition duly filed under Section 9 of the National Labor Relations Act, as amended, and subject to the approval of the Regional Director for the National Labor Relations Board (herein called the Regional Director), the undersigned parties hereby AGREE AS FOLLOWS:

1. SECRET BALLOT.—An election by secret ballot shall be held under the supervision of the said Regional Director, among the employees of the undersigned Employer in the unit defined below, at the indicated time and place, to determine whether or not such employees desire to be represented for the purpose of collective bargaining by (one of) the undersigned labor organization(s). Said election shall be held in accordance with the National Labor Relations Act, the Board's Rules and Regulations, and the applicable procedures and policies of the Board.

2. ELIGIBLE VOTERS.—The eligible voters shall be those employees included within the Unit described below, who were employed during the payroll period indicated below, including employees who did not work during said payroll period because they were ill or on vacation or temporarily laid off, and employees in the military services of the United States who appear in person at the polls, also eligible are employees engaged in an economic strike which commenced less than twelve (12) months before the election date and who retained their status as such during the eligibility period and their replacements, but *excluding* any employees who have since quit or been discharged for cause and employees engaged in a strike who have been discharged for cause since the commencement thereof, and who have not been rehired or reinstated prior to the date of the election, and employees engaged in an economic strike which commenced more than twelve (12) months prior to the date of the election and who have been permanently replaced. At a date fixed by the Regional Director, the parties, as requested, will furnish to the Regional Director, an accurate list of all the eligible voters, together with a list of the employees, if any, specifically excluded from eligibility.

3. NOTICES OF ELECTION.—The Regional Director shall prepare a Notice of Election and supply copies to the parties describing the manner and conduct of the election to be held and incorporating therein a sample ballot. The parties, upon the request of and at a time designated by the Regional Director, will post such Notice of Election at conspicuous and usual posting places easily accessible to the eligible voters.

4. OBSERVERS.—Each party hereto will be allowed to station an equal number of authorized observers, selected from among the nonsupervisory employees of the Employer, at the polling places during the election to assist in its conduct, to challenge the eligibility of voters, and to verify the tally.

5. TALLY OF BALLOTS.—As soon after the election as feasible, the votes shall be counted and tabulated by the Regional Director, or his agent or agents. Upon the conclusion of the counting, the Regional Director shall furnish a Tally of Ballots to each of the parties.

6. POST-ELECTION AND RUN-OFF PROCEDURE.—All procedure subsequent to the conclusion of counting ballots shall be in conformity with the Board's Rules and Regulations.

7. RECORD.—The record in this case shall be governed by the appropriate provisions of the Board's Rules and Regulations and shall include this stipulation. Hearing and notice thereof, Direction of Election, and the making of Findings of Fact and Conclusions of Law by the Board prior to the election are hereby expressly waived.

8. COMMERCE.—The Employer is engaged in commerce within the meaning of Section 2(6) of the National Labor Relations Act, and a question affecting commerce has arisen concerning the representation of employees within the meaning of Section 9(c). *(Insert commerce facts.)*

9. WORDING ON THE BALLOT.—Where only one labor organization is signatory to this agreement, the name of the organization shall appear on the ballot and the choice shall be "Yes" or "No." In the event more than one labor organization is signatory to this agreement, the choices on the ballot will appear in the wording indicated below and in the order enumerated below, reading from left to right on the ballot, or if the occasion demands, from top to bottom. *(If more than one union is to appear on the ballot, any union may have its name removed from the ballot by the approval of the Regional Director of a timely request, in writing, to that effect.)*

First.

Second.

Third.

10. PAYROLL PERIOD FOR ELIGIBILITY.—

11. DATE, HOURS, AND PLACE OF ELECTION.—

12. THE APPROPRIATE COLLECTIVE BARGAINING UNIT.—

If Notice of Representation Hearing has been issued in this case, the approval of this stipulation by the Regional Director shall constitute withdrawal of the Notice of Representation Hearing heretofore issued.

.... (Employer)	.... (Name of Organization)
.... (Address)	.... (Address)
By .... (Name and Title) (Date)	By .... (Name and Title) (Date)
Recommended:	
.... (Board Agent) (Date)	.... (Name of other Organization)
Date approved............................	
.... Regional Director, National Labor Relations Board.	.... (Address)
Case No.	By .... (Name and Title) (Date)

GPO 878 416

NLRB 601
(7-57)

UNITED STATES OF AMERICA
NATIONAL LABOR RELATIONS BOARD

WITHDRAWAL REQUEST

In the matter of _____   _____
                 (Name of case)   (Number of case)

This is to request withdrawal of the (petition) (charge) in the above case.

_____
(Name of Party Filing)

By _____
     (Name of Representative)

_____
(Title)

Date _____

Withdrawal request approved

_____
(Date)

Regional Director,
National Labor Relations Board.

GPO 920844

TOPICAL INDEX